D1547577

EFFECTIVE COLLABORATION

Effective Collaboration

Managing the Obstacles to Success

Edited by
Jens Genefke
and
Frank McDonald

First published 2001 by
PALGRAVE
Houndmills, Basingstoke, Hampshire RG21 6XS and
175 Fifth Avenue, New York, N.Y. 10010
Companies and representatives throughout the world

PALGRAVE is the new global academic imprint of
St. Martin's Press LLC Scholarly and Reference Division and
Palgrave Publishers Ltd (formerly Macmillan Press Ltd).

ISBN 0-333-94810-6

This book is printed on paper suitable for recycling and
made from fully managed and sustained forest sources.

A catalogue record for this book is available
from the British Library.

Library of Congress Cataloging-in-Publication Data
Effective collaboration : managing the obstacles to success / edited by
Jens Genefke and Frank McDonald
     p. cm.
   Includes bibliographical references and index.
   ISBN 0–333–94810–6 (cloth)
     1. Strategic alliances (Business) I. Genefke, Jens. II. McDonald, Frank,
   1951–

   HD69.S8 E33 2001
   658'.044—dc21   2001031522

10   9   8   7   6   5   4   3   2   1
10   09 08 07 06 05 04 03 02 01

Printed and bound in
Great Britain by Antony Rowe Ltd, Chippenham, Wiltshire

Contents

List of Tables

List of Figures

Acknowledgements

Early versions of all of the chapters were presented at the Fourth and Fifth International Conferences on Multi-Organisational Partnerships and Co-operative Strategy held at the University of Oxford in 1997 and 1998. The editors are grateful to David Faulkner, the organiser of the conferences, for helping us to contact the authors of the chapters. The chapters were written in the light of the comments, suggestions and corrections that were made when the original papers were presented at these conferences. The research reported in Chapter 3 was partly funded by the British Council and Birmingham Business School at the University of Birmingham. The Banking Centre and the International Business Group at Loughborough University Business School also provided assistance with the research. Chapter 7 is based on research funded by the Economic and Social Research Council (R000234910).

J. G.
F. M.

Notes on the Contributors

Richard Butler is Professor of Organisational Analysis and Head of the Graduate School at the University of Bradford Management Centre.

Carolyn Erdener is a Professor at Stuttgart Institute of Management and Technology. Previously she worked at the Department of Management at the Baptist University of Hong Kong.

Jens Genefke is a Professor in the Department of Management at the University of Aarhus. He previously worked as a business consultant and periodically returns to work in industry. Recently he completed three years working as a chairman of a board of six shipyards in Greenland. He publishes in Danish and English in the areas of organisation and management.

Jas Gill is a Research Associate at the School of Management, Royal Holloway, University of London. Previously he worked at the University of Bradford Management Centre. His research has focused on interorganisational cooperation and the role of trust.

Chris Huxham is a Professor at Strathclyde Graduate Business School at the University of Strathclyde. Her research work is focused on the practical implications of managing alliances and partnerships.

Frank Martin is Director of Global Integration, an international consultancy and training organisation. He is also a Fellow of the International Business Policy Centre at Kingston University.

Robin Matthews is Professor of International Business and Director of the International Business Policy Centre at Kingston University. He has published extensively on game theory and business and management topics.

Frank McDonald is Head of the International Business Unit at Manchester Metropolitan University Business School. He is researching the use of networks by firms as a means of developing international competitiveness.

Ian C. Morison is Professor of Banking and Finance at Loughborough University. He was Director of the Banking Centre at Loughborough

University from 1989 to 1992. From 1983 to 1988 he was Assistant General Manager and Corporate Affairs Director at the Midland Bank. Ian has written extensively on banking and related topics.

François Sauer worked with Professor Winch on the project using IT systems to improve the management of organisations and is now working at marchFirst in Kansas City.

David Sink is Professor of Public Administration at the University of Arkansas in Little Rock. His research has included collaboration to promote community development and has led to publications in journals such as *American Review of Public Administration, Human Relations, Public Administration Review* and *Policy Studies Journal*.

Jan Stiles is Lead Tutor in Strategic Management at Henley Management College.

Ingemar Torbiorn is a Professor in the Department of Psychology at Stockholm University.

Rehan ul-Haq is a Lecturer at Birmingham Business School, University of Birmingham where he is a member of the Marketing Group. Previous to this he worked at the Banking Centre at Loughborough University Business School. He has published over 40 articles and chapters in books in the areas of strategic management and strategic alliances in the banking sector.

Siv Vangen is a member of Strathclyde Graduate Business School and is, with Professor Huxham, working on a research programme on the practical management of alliances and partnerships.

Graham Winch is a Professor in the Business School at the University of Plymouth. His research is centred on the use of IT systems to improve the management of organisations and he has received a grant from the Economic and Social Research Council for work on this area.

Introduction

ANOTHER BOOK ON COLLABORATION?

Our 'excuse' for yet another book on partnership and cooperation is twofold:

1. Many other books on collaboration are structured along the lines of sector studies or general studies, or theoretical studies and empirical studies, or public and private sector issues. However, this book centres on the various connections between different topics common to most partnerships. Consequently, the focus of this book is not on a particular theoretical approach, or on studies of particular sectors, but rather on highlighting many of the common issues and problems associated with partnerships.
2. Much of the literature on partnerships is centred on the view that collaboration leads to improved performance, better resource deployment and the like. However, even if the potential for synergy and other benefits from partnerships is great, these benefits are not available for free. This book highlights the hard work that is necessary to make partnerships succeed and provides conceptual frameworks, case-studies and assessments on many of the key factors that influence the effective formation and operation of partnerships.

Therefore, we think that the book can be of help to those inclined towards thorough preparation before committing themselves to a partnership, and we hope it can be of help for those who have already joined forces with other organisations, but are meeting unforeseen obstacles in the process. Furthermore, academics and students interested in collaborative ventures will gain insights into the problems that are likely to be faced in making partnerships work effectively.

At least for the time being, it is impossible to calculate all the details that must be known to ensure that partnerships operate effectively and are thus able to deliver desired results. It is unlikely that a complete theory of collaboration will be put together in the foreseeable future. The ideas on how best to understand collaborative arrangements are a battlefield between different theories. Joining a partnership may mean more efficiency, but it also can lead to more dependence, which can be dangerous if partners are unreliable. Collaboration may permit better decision-making, but the decision time can be unacceptably long. Partnerships may increase profits or market share, or aid in the process of acquiring and developing new technology, but damaging conflicts can arise over the distribution of the gains. Moreover, the amount of management time and expertise that is necessary to formulate the conditions for effective partnerships and to operate them in an effective manner may limit the attractiveness of collaborative arrangements.

This means that every new partnership needs its own reflections. Like a puzzle, it is quickly completed when some essential pieces are brought together, but it is necessary to make judgements of the factors crucial for successful collaboration, and then test them for mutual consistency. Such testing demands knowledge from several theories such as organisation design, organisation development, transaction cost theory, and resource-based theory. The chapters in this book use these and other theories to aid in the process of understanding and evaluating partnerships. Some of the chapters are purely conceptual while others investigate the private and public sectors, partnerships in the not-for-profit sector and those involving collaboration between all of these sectors. Although the chapters investigate a variety of sectors the focus of the study is not on specifically sectoral or conceptual issues; rather, attempts are made to investigate the problems and possible solutions to them that arise in creating and effectively managing collaborative ventures.

THE RATIONALE FOR COLLABORATION

The benefits of collaboration between organisations may be viewed as a low-cost means to acquire useful assets such as high-quality inputs, knowledge about and access to markets and technology. The emphasis is on low-cost acquisition because all organisations have to make decisions about how they acquire assets, knowledge and technology. There are three basic choices – 'do it yourself', where organisations marshal resources to produce desired items for themselves; 'buy on the market', where organisations search markets and purchase based on their estimation of the best offer available; and 'collaboration', where organisations form some type of partnership with other organisations to produce the desired results. Therefore, the options for organisations range from acquisition by markets through various types of collaboration to vertically integrated firms. An important feature of such analysis is the highlighting of the fact that collaboration is not always the 'best' solution. In this book the focus is on the difficulties of managing partnerships in cases where collaboration is the 'best' solution, or of identifying management problems that render collaborative solutions that on first examination appear to be optimal, but which on closer examination are rendered sub-optimal because of incompatibilities between partners.

Assuming a given specification for the desired items, the choice of the best means of acquistion depends on the relationship between the production costs of acquiring items and the transactions costs of arranging for the acquisition of these items. These costs and the optimal solution are illustrated in Figure I.1.

In the example given in Figure I.1, transaction costs (shown by TC1 and TC2) are upward-sloping, indicating that as organisations move from markets towards vertical integration transaction costs rise. Production costs (shown by PC) are downward sloping, indicating economies of scale can be reached as the organisation moves from market provision towards vertical integration. If cost conditions were given by TC1 and PC, the optimal way to obtain desired items would be some type of collaboration. If transaction costs moved from TC1 and TC2, the optimal way to obtain desired items would move towards closer collaboration or even towards vertical integration. If the PC and TC curves had properties other than those shown in Figure I.1 (for example, an upward-sloping PC curve and/or a curvilinear TC curve), different optimal solutions would emerge.

Clearly the optimal way to acquire desired items depends on the position and slope of these cost relationships. Therefore, increasing internationalisation may alter production costs and transaction costs by providing new sources of supply that have different cost relationships from existing sources. The development of new technologies such as e-commerce can also alter these cost relationships and can result in evolution to new types of partnerships or a move to new types of market relations or revamped

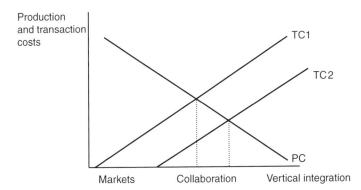

Figure I.1 The optimal solution for acquiring desired items.

vertical integration systems. The increasing focus on knowledge and relational assets as key requirements for organisations also has implications for collaborative ventures, because obtaining and utilising these assets nearly always involves cooperation between many agents.

Elaboration of these types of models to differentiate between the various types of market, collaborative and vertically integrated systems and the costs associated with these different types of organisations is possible. It is possible, at least in principle, to produce a specification of the optimal solution by consideration of the transaction and production costs of delivering required results and thereby to select the best means of acquiring the resources necessary to achieve desired outcomes. Consideration of the drivers for collaboration such as internationalisation, regulatory changes and technological developments can then be used to determine the 'best' system for collaboration, either from existing taxonomies of partnerships or by devising new forms of cooperation.

Much of the literature on collaboration is concerned with the characteristics of these cost relationships (especially transaction costs), the drivers for collaboration and the selection of the 'best' type of partnership, either from an existing portfolio of possible organisational systems or by creating new forms of cooperating. However, deciding whether collaboration is optimal and selecting the appropriate type of cooperation is only part of the management of collaborative ventures. Partnerships, once they have been established, have to be effectively operated. It is this aspect of collaboration that is the focus of this book. The various chapters examine different types of cooperation and are interested in the various costs connected to various types of partnership, but the focus is on how these factors affect the formation and evolution of collaborative ventures. From this analysis the chapters consider the factors that are important for the effective creation, development and operation of partnerships and also assess ways of overcoming or reducing the obstacles to the effective management of collaborative ventures.

THE COLLABORATIVE ARENA

This book then focuses on the factors in and around organisations that constitute the collaborative arena. A central theme is the view that every partnership has its own particular arena and that the composition of this arena determines the success or otherwise of the collaborative ventures. This common viewpoint of the book is developed in the first chapter by Huxham and Vangen. The aim of their work is to elucidate the type of problems that practitioners are meeting in practice. Their research uncovers a number of recurrent themes, and they identify common problems that cut across all the complexities raised by practitioners. They review the literature, explain their methodology, present lists of common problem-areas and end by providing 'top ten tips' for collaborators.

Huxham and Vangen establish a basis for a broader understanding of the forces involved in collaboration building, and the rest of the book aims at more specific questions that often arise. Some of the chapters are theoretical, some are case-studies, and some are based on empirical investigations. A wide variety of theoretical frameworks are used and the case studies range across a variety of industries in both the private and public sectors. Notwithstanding the diversity of approaches and industries that are covered, a set of common themes emerge from these chapters. These themes are covered under three main headings: collaborative intent, formation of partnerships and organisational differences.

COLLABORATIVE INTENT

In this section, Chapters 2 and 3 investigate the incentives for forming partnerships and the approach taken towards partners.

In Chapter 2, Stiles examines two different approaches to partnership: the cooperative (where partners join forces for reasons of protection or security) and the competitive (where they seek synergistic advantages such as the transfer of knowledge). This chapter shows that some factors are likely to influence the extent to which firms adopt cooperative and/or competitive intent and that other factors serve as barriers that can affect the implementation of the intent. This analysis leads to a taxonomy of five distinct types of collaboration.

In Chapter 3, ul-Haq and Morison explore why organisations join strategic partnerships. Their theoretical considerations lead them to categorise three possible purposes and it is shown and explained why the banks cluster in two of these categories.

FORMATION OF PARTNERSHIPS

The formation process is discussed in Chapters 4 to 7. The focus is on design and the critical factors that need to be considered in order to increase advantages and decrease misunderstandings and trouble.

Martin and Matthews discuss the forming of a new industry, natural gas vehicles, by an alliance between firms and government agencies.

They present a model that provides a methodology for solving the problems inherent in such alliances. They find the sole distinction between cooperation and non-cooperation too simple, and their findings suggest that it is possible to reconcile the conflicting goals of various stakeholders as long as there is a detailed mapping of payoff interdependencies and a strong inclusive leadership.

This line is followed up by Sink in Chapter 5. He theorises about partnerships with multiple members where the members of the alliance have unclear purposes and also vary greatly in size, organisation and interests. After a presentation of six 'stubborn' challenges for alliance-forming under these circumstances, he concludes – much like Martin and Matthews – that before alliance construction one ought to create a meta-domain – preferably based on a systems view.

Chapter 6 is devoted to coordination techniques between multiple partners. Winch and Sauer show how a professional partnership can be enabled through the use of integrated IT systems. Based on description of a rather complex healthcare system, they show how organising, associating and presenting information simultaneously from various perspectives can further the collective learning processes. This learning is important because the partner organisation – in its own best interests – ought to focus as much on the overall alliance system as on its own internal affairs.

In Chapter 7 Butler and Gill investigate a joint venture between two organisations to analyse how organisations build knowledge of potential partners. This is done as a means to develop a more general framework for thinking about the process of partner selection. They identify three types of trust, and show how the prospective partners used different knowledge-gathering techniques to assess each of the three types of trust. Generally speaking they find that there is a tendency towards a one-to-one correspondence between search types and trust types.

ORGANISATIONAL DIFFERENCES

This section of the book, Chapters 8 to 10, explores the countermeasures that are at the disposal of management when partners have trouble fitting their people and managerial systems together across organisational boundaries.

In Chapter 8, Erdener and Torbiorn present their analysis of staffing in international alliances. Their point of departure is that it is people that make as well as implement organisational strategies. Therefore, they stress the importance of the fit between strategic and human-resource approaches to the strategic formation of alliances. This leads them to focus on the need for a double view, maintaining the local operational efficiency in the partners while simultaneously securing the strategic fit. This objective cannot always be managed by focusing on the optimisation of only one of the strategies.

Power asymmetries are on McDonald's agenda in Chapter 9. Looking at the power big buyers can achieve over smaller sellers, he disputes the wisdom of using power over the supply chain to the full extent because such a course can undermine the ability of the partnership to deliver and maintain competitive advantage. His analytic schemes give a concrete understanding of the forces for, and the maximal level of, power employment within supply chains.

Chapter 10 by Genefke regards culture as a perceptual filter that directs the partners' awareness in specific directions. He decomposes the cultural concepts and shows what kinds of remedial action management can apply to align cultures that are in different states of misfit.

These three groupings of chapters are, of course, not independent. Figure I.2 seeks to provide a more comprehensive and integrated picture.

On the basis of a joint understanding of both the benefits, disadvantages and implementation problems of collaboration it can be argued that prospective partners ought to take account of intent as well as differences before the partnership is formed. Likewise it could be argued that inbuilt into all forms of partnerships are synergistic possibilities towards some types of intent and barriers towards others, and that some differences are so difficult to eliminate that the costs of sorting them out may outweigh the benefits and/or render the implementation of a smoothly operating partnership impossible. These factors, outlined in Figure I.2, accentuate

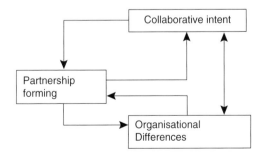

Figure I.2   Main factors influencing the development of collaborative understanding.

the need for a balanced view of how the forces inherent in partnerships act in unison.

Finally, Chapter 11 seeks to draw together the material presented earlier to provide a framework that permits analysis of the many complex and interdependent factors that affect the creation and effective operation of partnerships.

JENS GENEFKE
FRANK MCDONALD

1 What Makes Practitioners Tick? Understanding Collaboration Practice and Practising Collaboration Understanding

Chris Huxham and Siv Vangen

INTRODUCTION

A striking characteristic of research on interorganisational relations is the astonishing variety of disciplines, research paradigms, theoretical perspectives and sectoral focuses within which it takes place (Gray and Wood, 1991; Huxham and Cropper, 1997). An abundance of articles emanates from such disciplines as economics, strategic management, organisation theory, policy studies, international relations and management science, and research approaches range from strictly positivist hypothesis-testing at one extreme to highly phenomenological, ethnographic, participative or action research at the other, taking in case-studies, focus groups and documentation-based policy analysis somewhere along the way. Some approaches are rooted firmly in the private sector while others see only the social perspective. Yet others are rooted in very specific microsectors: housing, health, supply chain relationships, international joint ventures, local government, the environment, NGOs and urban regeneration are examples.

With the notable exception of Gray and Wood (1991) and Wood and Gray (1991), little attempt has been made to clarify the way in which this literature interrelates and the complexity of perspectives remains baffling. There is little cross-referencing of material from one discipline to another and many authors appear oblivious of the existence of *any* other relevant research. Not surprisingly, even the most basic terminology – such as 'partnership', 'alliance', and 'collaboration' – is subject to a wide variety of interpretations and while many authors make tight definitions for their own purposes, there is no consistency of usage across the field (Huxham, 1996a). Exactly what is the ultimate aim of much of this research is

1

unclear. Who or what it is intended to influence or contribute to, and how, is rarely made explicit. Much of this research may be argued to be theoretically weak. For example, conferences abound with presentations by practitioners, and academics *qua* practitioners, describing – with hindsight, and without conceptualisation – collaborative ventures in which they have participated. Nevertheless, there remains a significant volume of literature which would be argued to be of high quality by others researching from similar disciplines and research approaches.

While acknowledging that research from all perspectives has validity, our own guiding values have led us to focus our research on the practice of collaboration. Specifically, we have been concerned to find ways to understand and influence effectiveness in collaboration. To date, the research has tended to focus on the public and non-profit sectors with social issues as the subject of the collaborations. However, it is the issues concerned with convening, designing, managing, participating in and facilitating collaborations, rather than the sector or subject of collaboration, which are at the centre of our concern.

Our preoccupation with practice stems inevitably, to a large extent, from our own backgrounds. Our original base discipline of management science, our location in a business school, and within a university which has as its guiding motto 'A Place of Useful Learning', have all been heavy influences. Arguments in favour of collaboration abound. Trist's (1983) argument that serious social issues necessarily fall into the interorganisational domain and thus can only be tackled collaboratively is reason enough to justify its promotion in the social sector. In the private sector, many have argued that increasing globalisation makes international alliances inevitable (Lamming, 1993; Ohmae, 1993). Policymakers and management consultants have both joined the bandwagon and government incentives and books extolling the advantages of collaborations are widespread (see, for example: Bergquist *et al.*, 1995; Doz, 1994; Lewis, 1990; Lowndes, 1997; Lynch, 1993; Painter *et al.*, 1997; Turock, 1997). The pressures for collaboration are therefore great. As one public policy observer put it recently: 'In the UK, joint working is what you have to say you do even if you don't.'

However, there is a continual stream of evidence to suggest that practice of partnership is difficult to sustain effectively in any situation (Kanter, 1994; Webb, 1991; Wistow and Hardy, 1991). Attempts to involve the community in such partnerships are particularly fraught with difficulty (Hasting *et al.*, 1996; Himmelman, 1996; Taylor, 1995), and terminology such as 'divorce', 'instability', and 'inertia' arises frequently in the context of strategic alliances and joint ventures (Baumhauer and Naulleau, 1997;

Inkpen and Beamish, 1997; Medcof, 1997; Meschi, 1997). Potentially huge differences between the collaborating organisations in terms of aims, organisational (and sometimes ethnic) culture, structures, procedures, use of language, power and accountabilities, together with the sheer time required to manage the logistics of communication, all mitigate against success. For these and other reasons, many partnerships set up with the best of goodwill and intentions fail to live up to the expectations of those involved. Progress towards achieving aims seems painfully slow and is often accompanied by a huge sense of frustration. We have used the term 'collaborative inertia' to describe this (Huxham, 1996b). As one practitioner concerned with promoting collaborative responses to the problem of 'young offenders' put it:

> The Audit Commission report [on young offenders] said collaborative working is essential, but no-one says how ... multi-agency work is very slow – trying to get people moving collectively rather than alone is difficult ... there are lots of multi-agency conferences but everyone is talking about task and no one about process.

Given these difficulties, it is important for practitioners to understand how to act in such circumstances. It is also essential that policy-makers appreciate the ramifications of their policies and provide appropriate support for implementation.

Our concern is thus to understand how to develop, present and disseminate theory which will have a real, positive and reasonably direct influence on practice. In this chapter, we provide an overview of our approach to addressing this challenge to date. Our purpose is to provoke debate. We are not so arrogant as to believe that our approach is the only one possible for addressing practice, but we *are* arrogant enough to hope that others will incorporate our work into their approach too!

UNDERSTANDING COLLABORATION PRACTICE: RESEARCH APPROACH

Viewed from the broadest level, we have taken an integrated research approach in which development, presentation and dissemination of practice-oriented theory are all part of the same research activities. Theory about the practice of collaboration is derived from data drawn from the practice of collaboration and used directly to inform the practice of collaboration. Nevertheless, it is possible to distinguish the data collection and methodological aspects of theory-building from the theory itself and from the mechanisms for transferring that into practical usage. This and the following sections describe each of these aspects of our approach in turn.

Our understanding of the issues that practitioners of collaboration have to grapple with, and of the value of theory and methods in assisting them, has been built over a prolonged research period involving many projects, both large and small. Inevitably, the approaches used, and our understanding, have evolved during this. Our approach has been inspired by the action research paradigm described by Eden and Huxham (1996), though it does not all strictly fit within the criteria for action research presented there. An important aspect of the approach is that it has been inductive rather than deductive, with research output being almost entirely emergent (Burell and Morgan, 1997; Glaser and Strauss, 1967).

Much of the research data has been gained through interventions in which we act as 'consultants', facilitators or workshop leaders. Many of these have been one-off, half-day, or single-day affairs, but other projects have run over many months or years. During these interventions, the expressed experiences, views, action-centred dilemmas and actual actions of participants have been recorded in a variety of ways. These include: cognitive maps (stored on computer using the software *Decision Explorer*; Banxia, 1996) containing individuals' views expressed in interviews; cause maps prepared for and developed during group decision support workshops containing the combined views of collaborative group members; video recordings of workshops; notes from meetings with people involved in collaborative initiatives; models of aspects of collaborative practice developed with people involved in collaborative initiatives; flipchart responses developed during awareness-raising workshops; notes taken while observing meetings or workshops; post-event evaluation questionnaires; notes from follow-up phone calls; notes of comments made by those who have listened to our presentations or read articles we have written; and documents produced by organisations or collaborations such as minutes or strategy documents.

In addition to these formal interventions, we have, over the years, had many informal conversations with practitioners involved in collaboration. These have been during telephone calls or visits from practitioners who have made contact with us having seen an article we have written; they followed presentations we have made; and they have arisen in the course of other conversations when a practitioner happens to discover that this is an area in which we have some expertise. Typically, practitioners provide rich, if short, snippets of description of their experiences and feelings. Typically, we respond with an interpretation of the experience based on our theoretical understanding. If they find the theory enlightening, or if it does not quite match their experience, they usually elaborate further on their experience. Frequently we are able to make notes of such conversations. We are thus able to gain data that is volunteered rather than generated during more formal intervention. We are also able to record reaction to our theory-based interpretations.

A third type of data is based upon our own understanding and synthesis of the situations we are researching. On the one hand, this refers to our synthesis of the stories of many participants into a view of what might actually be happening in a particular situation. In some cases, this may happen serendipitously and over prolonged periods as we come into contact with more and more of those involved. For example, in this way, we have been able to build up a picture of the membership structure of particular collaborations that any individual would have found difficult to explicate (Vangen and Huxham, 1997). On the other hand, we regard the notes made at meetings between fellow researchers and ourselves, as we try to analyse and conceptualise the situations we have been involved in, as important pieces of data in their own right.

Within the longer-running projects it has been possible to collect comparable data over time, and thus to track the way the project develops (for example, Huxham, 1993). The use of computer-based cognitive and cause maps are particularly valuable in this respect. Importantly, however, we are also able to pool the data gained from all of the interventions in which we have been involved. Since we are searching for emergent theory, it does not matter that the data is not gathered in a consistent way. We are not aiming to triangulate in the normal sense of the word, but to build a rich picture of what can (rather than does) happen in collaboration practice. The difference between the settings in which the data is collected therefore serves to enrich the picture. Although this data is collected and recorded in many different ways, we are always careful to represent as faithfully as possible the way in which practitioners express their points. Often it is necessary to paraphrase and sometimes the original statement is converted into an imperative form to imply an action orientation, but the aim is to capture as much as possible of the original language used. Subtleties in perspective and expression serve to enrich the picture further.

Gradually we are accumulating an ever-increasing base of data relating to many different aspects of collaboration, which can be considered from many directions to allow us to focus on particular aspects of the collaboration story. For example, in order to build up a picture that focuses specifically on membership of collaborations, the data was reviewed and membership issues and examples extracted. These issues and examples were then grouped into clusters of related ideas. The theoretical elements that emerged were thus based on the issues implied by each of the clusters. Other mechanisms for 'slicing' are also used, but the broad principle remains the same. In the next section, we discuss the overall form of the theory developed.

UNDERSTANDING COLLABORATION PRACTICE:
THEORY DEVELOPMENT

Among the variety of research referred to in the introduction, two approaches in particular seem directed towards describing the practice of collaboration. One of these focuses on describing the collaboration process and conceptualises it in terms of phases in a life cycle. McCann (1984) and Gray (1985; 1989), for example, suggest that a progression through three sequential phases – problem-setting, direction-setting and structuring – is a natural process for collaborations, although this may be subject to interruptions, enhancements or impediments influenced by internal and external forces. Similarly, in the context of strategic alliances, Kanter (1994) argues that successful alliances generally unfold in five overlapping phases: courtship, engagement, housekeeping (in which they discover they have different ideas about how the alliance should operate), bridging, and old marrieds (in which each organisation realises that it has changed as a result of the alliance).

A second common approach is to try to identify attributes, conditions or factors that, if present, will determine the chances that the collaboration will perform well or badly. Some aim to provide relatively comprehensive, multi-dimensional pictures of the factors (see, for example, Doz, 1994; Faulkener, 1995; Gray, 1985; Kanter, 1994; Lorange and Roos, 1993; Long and Arnold, 1995; Pearce, 1997; Sink, 1996). Some authors have even gone so far as to present a ranked list of 'success factors'. Among the attributes, conditions or factors which are seen to contribute to good performance are inclusion of stakeholders, partner selection, mutual trust, consistency of position, shared vision, concrete goals, mutual interdependence of members, open communication, appropriate distribution of power, political influence, appropriate governance structure, and skilled convenors. Poor performance factors include personal agendas and individual egos, politicking, bridging work and social sectors, geographical distances, and cultural differences. Other researchers have devoted their attention more narrowly to in-depth investigations of the role of one particular factor in achieving successful collaboration. A great deal of effort, for example, appears to have been devoted to investigating the role of trust and of national culture in collaboration (see, for example, Barney and Hansen, 1994; Calton and Lad, 1995; Gill and Butler, 1996; Lyson and Mehta, 1996; McCalman, 1996; Pothukuchi and Park, 1996; Ring, 1997). A host of other factors, too numerous to mention in detail, have also been researched. Exactly what constitutes success or good performance is matter of research effort in own right (Cropper, 1996; Glaister and Buckley, 1998; Gray, 1996; 1997 and Pearce, 1997).

While some of this research is superficial or very narrowly focused, many researchers have provided descriptions of the processes and factors that provide rich pictures of the subtleties of the reality of collaboration practice in the area of focus. Taken together, the output from all of this work provides a broad and deep understanding about what environmental factors and what participant behaviour influence the chances that a collaboration either will be a positive experience and make a positive impact or else will regress into a state of collaborative inertia. As a whole, the research demonstrates that these performance factors are extremely complex under the surface.

Taking account of the above research, we have approached theory-building in a slightly different fashion. We have been concerned to build a holistic picture of collaboration practice that will be recognisable by practitioners and also capture the complexity implied above. The way in which we have developed this picture has been heavily influenced by the data collection processes described in the last section.

The starting point for this picture has been the identification of issues that are perceived by practitioners to cause anxiety or reward in collaboration. As a first stage in most of our interventions, interviews or group exercises have been used to collect individuals' views and experiences of collaboration. The points raised by participants have been grouped into clusters of like ideas and each cluster given a label by them. While some of these clusters are context-specific, many are raised repeatedly by every group. We refer to these as themes in collaborative practice (Huxham and Vangen, 1996a, b). The themes represent practitioners' 'first thoughts', sparked by very general questions. They are, however, a valuable indicator of their concerns. The themes appearing most frequently are: common aims; communication; commitment and determination; compromise; appropriate working processes; accountability; democracy and equality; resources; trust; and power.

Although there is a degree of congruence between these theme labels and performance factors identified by other researchers, the particular way in which they represent collaboration practice explicitly derives from a practitioner perspective. We have taken these theme headings to be our agenda for more detailed research. By considering the data pool referred to in the last section, we have begun to build up a picture of the interrelated issues that underlie each theme heading. We have thus begun to develop a deeper understanding of the nature of the themes in general. A number of general conclusions emerge from this:

1. When stimulated to do so, most practitioners who have experienced collaboration can articulate the problems that they have faced and identify factors that 'ought to' make it work better. Typically they express the latter as 'if only' wish lists or highly prescriptive 'you must' lists, for example: 'If only we could get down to agreeing on what we are aiming for in this collaboration…,' or 'You must have a clear and agreed aim…'

2. The deeper analysis of the data has revealed that the issues underlying the themes are less straightforward in a number of respects than these initial practitioner views would suggest:

    (a) Individuals often address an issue from a variety of angles, so the collective picture can be quite complex. For example, while some practitioners express views about democracy and equality from the perspective of inclusion of those with a stake in the issue, others express concerns for democratic discussion and yet others focus on accountability issues.

    (b) The complex picture often actually contradicts the common initial view. For example, through analysis of data about the aims of various parties it has been possible to demonstrate that the motivation of each for involvement in a collaboration is necessarily going to be different from that of the others (Vangen *et al.*, 1994). Thus (in contradiction to the example statements in point 1) any attempt to collaborate which relies upon agreement of a clearly stated aim is highly likely to get into difficulty.

    (c) Many of the wish list items are themselves in tension with each other (Huxham, 1996b). For example the prescription for collaborative groups to be accountable is in tension with the prescription that they need a degree of autonomy; the prescription for strong leadership tends, in practice, to be in tension with the prescription of ensuring that no one dominates.

    (d) Many of the wish list items are difficult to achieve in practice. For example, while the prescription that trust between partners is essential may have some validity, it does not acknowledge the difficulties often inherent in building trust if it does not exist.

    (e) The themes themselves are highly interlinked. For example, issues concerned with perceived power imbalance are clearly related to those of trust. Similarly, issues of democracy in the collaborative process are clearly related to those of commitment to participate, which are in turn related to those of common aims.

3. Since practitioners generally do not conceptualise this complexity, research which is based solely on asking people about their experiences is unlikely to get beyond the superficial picture. The deeper picture can only be gained either by capturing the considerations people make at the point of action and what they actually do or by combining the views, experiences and incidents described by many people.

4. Analysis of the research data has also revealed complexities in dimensions that have not directly emerged from practitioners as themes but which cut across all of them. For example, the analysis of data about membership of community collaborations revealed that they are ill defined, complex and dynamic structures in which it is difficult for participants to agree on who is a member at any point in time, and in which there is little consistency in membership over time (Vangen and Huxham, 1997). This is significant because it impacts upon all of the other factors that make collaboration difficult; for example, continually shifting membership adds another degree of difficulty to the problem of agreeing aims.

Our theory therefore describes collaboration in terms of a framework of theme labels constructed partly out of practitioner perceptions of key issues and partly out of key issues that emerge across the practitioner-generated themes. The intention is to build up a picture, for each theme, of the key issues that underlie the practice of collaboration. This means identifying and clarifying contradictions, tensions and difficulties in each theme area. The issues are viewed not as performance factors, but simply as aspects of the nature of collaboration that may arise and need to be managed. The intention is not to describe specific phases in collaboration (though it explicitly recognises their dynamic nature); rather, the themes are seen as having relevance at all times. The themes are highly interrelated, with issues in each one affecting issues in all of the others. It is not possible to provide detailed illustration of the theory here, but the following extremely brief précis of issues in the 'aims' theme may serve to give a sense of it.

Typical expressions from practitioners (which are mirrored in much of the research literature) on the subject of aims extol the virtues of having: 'common aims'; 'agreed aims'; 'compatible aims'; 'well-defined and tangible purpose'; 'shared vision'; and/or 'shared values'. In contradiction to this, we paint a picture that argues that there *will* be a mass of different aims that individuals and organisations *will* be aiming to pursue through the collaboration, and that many of these will not be obvious because they will form parts of hidden agendas. Tensions arise concerning how far it is wise to bring these out into the open and about the extent to which, and level of detail in which, it is necessary to agree on aims before beginning to take some joint action. The theory recognises that *managing* (rather than agreeing) aims is a central, continuous and inherently difficult aspect of collaboration practice, rather than a precursory task to be got out of the way so that the main business of getting on with the job can be accomplished.

Our theory-building agenda is therefore concerned with further exploration of the issues underlying the themes and, hence, with providing theoretical conceptualisations of collaborative practice which are valid from a perspective both of rigorous research methodology (Eden and Huxham, 1996) and of being meaningful and useful to practitioners. It is fundamental to this approach that the theory must be grounded in action-oriented data (Eden and Huxham, 1996; Glaser and Strauss, 1967), but research output of others can be incorporated to reinforce or question the developing conceptualisation, to suggest new lines of exploration or, where cases are referred to, to act as an additional source of data. To date, a basic level of underlying theory has been captured in all theme areas to a degree that allows a holistic picture of collaboration practice to be elucidated (Huxham and Vangen, 1996a). For some themes, a detailed picture is emerging (Vangen *et al.*, 1994; Vangen and Huxham, 1997), but the theory underlying others is, as yet, underdeveloped.

PRACTISING COLLABORATION UNDERSTANDING: USING DESCRIPTIVE THEORY

The themes-based theory deliberately aims to paint a complex and highly interrelated picture of collaboration, in which there are no simple prescriptions for best practice. We have argued elsewhere (Vangen and Huxham, 1997) that a significant challenge in providing useful support to practitioners involved in collaboration is to find a way to address the tension between practitioners' typically expressed needs for 'simple pictures' and 'quick (directive) fixes' and the frustrations they express when they realise that the quick solutions do not begin to give a handle in helping them to deal with the particular difficulties of their situation.

Our response to this challenge is to argue for a dual approach. One line of attack is to try to find ways to present the complexity that will be instantly meaningful. Our second is to try to find mechanisms which allow practitioners to access the more complex picture only as and when it becomes relevant to their practice; that is, when they are ready to receive it.

Our research demonstrates that it is possible to convey at least an overview of the complex picture in a way that does immediately capture attention. Even though practitioners are not generally able to articulate the complex picture, they do usually recognise it. For example, participants at recent workshops commented that the picture presented by one of the authors was 'horribly real' and 'spot-on – exactly what happens in my area'. Similarly, an article which provides, in straightforward language, an overview of the themes and the tensions underlying them, has been described by the managers of one alliance as 'the best tool so far to help with collaborative practice' (Huxman and Vangen, 1996a). Clearly, the particular language used to present the picture is important, but the use of the practitioner-generated themes, as the mechanism for breaking down the overall picture into manageable though clearly interrelated chunks, also seems critical. Within this framework, the ability to highlight dilemmas that are subtle enough not to be obvious, yet nevertheless derive from real experiences, seems crucially important. It is interesting to note that we are rarely able to gain ownership of the picture from practitioners who have not experienced the pain of collaboration directly.

For those who have experienced the pain, the enlightenment provided by the themes-based theory often appears to be highly empowering. This seems to be not because they immediately have a better sense of how to act, but rather because it clarifies the activity they are involved in, legitimises the pain that they are experiencing and addresses their sense of isolation. Our data suggests that many people involved in collaborations do not recognise these as special organisational forms that are inherently more problematic to manage than their day-to-day activities and hence cannot understand why they are finding the collaborative task so frustratingly difficult to progress. The use of conceptual labels can be helpful in this respect. For example, the director of an alliance commented that 'collaborative inertia *is* a piece of terminology that is instantly recognised by any group I talk to'.

Our attempts to find ways to allow practitioners to access a greater level of complexity as and when they need it have, to date, borne less fruit. Clearly, if we – or anyone else with a ready grasp of the theory – can be involved as 'consultants' or 'facilitators' it is possible for us to inject whatever aspect is needed at the appropriate moment. In effect, therefore, the challenge that we have tried to address is how to develop an 'expert system' that can produce informative theory at the point of need. Design principles for such a mechanism have been developed, but are beyond the scope of this chapter.

PRACTISING COLLABORATION UNDERSTANDING: FROM DESCRIPTION TO PRESCRIPTION

We have fairly clear evidence from practitioner response that the theme-based theory has value, at least to some practitioners, simply through increasing awareness and relieving pain and isolation. However, to be really useful, the theory needs to be able to inform action. Although descriptive, the theory does indeed imply managerial action, though by its very nature the theory will never produce highly prescriptive recommendations. Instead, prescription comes through identification of areas in which careful management is needed and in which it will be necessary to weigh up tensions and to nurture implementation of chosen courses of action. Philosophically, the theory leaves the user to design his or her own courses of action, while recognising that he or she may need facilitative help to do that. Where we have needed to write in a more prescriptive style, and indeed when we have been asked for advice, our aim has been to present this in ways which reflect the complexity and tension in the themes. By way of illustration, the following extract is from a chapter in a handbook for voluntary sector managers:

> If you are feeling vulnerable, it is worth remembering that the apparently powerful organisations would probably not be wanting to collaborate with you if you did not have something to offer over and above what they can provide themselves. If you can identify what this is, it can put you in a good negotiating position. On the other hand, if you are collaborating with organisations which are smaller than yours, it is worth remembering that they may be feeling much more vulnerable than you at first imagine. If you wish the partnership to be on roughly equal terms, you may need to find ways to demonstrate this to them. Paying attention to communication and especially to careful use of language is essential. (Huxham and Vangen, 1996b: 12)

A recent request (which could not be thwarted!) to provide 'top ten tips for collaborators' resulted in the following, derived directly from the theme-based theory:

1. Don't do it unless you have to! Joint working with other organisations is inherently difficult and resource-consuming. Unless you can see the

potential for real collaborative advantage (that is, that you can achieve something really worthwhile that you couldn't otherwise achieve) it's most efficient to do it on your own.

But if you do decide to go ahead.

2. Budget a great deal more time for the collaborative activities than you would normally expect to need.
3. Don't set up an alliance and then delegate the task of making it work to junior staff. Alliances need to be continuously nurtured by you or your most able and committed staff.
4. Remember that the other organisations involved are unlikely to want to achieve exactly the same thing as you and make allowances. Be prepared to compromise.
5. Try to begin by setting yourselves some small, achievable tasks. Build up mutual trust gradually through achieving mutual small wins.
6. Pay attention to communication. Be aware of your own company jargon and professional jargon and try to find clear ways to express yourself to others who do not share your daily world. If partners speak in ways that do not make sense, don't be afraid to seek clarification.
7. Don't expect other organisations to do things the same way you do. Things which may be easy to do in your organisation may require major political manoeuvring in another.
8. Ensure that those who have to manage the alliance are sufficiently briefed to be able to act with a high degree of autonomy. They need to be able to react quickly and contingently without having to check back to the 'parent' organisations.
9. Recognise that power plays are often a part of the negotiation process. Both understanding your own source of power and ensuring that partners do not feel vulnerable can be a valuable part of building trust.

In summary:

10. Always be sensitive to the needs of, and constraints on, your partner. Then, with commitment, determination, and stamina, you can achieve collaborative advantage.

Though hugely constrained in format and produced in a very short space of time, they do represent a reasonable reflection of the themes. It would be interesting to know what ten tips other theoretical approaches would generate.

References

BANXIA (1996) *Decision explorer user guide*. Banxia Software, Glasgow.

BARNEY, J. and HANSEN, M. (1994) Trustworthiness as a source of competitive advantage. *Strategic Management Journal*, *15*, 175–90.

BAUMHAUER, C. and NAULLEAU, G. (1997) A new theoretical and managerial perspective on collaboration dynamics and inertia. Presented at the Fourth International Conference on Multi-Organisational Partnerships and Cooperative Strategy at Oxford University, July.

BERGQUIST, W., BETWEE, J. and MEUEL, D. (1995) *Building Strategic Relationships*. Jossey Bass, San Francisco.

BURELL, G. and MORGAN, G. (1997) *Sociological Paradigms and Organisational Analysis*. Heinemann, London.

CALTON, J. and LAD, L. (1995) Social contracting as a trust-building process of network governance. *Business Ethics Quarterly*, *12*, 15–27.

CROPPER, S. (1996) Collaborative working and the issue of sustainability. In Huxham, C. (ed.), *Creating Collaborative Advantage*. Sage, London, 80–100.

DOZ, Y. (1994) Partnerships in Europe. In de Witt, B. and Meyer, R. (eds), *Strategy: Process, Content and Context*. West, Minneapolis, 213–31.

EDEN, C. and HUXHAM, C. (1996) Action research for the study of organizations. In Clegg, S., Hardy, C. and Nord, W. (eds), *Handbook of Organisation Studies*. Sage, London, 526–42.

FAULKENER, D. (1995) *Strategic Alliances: Co-operating to Compete*. McGraw-Hill, London.

GILL, J. and BUTLER, R. (1996) Cycles of trust and distrust in joint-ventures. *European Management Journal*, *14* (1), 81–9.

GLAISTER, K. and BUCKLEY, P. (1998) Measures of performance in UK international alliances. *Organization Studies*, *19* (1), 89–118.

GLASER, B. and STRAUSS, A. (1967) *The Discovery of Grounded Theory*. Aldine, Chicago.

GRAY, B. (1985) Conditions facilitating interorganizational collaboration. *Human Relations*, *38*, 911–36.

GRAY, B. (1989) *Collaborating. Finding Common Ground for Multi-party Problems*. Jossey Bass, San Francisco.

GRAY, B. (1996) Cross sectoral partners: collaborative alliances among business, government, and communities. In Huxham, C. (ed.), *Creating Collaborative Advantage*. Sage, London, 57–79.

GRAY, B. (1997) Assessing interorganizational collaboration: multiple conceptions and multiple methods. Paper presented at the Fourth Annual Conference on Multi-organisational Partnerships and Co-operative Strategy at Oxford University, July.

GRAY, B. and WOOD, D. (1991) Collaborative alliances: moving from practice to theory. *Journal of Applied Behavioral Science*, *27* (1), 3–22.

HASTING, A., McARTHUR, A. and McGREGOR, A. (1996) Less than equal? Community organisations and estate regeneration partnerships. Policy Press, Bristol.

HIMMELMAN, A. (1996) On the theory and practice of transformational collaboration: from social service to social justice. In Huxham, C. (ed.), *Creating Collaborative Advantage*. Sage, London, 19–43.

HUXHAM, C. (1993) Collaborative capability: an intra-organisational perspective on collaborative advantage. *Public Money and Management, 12*, July–Sept, 21–8.

HUXHAM, C. (1996a) Collaboration and collaborative advantage. In Huxham, C. (ed.), *Creating Collaborative Advantage*. Sage, London, 1–18.

HUXHAM, C. (1996b) Advantage or inertia: making collaboration work. In Paton, R., Clark, G., Jones, G., Lewis, J. and Quintas, P. (eds), *The New Management Reader*. Routledge, London, 238–54.

HUXHAM, C. and CROPPER, S. (1997) Integrating research and practice in interorganizational collaboration. Workshop presentation, annual meeting of the Academy of Management, Boston, MA, August.

HUXHAM, C. and VANGEN, S. (1996a) Working together: key themes in the management of relationships between public and non-profit organisations. *International Journal of Public Sector Management, 9*, 5–17.

HUXHAM, C. and VANGEN, S. (1996b) Managing inter-organizational relationships. In Osborne, S. (ed.), *Managing in the Voluntary Sector*. International Thompson Business Press, London.

INKPEN, A. and BEAMISH, P. (1997) Knowledge, bargaining power and the instability of international joint ventures. *Academy of Management Review, 40* (1), 177–202.

KANTER, R. M. (1994) Collaborative advantage: successful partnerships manage the relationship, not just the deal. *Harvard Business Review*, July–August, *72*, 96–108.

LAMMING, R. (1993) *Beyond Partnership: Strategies for Innovation and Lean Supply*. Prentice-Hall, London.

LEWIS, J. (1990) *Partnerships for Profit: Structuring and Managing of Strategic Alliances*. Free Press, New York.

LONG, F. and ARNOLD, M. (1995) *The Power of Environmental Partnerships*. Dryden Press, Fort Worth, TX.

LORANGE, P. and ROOS, J. (1993) *Strategic Alliances: Formation, Implementation, and Evolution*. Blackwell, Oxford.

LOWNDES, V. (1997) Change in public service management: new institutions and new managerial regimes. *Local Government Studies, 23* (2), 42–66.

LYNCH, R. (1993) *Business Alliance Guide: The Hidden Competitive Weapon*. Wiley, New York.

LYSON, B. and MEHTA, J. (1996) Contract, opportunism, and trust: self-interest and social orientation. Paper written for the ESRC Contracts and Competition Research Programme. University of East Anglia, Norwich.

McCALMAN, J. (1996) Lateral hierarchy: the case of cross cultural management teams. *European Management Journal, 14* (5), 509–17.

McCANN, J. (1984) Design guidelines for problem solving interventions. *Journal of Applied Behavioral Science, 19*, 177–92.

MEDCOF, J. (1997) Why too many alliances end in divorce. *Long Range Planning, 30*, 718–32.

MESCHI, P.X. (1997) Longevity and cultural differences of international joint ventures: toward time-based cultural management. *Human Relations, 50*, 211–28.

OHMAE, K. (1993) The global logic of alliances. In Bleeke, J. and Ernst, D. (eds), *Collaborating to Compete: Using Strategic Alliances and Acquisitions in the Global Marketplace*. Wiley, Chichester, 35–54.

PAINTER, C., ISAAC-HENRY, K. and ROUSE, J. (1997) Local authorities and non-elected agencies: strategic responses and organizational networks. *Public Administration, 75,* 225–45.

PEARCE, R. (1997) Towards understanding joint venture performance and survival: a bargaining and influence approach to transaction cost theory. *Academy of Management Review, 22* (1), 203–25.

POTHUKUCHI, V. and PARK, S. (1996) The influence of culture in cross-border alliances. Paper presented at the annual meeting of the Academy of Management, Cincinnati.

RING, P. (1997) Process facilitating reliance on trust in interorganizational networks. In Ebers, M. (ed.), *The Formation of Inter-organizational Networks.* Oxford University Press, 106–21.

SINK, D. (1996) Five obstacles to community-based collaboration and some thoughts on overcoming them. In Huxham, C. (ed.), *Creating Collaborative Advantage.* Sage, London, 101–9.

TAYLOR, M. (1995) *Unleashing the potential. Bringing residents to the centre of regeneration.* Joseph Rowntree Foundation, York.

TRIST, E.L. (1983) Referent organizations and the development of interorganizational domains. *Human Relations, 36,* 269–84.

TUROCK, I. (1997) *Picking winners or passing the buck: competition in area selection in Scotland's new urban policy.* Scottish Council for Voluntary Organisations, Edinburgh.

VANGEN, S. and HUXHAM, C. (1997) Creating a TIP: issues in the design of a process for transferring theoretical insight about inter-organisational collaboration into practice. In Montanheiro, L., Heigh R. and Morris, D. (eds), *Understanding Public and Private Partnership.* SHU Press, Sheffield, 25–31.

VANGEN, S., HUXHAM, C. and EDEN, C. (1994) Performance measures for collaborative activity. Presented to the annual conference of the British Academy of Management, Lancaster University, September.

WEBB, A. (1991) Co-ordination: a problem in public sector management. *Policy and Politics, 19,* 229–41.

WISTOW, G. and HARDY, B. (1991) Joint management in community care. *Journal of Management in Medicine, 5,* 40–8.

WOOD, D. and GRAY, B. (1991) Towards a comprehensive theory of collaboration. *Journal of Applied Behavioral Science, 27* (2), 139–62.

2 Managing Strategic Alliances' Success: Determining the Influencing Factors of Intent within Partnerships

Jan Stiles

INTRODUCTION

Collaborative partnership as a form of business operation has increased rapidly in recent years. Estimates of the annual growth in the early 1990s averaged between 27 and 30 per cent for industrialised countries (Anderson, 1990; Bleeke and Ernst, 1991). This surge in interest has been fuelled by a number of factors. Increasing levels of competition, the emergence of new markets, technological developments, and the maturity and homogenisation of markets have all helped to push back industrial boundaries and have facilitated globalisation of markets. Within this new and volatile environment, collaboration can offer a low-cost and flexible opportunity for an organisation to maintain, or improve, its competitive position. It can also facilitate multiple options to be explored as opposed to the high cost and restrictions of an acquisition or merger (Doz, 1992).

As the concept of partnering has developed, partnerships have grown to become increasingly complex, frequently resulting in multiple collaborative networks with both vertical and horizontal links (Faulkener, 1992; Hamel, 1990; Harrigan, 1986; Wheatcroft and Lipman, 1990). Many businesses now perceive collaborative ventures as critical in their plans to establish strategic business networks and as valuable strategic weapons with which to do battle in the increasingly competitive business environment (Geringer, 1991; Joynt, 1990; Lei and Slocum, 1992; Lei, 1993; Takec and Singh, 1992).

Definitions of strategic alliances are varied. An alliance may be seen as the 'joining of forces and resources, for a specified or indefinite period, to achieve a common objective' (Takec and Singh, 1992). This definition

17

reflects the traditional view of partnerships being based upon creating value for the participant firms. Other definitions, however, identify a more competitive aspect to the relationship. Lei and Slocum (1992) define alliances as 'co-alignments between two or more forms in which the partners hope to learn and acquire from each other the technologies, products, skills and knowledge that are not otherwise available to their competitors'. For the purposes of this chapter the following definition of strategic alliances is used:

> *Coalitions between two or more firms, either formal or informal, that share compatible goals, acknowledge a high level of mutual interdependence, involve partial or contractual ownership, and which are formed for strategic reasons.*

COOPERATIVE ASPECTS OF STRATEGIC ALLIANCES

Some of the benefits that may be attributed to a partner relationship stem from the pooling of resources and/or capabilities, and the mutual dependence aspects of the relationship, which can be used for strategic advantage (Lorange and Roos, 1992; Lynch, 1990; Mohr and Nevin, 1990; Mohr and Spekman, 1994). Further, depreciation of resources and capabilities over time may result in an individual firm's competitive advantage, and its consequent returns, being eroded. Cooperation can then provide the opportunity to upgrade both firms' positions, comparatively more rapidly than could be achieved individually, through the pooling of their resources and capabilities (Grant, 1991). It has been argued that this pooling can result potentially in a greater degree of benefit than the proportional apportionment. Inter-organisational cooperation can also result in a reduction in transaction costs and therefore enable competitive advantage through increased economic efficiency (Hennart, 1988; Kogut, 1988; Williamson, 1975). These costs may include financial costs, but also extend to non-financial costs such as the loss of specific knowledge, and costs associated with uncertainty, or supplier/buyer power. Cooperative partnerships may, therefore, be seen as providing protection or security to firms where the option of using the market system is viewed as a high-risk solution and therefore a problematic one.

An alliance partnership can also allow a firm to effectively replicate a particular process within the partner firm and thus efficiently transfer know-how, which may be otherwise encumbered by the hazards which surround the pricing of information (Kogut, 1988). The advantages associated with this stem from the expanded market/capacity/efficiency potential which an alliance partnership can offer once both firms involved gain the benefits associated with the particular process which has been transferred (Berg *et al.*, 1988; Kogut, 1988; Mohr and Spekman, 1994). From this perspective it may be argued that strategic alliances designed to exploit each player's unique characteristics to maximum effect will produce the greatest competitive advantage (Grant, 1991).

INTERNALLY COMPETITIVE ASPECTS OF STRATEGIC ALLIANCES

The concept of skill-building as an explicit goal can, however, also be viewed from a competitive perspective. The subsequent loss of the core competence or capabilities which provide a firm with its individual competitive advantage can result eventually in the removal of the reason behind the partnership, and in termination of the relationship (Hamel, 1990; Hamel, 1991; Lyons, 1991). It may further result in a loss of market positioning for the weaker firm, as the stronger partner uses the skills and/or resources appropriated from its partner to advance its position (Badaracco, 1991; Hamel, 1990; Hamel, 1991). Competitive tactics used by a partner firm can also induce a level of dependency in a weaker firm. This can skew influence and control within the relationship and is often a precursor to a merger or acquisition attempt by the dominant player (Devlin and Bleackley, 1988; Hamel, 1990; Hamel, 1991; Lyons, 1991).

The strategic alliance relationship may encourage a partner firm to concentrate its resources on a specific aspect of production, with an effective 'de-skilling' of competencies or processes crucial to the overall process. This can create an external dependence for such things as components, supplies, designs, skills and technologies (Lei and Slocum, 1992). While the alliance partnership continues, this dependency can encourage distortions in the control of the partnership and may again speed the decline and possible takeover of the partnership by the dominant party (Hamel, 1990; Hamel, 1991; Lorange and Roos, 1992; Lorange *et al.*, 1992; Lynch, 1991). As explicit competition within the market is reduced through alliance formation, 'development inertia' can also infest the industry as lower levels of competition in the market reduce the incentive for innovation (Lei and Slocum, 1992). Thus the implicit impact of the alliance partnership may be evidenced in generally lower development aspects within the industry. The ultimate implications of this may be a reduction in the ability to prolong the product's life cycle within the industry, or restrictions in the development of a new product life cycle prior to decline.

Finally, the alliance relationship may result in a means of more accurately calibrating a partner's strengths and weaknesses than would otherwise be possible. As a consequence the competitive risk in future collisions with the partner may be significantly altered. In this respect the alliance may, again, be viewed as an internally competitive tool rather than a cooperative one.

Thus the cooperative and competitive aspects of the strategic alliance can have major implications both for the individual partners and for the future of the alliance relationship. From the cooperative perspective they can facilitate rapid upgrade in resources and create synergistic benefits from the pooling of resources and/or capabilities. They can also help to reduce costs and encourage efficiency through the transfer of knowledge and capabilities, which might otherwise not be effectively transferable through the market system. From the competitive perspective, however, the alliance may result in a loss of core competencies and capabilities, encourage alliance dependency and loss of control, and introduce a form of development inertia into the industry. This may ultimately have implications for the potential life cycle and for the balance of future competition within the industry.

The influence of these different perspectives can have significant implications for firms considering entering a partnership. As Lei and Slocum (1992) state, 'although collaboration and competition do go hand-in-hand, how managers approach this duality can significantly affect the firm's propensity for learning and developing new skills'. The cooperative–competitive distinction does not, therefore, necessarily denote alternative forms of alliance arrangements. It may be argued that it simply reflects different combinations of alliance 'drivers' by each participating firm, and the consequent motivational differences that these induce. Thus it may be argued that although cooperative and competitive intents or abilities may coexist for each partner within a relationship, how these are emphasised or operationalised together will dictate the overall potential and character the alliance will ultimately adopt. It is therefore important to examine these two perspectives further to try to develop a better understanding of what characteristics of the firm or the particular relationship can influence the degree of cooperative and/or competitive intent within a partnership.

A FRAMEWORK FOR UNDERSTANDING COMPETITIVE/COOPERATIVE INTENT

Previous research on alliances has tended to bias investigations towards either the cooperative or the competitive aspects of the phenomenon. It is argued here, however, that prior identification of the factors which influence the degree of competitive and/or cooperative intent in an alliance relationship would enhance understanding of alliance formulation and operation and enable managers to plan their strategic partnerships more effectively.

The resource-based view can be used to provide a theoretical basis for research in this area. Resource-based theory focuses upon the resources and capabilities of the firm as providing the foundation for its long-term strategy (Grant, 1991). An underlying characteristic of this view is that resources and capabilities are heterogeneous, and as a consequence of this each firm develops its own unique character, resulting in sustainable performance differences (Penrose, 1985). This theory usefully draws upon transaction cost theory by considering the alliance in terms of transaction options. Further, econometric studies appear to support the theory that firm-specific resources and capabilities act as a driving force for the firm's diversification strategy, as it underlines the firm's emphasis on growth in its attempts to transfer intangible capital among related activities. It has, therefore, a recognised application to alliance operations as a key diversification and/or growth strategy that provides a contribution not only to the formation process but also throughout the continuing process of the alliance relationship (Mahoney and Pandian, 1992), thus incorporating the ability to compliment the dynamic element, which characterises this form of business operation. A further strength of this paradigm is its ability also to fit comfortably within the context of organisational economics while remaining complementary to industrial organisation theory, thus providing a unifying theory within business management research. Finally, the theory appears to provide an unbiased basis from which to view the cooperative/ competitive aspects of intent. It may be suggested, therefore, that resource-based theory can help to provide further insights relevant to this form of investigation.

Previous research suggests certain factors likely to influence the extent to which firms adopt a cooperative and/or a competitive intent. Four factors are considered in this chapter.

The Level of Mobility

The level of mobility of the key resources and/or capabilities of the firm from one partner to the other may be seen as a factor influencing intent within a strategic partnership. Not all resources are easily or equally transferable (Grant, 1991; Peteraf, 1993). At one extreme mobility may be high; at the other extreme, such things as 'tacit' knowledge, encompassing such aspects as specific market knowledge, skills, and experience of operations, may prove much more difficult to transfer (Hennart, 1988; Kogut, 1988; Teece, 1986). Thus the 'capture' of some key capabilities or resources can prove more difficult than others, and may necessitate the transfer of key personnel with the implicit knowledge required. It may be argued, therefore, that the level of mobility of a partner's key resources or capabilities may have an influence upon the intent with which a firm enters an alliance partnership. This suggests a research question around the mobility factor considering:

Research Question 1   To what extent does the mobility of the resources or competencies of a partner firm key to the relationship influence the cooperative or competitive emphasis within the intent of an entrant firm?

The Level of Imitability

Where the key resources and/or capabilities of a partner firm are perceived as highly immobile, an alternative approach may be to adopt a policy of replication or imitation (Grant, 1991). However, the emphasis upon this approach will be significantly influenced by the cost/benefit involved – in both financial and temporal terms. It may also be influenced by the ease of imitation, as some capabilities are more easily imitated than others, particularly those based upon highly complex organisational routines or those fused into the firm's corporate culture. Where there are many obstacles or a high cost associated with imitation it may be argued that firms will be less likely to enter a partnership with a competitive intent. The research question associated with this aspect is, therefore:

Research Question 2   To what extent does the ease of imitability of key resources or capabilities of a partner firm influence the competitive and/or cooperative intent of an entrant firm?

The Level of Uniqueness

It has been argued previously that all resources and capabilities are, to varying extents, unique, in that the productive values of the resources and capabilities are basically heterogeneous. This heterogeneity can result in varying levels of efficiency, superiority and utility for the firm concerned (Barney, 1991; Penrose, 1985; Peteraf, 1993). As superior resources are also limited in supply, this level of uniqueness can act as a driving force for alliance partnerships, because the more unique a key capability or resource appears to be, the more value it is likely to add (Mahoney and Pandian, 1992; Peteraf, 1993). It may, therefore, be suggested that the level of uniqueness must have an influence upon the intent with which firms enter and operate an alliance partnership. Thus a further research question stemming from this is:

Research Question 3   To what extent does the level of uniqueness of key resources or capabilities of a partner firm influence the intent with which the entrant firm enters and operates within the alliance partnership?

Value to the Partner Firm

The concept of value needs, however, to be considered further. Although the resources and capabilities have a value, different values may be implied for the same capabilities and resources between different firms. This may be due to the different supporting resources of an individual firm. It may also stem from the different forms and ways in which these resources or capabilities may be applied by an individual firm. Differences will, therefore, exist in the perceived value to be gained from acquisition of a particular resource or capability (Hennart, 1988; Peteraf, 1988). This value may be measured in terms of current or long-term sustainable value (Grant, 1991). It may, therefore, be suggested that a further question in respect of this research is:

Research Question 4   To what extent will the perceived value of a partner firm's key resources and capabilities induce a competitive or a cooperative intent on the part of an entrant firm?

The four key factors above appear to encompass the main aspects, which influence the cooperative/competitive intent of an entrant firm. However it may be argued that these simply form a theoretical intent. Previous literature on alliances also suggests that in order for the identified intent to be realised an additional four factors require consideration; these are:

The Level of Transparency of the Partner Firm

The extent to which a partner firm allows the entrant firm access to its key resources or capabilities has been defined as 'transparency' (Grant, 1991; Hamel, 1990; Hamel, 1991). There has to be a degree of sharing in any partnership, even those who are characteristically protective need to offer enough to provide an incentive for the partnership to occur. However, the level of openness assumed by each partner may differ. Where the level of transparency is high, because of either agreement, ineptitude or inability by the partner firm to protect itself, access to information and information sharing is relatively straightforward. In consequence a higher transfer of skills or competencies than was either agreed or wanted may occur (Hamel, 1990). On the other hand, where access is very restricted, either because of deliberate mistrust of the partner firm or because of environmental restrictions such as regulatory barriers or political disagreement, transference of even highly valued or imitable skills may prove problematic to the entrant firm. In consequence a further question, which may be posed, is:

Research Question 5   To what extent does the level of transparency of a partner firm support the competitive or cooperative intent of an entrant firm?

The Level of Complexity

The level of complexity or involvement by one partner with another can vary significantly. At one extreme, partnerships may be simple marketing agreements which operate at arm's length with little additional involvement between the two parties concerned, while at the other extreme the partners may be tied firmly together in a wide-ranging alliance or joint venture with possibly cross-equity investment, a sharing of resources, functions and interlinking systems. The latter form of partnership can impose a high level of interdependence within the relationship, thus making it more difficult for either partner to terminate the arrangement (Stiles, 1994). Additionally, many organisations today may be part of a larger, highly complex multiple systems or 'spider's webs' of alliances (Faulkener, 1992; Harrigan, 1986). In this respect firms may be tied not only to the direct partner but also to a larger network the departure from which could result in significant losses. In these circumstances the level of complexity may be seen as influencing the behaviour of the partnership. As such, a further research question to consider is:

Research Question 6   To what extent does the complexity of the alliance influence the pursuit of a cooperative or competitive intent by the entrant firm?

The Level of Cultural Compatibility

Cultural differences have been noted in the past as being one of the major reasons why partnerships disintegrate (Alcar Group, 1988). Different ways of working, different systems and approaches, and different perspectives can all create tensions within an alliance and add to the complex management issues this type of organisational arrangement can induce. Where cultural dissimilarities exist in either a corporate or a national context it may be argued that partner firms will be less likely to feel committed to ensuring the partnership continues and may, therefore, be encouraged to take the opportunity to adopt a value appropriation view to the partnership. In contrast, where a high level of cultural compatibility exists commitment to the partnership is likely to be high and a long-term relationship, encouraging a cooperative emphasis, is more likely to be preferred. This may be considered in respect of the research as:

Research Question 7 To what extent does the cultural compatibility of the partners encourage a more cooperative or a more competitive view of the relationship?

The Level of Experience

As experience of working within the alliance develops, confidence tends to increase, as do the particular skills and flexibility necessary to influence and manipulate the relationship. Previous research has also revealed that this has a direct and positive effect upon the success rate of the venture (Pekar and Allio, 1994). In comparison, relatively inexperienced firms demonstrate weak alliance strategy development (Pekar and Allio, 1994). It may therefore be suggested that as firms develop their expertise and management skills in alliance partnerships this increases their abilities and success rates in this form of operation. It may be further argued that this level of experience is therefore an influencing factor in the extent to which firms are able to drive a competitive intent within the relationship. In terms of the research it is therefore important to consider:

Research Question 8 To what extent does the level of experience of partnering relationships influence the ability of an entrant firm to exercise a competitive rather than a cooperative intent?

RESEARCH AREA

The service sector was initially chosen as the focus for the research. This sector has recently seen significant and growing importance within industrial economies (Jones, 1989). Strategic alliances in this sector also appear to be increasing and are expected to remain an important factor in this sector in the foreseeable future (Segal-Horn, 1989; Goodman, 1990). The majority of analytical frameworks used to develop understanding of managerial decision-making and capabilities have been based upon consideration and an analysis of data collected from the manufacturing sector (Campbell and Verbeke, 1994). Additionally, service sector firms have different characteristics with different patterns of organisational restructuring evident in their metamorphosis in comparison with manufacturing organisations (Campbell and Verbeke, 1994). It may therefore be argued that the key factors and challenges facing organisations of these types need to be addressed on a separate basis from those researched in more traditional manufacturing firms. It therefore seems to be both appropriate and of significance to focus upon applying the research question to firms within this sector

In determining a specific subgroup for the research an initial distinction was made between those services which are naturally networked and those which are proximity-based. The concept of the networked organisation related to those service firms which can rely primarily upon use of a network regardless of their individual geographical proximity to the point of sale in providing their particular service. In contrast, however, for those firms which still have a need to be proximity-based, that is, those for which a network may provide some secondary benefit, the primary need for the service is to remain at the point of sale. Consequently, for such organisations the ability to create a distance between the provider and the product and therefore bridge this through the use of a partner organisation is still not a realistic option. Thus inseparability in this respect is still fixed.

A further distinction was made between firms, reflecting sole or complete capability of a particular process independent of those around it. Many organisations provide services that may simply be outplacements of an activity which was originally integrated into a parent firm's operations and which may still be tied to that parent operation as part of its integrated solution for its existence. As such, a firm in this situation cannot operate on an independent basis. Depending upon its potential, its bias towards adoption of a flexible or fixed approach will be strongly governed by the parent organisation. An organisation of this type cannot, therefore, be considered an objective example in terms of its ability to select, or enter, a potential strategic relationship. In direct comparison, other organisations may be seen to operate on an independent basis. The choice of customer for these firms will, therefore, be based solely in terms of costs, potential revenues, expectations of future business and long-term strategic objectives.

Networked	Advertising Marketing	Transportation, telecommunications, banking, finance and insurance distance learning education
Proximity-based	Hospital cleaning, laundry, catering, personal services	Retail, medical services local education and welfare, hotels, legal services
	Part of integrated solution	**Sole capability**

Figure 2.1   Classification of sub-groups within service-related industries.

Bringing these four aspects together, the consequent segmentation produced by these four distinctions then provides a clearer focus for the research into service-related industries (see Figure 2.1) On this basis, the industrial groups studied included telecommunications, insurance and airlines, which qualified as being both networked and having sole capability characteristics.

THE RESEARCH METHOD

Existing literature on alliances was initially reviewed to help to advise the research and assist in the formulation of the key research questions outlined earlier. A semi-structured interview framework was then developed from this and, following initial piloting and minor revisions to this, thirty interviews were conducted with key alliance managers in order to gain adequate depth in the study. The interviews were collected over a period of 14 months, each lasting between 2 and 4.5 hours in length. Overall the interviews encompassed consideration of 101 alliance relationships, although each interview focused upon a particular partnership in depth. Where relevant, two managers from the same company involved in a particular alliance attended the interview. Interviewees were selected by key informant technique and were asked to rate themselves on a scale of 1 to 5 in terms of their expertise and ability to respond to the questions on the alliance in order to ensure consistency between the interviews collected.

Interview questions were designed to focus upon the key issues identified in the conceptual framework, some of which were based loosely upon those previously tested for investigation into alliance management by Hamel (1990). Additionally, the questioning allowed the interviewee to include additional comment and information that could advise the study. The overall structure of the interviews included consideration of the following key areas:

- the overall context and goals of the partnership;
- the basis for collaboration;
- the aspects associated with complementarity and bargaining power;
- the form and structure of the alliance partnership;
- the input and output contributions of the partners involved;
- the costs and benefits of the relationship;
- the relation in terms of the competitive/collaborative element;
- the criteria used to measure 'success';
- the anticipated outcomes of the alliance; and
- the past experience of the participating firm in terms of previous partnerships.

THE RESEARCH FINDINGS

Analysis of the interviews showed the following:

The Level of Mobility

It has been assumed in the literature considered earlier in this chapter that certain aspects of the firm such as complex operational experience or processes might be viewed as immobile by the entrant partner and that the concept of partnering may be stimulated by these non-transferrable characteristics. The primary research evidence suggested, however, that in service sector organisations technological and skills development are not viewed as a major hurdle or a major stimulus to partnering unless the industry is experiencing significant levels of technological speed and/or uncertainty. Rather, the key motivating factor for partnering in service industries relates to the other identified need to create a defence from competition by gaining market presence, specific market knowledge and market share and to leapfrog political barriers. Technical and skills transfer, and product development, can then in the more productive relationships provide additional synergies, as illustrated in the following quotation taken from one of the airline industry players interviewed: 'We started with route cooperation then used each other's systems more. Later came code sharing and handling facilities.'

A number of key characteristics of mobility were identified which largely agreed with current literature. Where a partner firm's resources and/or capabilities were viewed as key to a relationship by the entrant firm, and were mobile without undue cost or difficulty, evidence suggested that this was likely to emphasise a more competitive approach to the relationship by the entrant firm. This was providing no additional, immobile key factors existed, as the following statement from the interview data illustrates: 'It happens often that they will take our skills and competencies; fine – we also enter partnerships to gain insurance skills and competencies to compete independently.'

It was also found that in these circumstances the relationship was likely to move towards acquisition or termination within a given period. However, where immobile key factors existed in part, these tended to act as a barrier to the competitive approach and could engender a more stable, cooperative and synergistic characteristic to the partnership. This appeared to be the most common occurrence for partnerships in this sector, as the following statement demonstrates: 'The key strength for us is that they [the partner] have the graphics needed for the project.'

Where all key factors were wholly immobile the relationship tended to continue to operate on a cooperative level. Evidence from the research suggested, however, that further synergistic development outside joint product development appeared to be limited in these cases. Further, the high degree of immobility within the relationship influenced continuation of the partnership as long as the environmental and technological conditions, alongside existing customer demand or potential customer need, existed for the joint product or service offering involved. However, where acquisition of a key resource and/or capability was the ultimate intent of a partner, but was obstructed because of a lack of mobility, and where no other factors were viewed as key, or where the key objectives for the partnership became obsolete, the relationship was likely to terminate through either dissolution or acquisition.

In relation to 'research question 1' posed above, it may, therefore, be suggested that the mobility of the resources or competencies of a partner firm key to the relationship does significantly influence the cooperative and the competitive emphasis within the intent of the entrant firm. However, the extent to which this occurs will be influenced by the complexity and rate of development of the technological environment and the particular dynamics and characteristics of the industry.

The Level of Imitability

Previous literature suggested that the level of imitability of key skills and capabilities of a partner firm could influence intent to compete internally within a relationship by the entrant partner. This occurs where the key skills and competencies, which are core to the partnership, are not complex, fused to the corporate culture or of prohibitive cost to transfer. Alternatively, where these barriers occur this would be a factor in encouraging a more cooperative approach to the partnership.

Initial evidence from the population sample suggested that of the above factors noted, where mobility was assumed to be problematic, only that relating to cost appeared to be significant in determining a competitive/cooperative intent in terms of imitability. Further influences noted including speed and the extent of change and influence of the competitive environment, the need for cultural understanding and consequent reputation of a local partner, while to a lesser extent exchanged equity investment between the two partners also appeared to be significant.

Further analysis of the data also suggested that the characteristics of the imitability factor could not be considered as an independent influence in isolation but were strongly related to, and mirrored, those of mobility. It may be argued, therefore, that imitability may be seen as a more externally oriented extension of the mobility factor, and that these aspects together act as, or are part of, the same continuum of influence, condoning or reinforcing the cooperative/competitive emphasis. Thus complexity of process and fusion to the corporate culture are internal aspects, which, although not considered by respondents in terms of imitation alone, may be part of the influence upon responses to the overall mobility/imitability question.

Where a key objective identified within a partnership was viewed as immobile, imitation could occur where low cost and relative ease in relation to the dynamics of the competitive environment allowed. Where this was possible and no other immobile objectives were key to the partnership, this did appear to encourage a competitive approach to the relationship, as the respondents in this category indicated that this preceded either the end of the partnership or, in some cases, significant changes to the arrangement. In both cases where this occurred the partnerships were dissolved later, as is illustrated in the following statement from one of the interviews: 'Success is measured in increased number of passenger seats sold. ... We may move away from the partnership if we can pull over a massive demand for seats to the US.'

The most common result, however, was for a mixture of mobile and immobile objectives to remain. In this context partners combined both transfer and imitation to create learning within the relationship. This confirms the argument that a high competitive/high cooperative influence is occurring within the partnership.

In response to 'research question 2' posed above, on imitability, it may therefore be suggested that the ease of imitability of key resources or capabilities of a partner firm does significantly influence the competitive/cooperative intent of an entrant firm. However, this should be viewed as an extension of the mobility factor, rather than an entirely separate variable.

The Level of Uniqueness

The level of uniqueness of a core skill or competence, literature noted earlier in this chapter suggests, can influence a partner to adopt a more cooperative or a more competitive stance in the relationship in response to the risk of losing control or power within the partnership. Analysis of the research data collected in the sample indicated that uniqueness could occur to varying extents within a relationship and was likely to focus on aspects associated with increasing market presence, or skills and technology development. The research also showed that the level of uniqueness of a key objective of an entrant partner would be influenced by a number of different factors, particularly the reputation, size, network involvement and cultural symmetry of a partner firm in addition to the particular type of skills and technology it owns. Thus uniqueness was related to both internal and external characteristics of a partner firm and acted by delimiting the alternative options of an entrant partner, either through the external influence the partner firm had already established or through the internal core competencies it controlled.

Further, from the analysis undertaken, the concept of uniqueness could be seen to act as a contributing element in the creation of a competitive stance within a partner relationship. Where one partner identified a level of uniqueness in the key objective it was pursuing, evidence showed that this was likely to result in a highly competitive approach to the relationship, resulting in a takeover of the partner firm where suitable conditions and financial resources existed to do so. Thus in these circumstances power and control were transferred directly into the hands of the acquiring partner, as is illustrated in the following: 'We were seeking to differentiate. With the Australian partnership they had specific skills we needed. … The owners didn't want to sell out straight away, but agreed that after three years we buy them out. …'

Where a level of uniqueness of objectives existed for both firms, however, evidence indicated that these relationships tended to pursue more stable, long-term approaches to the partnership with no evidence of intent to buy out the partnership and no efforts existent to gain synergies from the relationship. It could fairly be deduced from this that the partnership was viewed as the most appropriate means of operation and provided a positive contribution to both parties. In some cases noted, a highly beneficial partnership was recognised in this respect. Consequently it can be fairly assumed that in this type of situation a level of cooperation occurred in relation to the sharing of the respective skills or resources of the participants, as the following quotation demonstrates: 'Both are equal partners; each had one element which is needed by the other for them to work. This provides a good symmetry – neither is dominant.'

In contrast, where little uniqueness was identified on either side there was an increased likelihood of early termination of the partnership, as the respective partners had less to prevent them from considering alternative relationships.

It is therefore argued that a high level of uniqueness of a resource or capability identified as key by an entrant firm can significantly influence the level of competitive and cooperative activity within the relationship. Where equally significant levels of uniqueness exist on either side it can also encourage stability of the venture, and in that context both a competitive and a cooperative approach may be generated. However, where little uniqueness is identified in respect of the key objectives of either partner there is an increased likelihood that termination or disbandment of the partnership may occur at some stage in the relationship. Consequently, in terms of 'research question 3' posed above, it is argued here that the level of uniqueness of a key resource or capability of a partner firm can influence the cooperative/competitive intent with which the entrant partner enters and operates within an alliance partnership.

The Level of Value

It had been suggested that the value of a key resource or capability of a partner firm would influence the level of competitive and/or cooperative emphasis an entrant firm will place on the relationship, and, further, that this would in itself be influenced by the particular characteristics of the entrant firm and the ability it would have to apply, and thus gain value, from the integration of the key resource or capability into its own organisation.

Analysis of the research data from the survey supported this argument, highlighting an emphasis upon the *relative* value as perceived by the entrant firm in terms of the intent a firm may have to competitively adopt the key skill or competence and integrate this within its own organisation. Limiting factors on a competitive intent in this context for service sector firms appeared to include such aspects as necessary scope, cost, size, speed and handling of regulatory barriers in order to gain the potential benefits that have been identified. These factors also appeared to be stronger in areas associated with the achievement of market presence, including such aspects as the need for market presence, competitive defence, and market size, and were also associated with the development and/or broadening of a product or service. This was likely to relate to the fact that an advantage of a partnership cannot be expected to be limited to a particular relationship, but needed to be extended to the network of partners to which entry into a collaborative venture involves: 'The network we are now in makes us more attractive; this leads to greater value.' This, then, is more difficult to reproduce on an individual basis and therefore tends to promote a more cooperative view of objectives in this area.

Further difficulties where transference of the value of a resource or competence existed related to financial improvement and risk-spreading. In this area, again, the value was likely to relate to the size of the overall partnership and the scope that this resulted in: 'It has cost us very few international customers but we have been able to get a worldwide distributor through [our partner] so this is value-added success around the world.'

In comparison, the value of aspects associated with skills and technology development were considered to be more related to individual, rather than mutual, value added. In this area these factors were viewed as more appropriate for successful transfer and development within an individual firm. This is likely to relate to the lower cost involved and the ability of a partner firm to develop these in an arguably more manageable form. Further, fewer limiting factors had influence here than in wider areas such as market presence. Additionally, value in these terms can act as a secondary value-added activity within the ongoing relationship.

With reference to 'research question 4' posed above, therefore, some slight qualification is required. Consequently it can be stated that the extent of the relative perceived value of a partner firm's key resources and capabilities can contribute towards a competitive or cooperative intent on the part of the entrant firm.

THEORETICALITY TO REALISABILITY

It has been found that the above influences do affect the extent to which a cooperative/competitive intent can be pursued by an entrant partner within a service sector alliance. However, literature reviewed earlier in this chapter has also indicated that this intent cannot be realised without the positive support of four other factors that are now considered.

The Level of Transparency

The level of transparency or openness with which a partner firm allows an entrant firm access to its key skills or competencies, the literature suggests, influences the extent to which the intent of the entrant firm can be realised (Hamel, 1990). The primary research suggested that, in the service sector organisations surveyed, factors influencing transparency were viewed at two distinct levels. These included:

- initial or strategic influences such as the perceived permanence of the partnership;
- the level of trust between the parties involved;
- the extent to which equity investment is exchanged and therefore reinforces the long-term perception of the relationship; and
- the mutual recognition of joint objectives and benefits which can be realised from a level of openness and exchange.

At a more operational level, however, firms had also to provide:

- good communication channels which could be enhanced by regular meetings and discussion;
- staff exchanges; and
- a clearly understood and supportive structure to the partnership.

From the data it appeared that different levels of transparency were identified across the sector, with the majority of firms recognising that the transparency of their partner was as expected. A smaller percentage found that transparency was either higher or lower than they had expected. Overall, firms within the telecommunications sector appeared to consider they had a slightly lower level of transparency from their partners than firms in the other sectors surveyed, as can be illustrated by the following quotation: 'We have generally achieved what we want but it has taken longer than expected to get things up and running. ... There has been a greater need for communication.' This is likely to be a reflection of the competitive dynamics and defensive reactions of firms operating in this sector.

However, according to alliance literature noted earlier in the chapter, transparency is supposed to include consideration of both intended and unintended transfer. Therefore much will depend upon the initial targets or levels of intent established by the entrant partner. Where these are initially relatively conservative or uninformed it may be assumed that the potential for further gains would be higher once the relationship is underway. In contrast, where an entrant partner with ambitious, experienced or challenging expectations of openness of the partner firm exists it is possible that fewer additional unexpected benefits may be realised and, consequently, the level of unintended transfer may be lower. These factors are, however, closely associated with learning and experience, which will be considered later as additional aspects influencing realisability.

Consequently, in terms of 'research question 5' posed above, it is suggested here that the level of transparency of a partner firm can enable the competitive and/or cooperative intent of an entrant partner to realised. However, the extent to which this is seen to occur will depend upon the original expectation level set by the entrant partner

The Level of Complexity

Previous literature had suggested that an increased level of complexity in terms of the linkages it created, either inside the immediate partnership or as part of a network entry, would inhibit a firm from pursuing a competitive, acquisitive approach owing to the cost of disentanglement. From the research it appeared that the level of complexity within a relationship did appear to influence the cooperative and/or competitive realisation of cooperative/competitive intent of an entrant partner. Where little complexity existed, a narrow competitive or cooperative intent did appear to be realised.

Where these established linkages were associated with such aspects as a broader network, specific equity, joint function, training and/or managerial responsibilities, these appeared to emphasise a largely cooperative intent. However, where interlinkages had been established and developed over time, additional competitive *learning* within the relationship could also be enabled through the interaction the linkages create, as can be illustrated by the following quotation from one of the interviewees: 'We catch the synergies – that is, mutual development of IT systems, mutual approach to suppliers … Makes us more attractive, leads to greater value.'

None of the partnerships with significant amounts of linkages in the sample related to those where disbandment following individual acquisition of skills or competencies occurred. It may be suggested, therefore, that an increased amount of complexity does not encourage a purely *value appropriation* approach where termination of the relationship would follow.

With reference to 'research question 6' posed above, in this respect it is therefore suggested that the level of complexity of the alliance arrangement does support the pursuit of a cooperative and/or competitive intent depending upon the extent and type of interlinkages established.

The Level of Cultural Compatibility

The level of cultural compatibility within a partnership had been suggested as an influencer of the extent to which the partners can implement a cooperative and/or competitive intent. From the research investigation it was found that this does appear to occur in the service sector firms included in the survey. Where a high level of compatibility occurred in terms of both national and corporate culture, pursuance of a dynamic, long-term learning or synergistic relationship appeared to be emphasised. In contrast, where little compatibility in these terms existed a competitive/acquisitive or appropriation approach appears to have been preferred, as the following quotation illustrates: 'Culturally [the partners] are very different, we are very conservative. We know there are large cultural differences. The aim is to see about a merger; it is a way of working out if you have a future with another company.'

It is noticeable that for firms who found compatibility in respect of either corporate or national culture problematic, this was due to factors which had influenced the choice they had, rather than to a deliberate mismanagement of the selection process. Factors noted in this respect included the limited options available for, or compatible with partnering, the relative size of a partner, the level at which the agreement was made and the consequent management of this lower down, in addition to geographical focus, language and structural issues.

Where differences were seen to exist in terms of culture, this was viewed as an incentive to acquire the other partner and therefore to either infiltrate or control the partner's culture. Alternatively, for other organisations, training efforts were initiated: 'We incorporate a programme of training to educate the employees on cultural differences – cultural awareness training.' The differences were also viewed by one respondent as a means of broadening the entrant partner's cultural understanding. However, it should be noted that this last approach can be considered relatively high-risk, because the partnership was later disbanded.

In response to 'research question 7' posed earlier, it may therefore be suggested that cultural compatibility of the partners does influence the extent to which a cooperative/competitive intent can be pursued within a partnership.

The Level of Experience

In line with the literature that suggested a link between experience and success in alliance partnerships, an influence did appear to stem from this aspect.

Where entrant firms had significant amounts of experience in similar forms of partnering this did appear to contribute towards a more productive, long-term and/or dynamic relationship. In contrast, where previous experience was significantly limited a more competitive and also in some situations less successful relationship could occur.

Length of experience, however, should not be considered as the only determinant that influences success in this respect. The extent to which the learning of the past had been communicated and used practically in the organisation was also significant and depended upon the type of structure and systems put in place, alongside the deliberate intentions of the organisation to facilitate this. It could also be impacted by the size of the organisation. Where the organisation was relatively small or informal, information transfer appeared to occur more easily than in larger organisations which could lose the learning initiative and revert to a level of reinventing the wheel as each new potential partnership approaches, as the following quotation from one of the interviewees demonstrates: 'Where people who work for you have experience of bad alliances this is a good learning experience we can use. We do have a meeting which is supposed to look at problems with past ventures as part of its meaning; however, I think information on mistakes or where things go wrong with alliances is very badly shared, although we are trying to learn – we are just not very good at it yet.'

With reference to 'research question 8' posed, it is therefore suggested that, bearing in mind the qualifications that have been made to the level-of-experience aspect, the level of experience of partnering relationships can enable the ability of an entrant firm to exercise a competitive and/or cooperative intent.

MODEL OF THEORETICAL COOPERATIVE/ COMPETITIVE INTENT

As a result of the above evaluation, a model of cooperative/competitive intent can now be considered (see Figure 2.2).

Competitive Influencers

The research suggests that a competitive intent (to acquire a key skill or competence from a partner) is likely to occur where the skills or competencies associated with the pursuance of a key objective are viewed as relatively mobile, or are easily transferable from the partner firm to the entrant partner. Where this is not the case, a partner firm may still decide

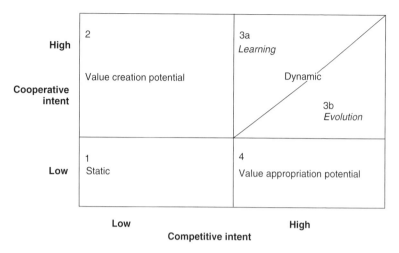

Figure 2.2   The cooperative/competitive matrix.

to pursue a competitive, acquiring approach, provided that the cost of buying in or imitating the competence or skill which would fulfil the objective is considered to be realistic. Further contributing competitive stimuli have also been recognised where the skills or competencies relating to a key objective are considered unique and/or valuable to an entrant partner (see boxes 4 and 3 in Figure 2.2).

However, a number of factors have been identified which can act as limiters to this competitive stance. These include such aspects as cost, time needed, and operational barriers to overcome in order for the acquiring firm both to internalise and gain sufficient value from a key skill or competence. These aspects must also be considered in relation to the existing dynamics in the competitive environment, the reputation of a partner firm and/or the network links they facilitate. They are also dependent upon assessment of the relative value which may be lost if such an approach threatens the existing partnership.

The extent to which these factors are considered to be significant or otherwise when combined will dictate the extent to which a competitive approach to the relationship is adopted. Where the competitive approach is significant and no cooperative emphasis is noted it may be said to adopt characteristics associated with *value appropriation* (see box 4 in Figure 2.2). In this case it is likely that the partnership will terminate once transfer of skills or competencies has been achieved. However, where the above barriers to skill or competence acquisition are significant, this will encourage the partnership to move towards a more cooperative approach should benefits of cooperation be identified in this respect (see box 2 in Figure 2.2).

Cooperative Influencers

Where greater value is considered to be generated from the mutual partnership rather than by transference of identified key skills and competencies to the entrant partner, and/or where transfer or imitation is severely limited, a highly cooperative *value-creating* relationship is likely to be encouraged. In this case the partnership focuses upon gaining benefit from mutual synergistic benefits within the partnership (see box 2 in Figure 2.2). However, evidence from the data collected also suggests that if the skills or competencies contributed by the partner firm are not considered unique or of significant value then the cooperative emphasis will be reduced.

Combined Cooperative and Competitive Influencers

Where a number of objectives exist for the entrant partner and these combine both highly competitive and highly cooperative intents (see box 3 in Figure 2.2) this may have one of two consequences:

Where the overriding skills and competencies to achieve key objectives emphasise aspects associated with the cooperative approach identified in box 2 in Figure 2.2, but further objectives also reflect an element of high competition, this is likely to result in a *dynamic learning* position (see box 3a in Figure 2.2). Here the cooperative synergies and mutual value-added benefits of the partnership which are prioritised block evolutionary pressures on the partnership and create stability for as long as these are seen as relevant and beneficial to all parties concerned. However, the competitive intentions of the lower level objectives, either identified on entry or recognised once the relationship is established, will induce a learning intent where mutual benefit is identified and transfer of some skills and competencies is achieved during the partnership.

An alternative situation can be identified where the key skills and capabilities identified as attractive by an entrant partner are associated with the highly competitive areas of the relationship (as in box 4 in Figure 2.2), and are viewed as significantly important to the entrant company on an independent basis. In addition, lower-level objectives of the entrant partner, either established on entry or during the development of the relationship, highlight significant synergistic characteristics representative of those indicated in box 2 in Figure 2.2. In this situation the partnership will reflect characteristics associated with *dynamic evolution*. This means that there is an increased likelihood that the relationship will continue to evolve towards acquisition of the partner firm by the entrant partner in order for the dominant partner to gain the advantages of both synergy and skills/competence acquisition identified (box 3b in Figure 2.2).

A further area of combined cooperative and competitive intent is indicated in box 1 in Figure 2.2. Here both cooperative and competitive emphases are of low significance, and consequently no notable mutual value creation or individual value appropriation incentives are apparent and the relationship is seen as *static*. In situations such as these, evidence indicates that relationships are likely to be disbanded.

From the above analysis it can be seen that the different combinations of influences upon intent can result in different approaches to the partnership. Figure 2.3 highlights these approaches in relation to the different combinations of influences as outlined in the cooperative/competitive matrix.

These approaches cannot, however, be realised unless levels of transparency or openness of the partner firm, cultural compatibility between the firms, complexity of the partnership, and certain levels of experience of the entrant partner are taken into account. Thus the realisability aspect is critical in determining whether the identified intent of a partner firm is realised therefore the intent, once identified, needs analysing further on this basis.

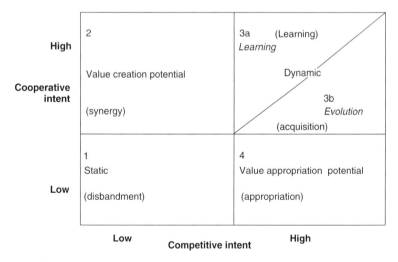

Figure 2.3   Cooperative/competitive intents identified.

CONCLUSION

Increasing amounts of research into strategic alliances have discovered that both a competitive and a cooperative intent can exist within an individual partnership, the implications of which can influence both the success and the ultimate destiny of the relationship. This cooperative and/or competitive intent of an individual partner firm should not, however, be viewed simply in terms of opposing options. Rather it should be viewed as a combination of characteristics, which, together, can help to explain the motivation of the partners involved, and consequently the ultimate form, duration and level of success a particular alliance is likely to reflect.

It has been argued here that the theoretical intent of each partner can be clarified by considering the relationship in terms of specific criteria, including the level of mobility, imitability, uniqueness and value of the key skills or competencies that each partner brings into the relationship. It has further been shown that the realisability of the cooperative/competitive intent requires additional factors relating to the level of transparency, complexity, cultural compatibility and experience of previous alliance partnering to be taken into account in order to operationalise the theoretical intent identified.

The framework for evaluating realisable cooperative/competitive intent within a relationship is aimed at assisting firms in their evaluation of, and management of, a partner within an alliance arrangement. The ability to understand the aims and objectives of both partners, to ensure the relationship is continually used to its best advantage, and the pitfalls avoided or at least identified and weighed constantly against the benefits of the partnership, is of paramount importance for the ultimate success of the relationship. It is argued here that the framework outlined above can provide a means of considering and re-evaluating these factors in a structured and logical form within this type of organisational behaviour.

References

Alcar Group (1989) Case study developed by Alcar Group Inc., Boston, MA.

ANDERSON, E. (1990) Two firms, one frontier: on assessing joint venture performance. *Sloan Management Review, 31* (2), 19–30.

BADARACCO, J.L. (1991) *The Knowledge Link*. Harvard Business School press, Boston MA.

BARNEY, J.B. (1991) Firm resources and sustained competitive advantage. *Journal of Management, 17*, 99–120.

BERG, S.V., DUNCAN, J. and FRIEDMAN, P. (1988) *Joint Venture Strategies and Corporate Innovation*. Oelgeschlager, Gunn & Hain, Cambridge.

BLEEKE, J. and ERNST, D. (1991) The way to win in cross-border alliances. *Harvard Business Review* (Nov./Dec.), *69*, 127–13.

CAMPBELL, A.J. and VERBEKE, A. (1994) The globalization of service multi-nationals, *Long Range Planning*, *27* (2), 95–102.

DEVLIN, G. and BLEACKLEY, M. (1988) Strategic alliances – guidelines for success, *Long Range Planning*, *21* (5), 18–23.

DOZ, Y. (1992) The role of partnerships and alliances in the European industrial restructuring, in Cool, K. Nevan, D. and Walters, I. (ed.), *European Industrial Restructuring in the 1990s*. Macmillan, London, 77–89.

FAULKENER, D. (1992) International strategic alliances: a proposed taxonomy. Paper given at BAM (British Academy of Management) Conference, 1992.

GERINGER, J.M. (1991) Strategic determinants of partner selection criteria in international joint ventures. *Journal of International Business Studies*, *22* (1), 41–62.

GOODMAN, R.L. (1990) Insurance: bold leaps in a game of inches. *McKinsey Quarterly*, (4), 112–31.

GRANT, R.M. (1991) The resource-based theory of competitive advantage: implications for strategy formulation. *California Management Review*, *33* (3), 114–35.

HAMEL, G. (1990) Competitive collaboration: learning, power and dependence in international strategic alliances (unpublished thesis).

HAMEL, G. (1991) Competition for competence and inter-partner learning within international strategic alliances. *Strategic Management Journal*, *12*, 83–103.

HARRIGAN, K.R. (1986) *Managing for Joint Venture Success*. Lexington, MA: Lexington Books.

HAY, M. and WILLIAMSON, P. (1991) *The Strategy Handbook*. Blackwell, London.

HENNART, J.F. (1988) A transaction costs theory of equity joint ventures. *Strategic Management Journal*, *9*, 361–74.

JONES, P. (1989), *Management in Service Industries*. Pitman, London.

JOYNT, P. (1990) Organizational research involving internal networks and external strategic alliances: a theoretical review of strategic alliances. Handelshoyskolen Bi Norwegian School of Management, Working Paper 1990/25.

KOGUT, B. (1988) Joint ventures: theoretical and empirical perspectives. *Strategic Management Journal*, *9*, 319–32.

LEI, D. (1993) Offensive and defensive uses of alliances. *Long Range Planning*, *26* (4), 32–41.

LEI, D. and SLOCUM, J.W. (1992) Global strategy competence-building and strategic alliances. *California Management Review*, *35*, 81–97 (Fall).

LORANGE, P. and ROOS, J. (1992) *Strategic Alliances Formation, Implementation and Evolution*. Blackwell, Oxford.

LORANGE, P., ROOS, J. and BRONN, P.S. (1992) Building successful strategic alliances. *Long Range Planning*, *25* (6, Dec.), 10–18.

LYNCH, R.P. (1990) Building alliances to penetrate european markets. *Journal of Business Strategy* (Mar./Apr.), *15*, 4–8.

LYONS, M.P. (1991) Joint-ventures as strategic choice – a literature review. *Long Range Planning*, *24* (4), 130–44.

MAHONEY, J.T. and PANDIAN, J.R. (1992) The resource-based view within the conversation of strategic management. *Strategic Management Journal*, *13*, 363–80.

MOHR, J. and NEVIN, J.R. (1990) Communication strategies in marketing channels: a theoretical perspective. *Journal of Marketing*, *54*, 36–51.

MOHR, J. and SPEKMAN, R. (1994) Characteristics of partnership success: partnership attributes, communication behaviour, and conflict resolution techniques. *Strategic Management Journal*, *15*, 135–52.

PEKAR, P. and ALLIO, R. (1994) Making alliances work – guidelines for success. *Long Range Planning*, *27* (4), 54–65.

PENROSE, E.T. (1985) *The Theory of the Growth of the Firm: Twenty Five Years Later*. Acta Universitatis Upsaliensis, Uppsala.

PETERAF, M.A. (1993) The Cornerstones of competitive advantage: a resource-based view. *Strategic Management Journal*, *14*, 179–91.

PETTIGREW, A. (ed.) (1988) *The Management of Strategic Change*. Blackwell, London.

SEGAL-HORN, S. (1989) The globalisation of service firms. In Jones, P. (ed.), *Management In Service Industries*. Pitman, London, 115–40.

STILES, J. (1994) Strategic alliances: making them work. *Long Range Planning*, *27* (4), 133–7.

TAKEC, P.F. and SINGH, C.P. (1992) Strategic alliances in banking. *Management Decisions*, *30* (1), 32–43.

TEECE, D.J. (1986) Firm boundaries, technological innovation and strategic management. In Thomas, L.G. (ed.), *The Economics of Strategic Planning*. Lexington Books, Lexington, MA., 79–108.

WHEATCROFT, S. and LIPMAN, G. (1990) *European Liberalisation and World Air Transport* . Economist Intelligence Unit, London, Special Report no. 2015.

WILLIAMSON, O.E. (1975) *Markets and Hierarchies: Analysis and Antitrust Implications*. Basic Books, New York.

3 The Forms and Purposes of Strategic Alliances in the European Banking Sector

Rehan ul-Haq and Ian C. Morison

THE NATURE OF STRATEGIC ALLIANCES

The use of strategic alliances to facilitate domestic and international business activity has increased rapidly over the 1980s and 1990s (Glaister and Buckley, 1994). There has been a commensurate increase in the academic interest in the formation, management and evolution of strategic alliances, from a number of different theoretical perspectives. This chapter considers the question of what constitutes a strategic alliance from the perspective of the transaction cost theory. Critiques of this approach can be found in Ramanathan *et al.* 1997.

Coase (1937) set out to explain why firms exist – that is, why market-based transactions do not in all situations result in the most efficient allocation of resources. The rationale of the firm as expounded by Coase (1937) and developed by Williamson (1970, 1975 and 1986) is, at its simplest, that the existence of transaction costs and uncertainty ('bounded rationality') may make it less costly, less risky or both to internalise inherently separate economic activities within the boundaries of a firm than for each such activity to be undertaken by a separate economic agent. The costs to be avoided include those of drawing up separate contracts specifying precisely the rights and obligations of every party to every economic transaction. The costs to be avoided include those of drawing up separate contracts specifying precisely the rights and obligations of every party to every transaction. Risks that are minimised include those of opportunistic behaviour by counter-parties to an insufficiently specified contract and of failing to find a market for the output of functionally specialised ('idiosyncratic') investments.

A strategic alliance may be defined by reference to legal and structural factors, the nature and purpose of the relationship and the strategic importance of the relationship. The legal, structural or ownership form that the alliance takes is outlined in Figure 3.1. A strategic alliance is based on a continuum between market-based, arms-length transactions or relationships

Market-based transactions relations	Informal cooperative ventures		Formal cooperative ventures	Joint ventures	Joint ownership	Strategic investment in partner	Intra-firm transactions, relations

←————— Strategic alliances —————→

Figure 3.1   Form of strategic alliances.
Source: Adapted from Lorange and Roos (1992).

and hierarchy, or intra-firm transactions or relationships. The range of alliance types moves from a formal cooperative venture through joint venture and joint ownership to strategic investment in a partner (see Figure 3.1 and ul-Haq, 1997 and 1998).

1. A formal cooperative venture exists where two or more independent firms formally agree to work together for their mutual benefit. This agreement may be supported by a formal document (such as the 17-page BNP–Dresdner Bank cooperation agreement) or perhaps by little more than a verbal agreement between the respective chairmen.
2. A joint venture is a separate company in which all the founding firms have an equity stake. A joint venture entity is usually governed by its own board of directors.
3. Joint ownership arises where two or more independent firms jointly own an asset, such as a manufacturing or bottling plant, to serve the interests of the owning firms.
4. A strategic investment in a partner typically involves one firm taking a small investment in another to support their agreement to work together. This often takes the form of a share swap, as a gesture of mutual commitment rather than as a precursor to a merger or to exploit formal ownership rights.

The nature of the resulting relationship between the partners is detailed in Figure 3.2. A strategic alliance is a subset of the relational-contractual part of the continuum (see Figure 3.2), and more specially the obligational-contractual part of the continuum. Firms that know each other, and have worked together or entered into one-off contracts in the past, can be deemed to have a pre-existing relationship by virtue of having freely entered into contracts (relational-contractual). By entering into strategic alliances, firms go a crucial stage further by obligating themselves to enter into future contracts/transactions with their alliance partners (obligational-contractual). The purpose of the relationship is sketched in Figure 3.3.

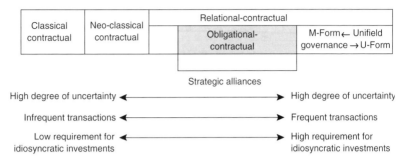

Figure 3.2   Nature of strategic alliances.
Source: Adapted from Williamson (1986).

Market-based transaction	Strategic alliances	Intra-firm transactions

Avoidance of transaction costs ⟶

Securing sources of supply, market outlets ⟶

Achieving economics of scale and scope ⟶

⟵ Retaining flexibility of sources of supply, market outlets

⟵ Avoiding diseconomies of scale

⟵ Avoiding cost (financial, cultural, etc) of mergers and acquisitions

Figure 3.3   Purpose of strategic alliances.
Source: Adapted from Glaister and Buckley (1994).

A strategic alliance represents an attempt to strike an optimal balance between the conflicting needs and purposes of economic activity outlined in Figure 3.3. It seeks to balance the various benefits to be received from collaboration against the external and internal forces, which may push the alliance in the direction of evolution (to a full merger, say), or to dissolution. The strategic importance of the relationship is outlined in Figure 3.4.

Another way of classifying alliances is to differentiate between non-strategic and strategic alliances. A strategic alliance is typically one which displays high levels of resource commitment, is (or is expected to be) of long or open-ended duration and whose purposes represent a core activity of a strategic nature for one or more of the partners.

Figure 3.4 Strategic importance of alliances.

A strategic alliance can therefore be defined as a durable relationship established between two independent firms, involving the sharing or pooling of resources to create a mechanism (corporate or otherwise) for undertaking a business activity or activities of strategic importance to one or more of the partners for their mutual economic advantage. A fuller discussion of this definition is contained in Hamilton *et al.* (1996).

Faulkner (1995) expands the work of Lorange and Roos (1992) and Williamson (1986) by classifying strategic alliances on three dimensions, which he defines as:

1. the scope of the alliance: focused (F) or complex (C);
2. the creation or otherwise of a new corporate legal entity: joint venture (JV) or non-joint venture (NJV) (subtitled 'flexible' and 'collaboration');
3. the number of alliance partners: two partners (2) or a consortium (greater than 2).

The two classification systems are mapped in Table 3.1.

Lorange and Roos have concentrated on the classification of the ownership structure along the classical markets–hierarchy continuum similar to Faulkner's JV and NJV classification, while Williamson (1986) discusses the nature of the relationship between alliance partners by using an obligational-contractual approach, which is a subset of relational-contractual arrangements. Faulkner's classification system complements this by expanding the number of axes to include the scope of the alliance – whether focused on a predefined set of objectives – for example, the transfer of specific knowledge from one firm to another (see Inkpen, 1995; Mowery *et al.*, 1996; Chong and Lee, 1997; Makino and Delios, 1997) – or complex, where separate firms agree to cooperate over a diverse range of activities. Examples include the geographically global and multidimensional alliance between Banque Nationale de Paris and Dresdner Bank (ul-Haq, 1996), and the Royal Bank of Scotland and Banco Santander alliance (Faulkner, 1994).

Table 3.1   Mapping classification

Lorange and Roos classes	Faulkner codes		Williamson
Formal cooperative ventures	FNJV2 FNJV > 2	CNJV2 CNJV > 2	
Joint venture	FJV2 FJV > 2	CJV2 CJV > 2	Obligational contractual
Joint ownership	FNJV2 FNJV > 2	CNJV2 CNVJ > 2	
Strategic investment in partner	FNJV2 FNJV > 2	CNJV2 CNJV > 2	

Source: Lorange and Roos, 1992; Faulkner (1998, see Appendix 3.A); Williamson (1986).

The Lorange and Roos, and Faulkner classification systems, coupled with a Morison, ul-Haq classification system is used to analyse a number of alliances. (see Appendix 3A and 3B)

BANKS AND STRATEGIC ALLIANCES

There are various reasons why it seems likely that the banking industry would offer some distinctive insights into the use of strategic alliances. In one respect, these would not appear to be natural forms of business organisation for banks, since banking is characterised by a high – perhaps uniquely high – degree of vertical integration. The main 'input' to the business of banking is money, and the information which accompanies that money; the main 'output' is the provision of financial services, to the self-same customers who provide the staple of money and information. The business of banking may be thought of as constituting a value loop, starting and ending with the bank's customers, rather than as a conventional value chain. The insurance industry, touched on indirectly in this chapter, has similar characteristics, which help to explain the prevalence of mutual, or customer-owned, enterprises in both sectors.

Thus the potential that strategic alliances offer to firms seeking to improve the management of their value chain linkages was traditionally of limited relevance to banking. Latterly, however, the picture has changed, as changing technology and market conditions have enabled and encouraged banks to question the appropriateness of their traditionally high degree of functional self-sufficiency. Two examples illustrate these changes.

Traditionally, lending was seen as an entirely integrated activity. Banks attracted customers, marketed loans to them, agreed the terms, wrote the loans, held the loans on their balance sheets until maturity, administered their own loan portfolios and exercised their rights against the borrower in the event of default. Each of these is, however, a separate economic event, capable of being undertaken by separate economic agents, which is increasingly what now happens. The firm which markets the loans may not write them; the firm which writes them may not administer them; and the firm which takes the loans onto its books may not hold them until maturity but instead securitise and sell them to a third party.

The second example is the processing of credit card transactions, traditionally seen as a core activity for major retail banks and undertaken in-house. Latterly, however, changes in the underlying technologies and cost functions have tilted the balance significantly in favour of outsourcing this activity to third-party specialists.

The resulting shift away from hierarchy towards market-based transactions has not, of course, involved the use of strategic alliances in all cases, but some of the more abiding arrangements for selling securitised loan portfolios and the relations between the major banks and card processors such as EDS may be so described.

It remains the case, however, that the most common instances of strategic alliances in the banking industry do not involve the exploitation of value chain linkages so prevalent in other industries. Rather, the main purposes identified in this study are typically concerned with the forging of multi-purpose alliances designed to enhance the global capabilities of the partners, or the creation of jointly owned strategic resources, such as clearing houses, ATM (Automatic Teller Machine) networks and credit card brands, or with the establishment of linkages between firms from different parts of the financial services industry, as a means of helping to meet the market's demand for a wide range of products from a single source. These we have termed 'global', 'infrastructure' and 'limited-transaction' alliances respectively.

Most of the alliances considered during our interviews were of the first and third type. It seems likely that respondents did not naturally think of infrastructure arrangements as constituting strategic alliances. Indeed, it may be stretching the term beyond acceptable usage to apply it to multilateral arrangements such as the Visa and MasterCard brands, the Link ATM network or the various clearing houses because the benefits of such arrangements accrue to so many firms that they are unlikely to represent a source of significant strategic advantage for any one of them. Whether these arrangements may be classified as strategic alliances or not, these infrastructure arrangements represent a particular feature of the banking industry which has received little attention in the banking-sector-related literature. The functional need for otherwise competing firms to cooperate intensively with one another in order to provide their core (money transmission) products requires some type of collaborative arrangements. Such cooperation traditionally went well beyond mere standard-setting or technical clearing arrangements and involved a huge array of collectively owned resources and collectively established rules and procedures.

Many of these arrangements have been terminated because of competition policy, notably in the UK with the extension of restrictive trade practices legislation to banking in the early 1970s. External competitor pressure also forced the London clearing banks to open up the main clearing houses to all credible participants in the early 1980s. The pursuit of distinctive competitive strategies by the major banks themselves led in the mid-1980s to the abandonment of the industry-wide development of EFTPOS – electronic funds transfer at the point of sale.

Interestingly, though, in many cases this breaking down of industry-level arrangements (benefiting all banks and therefore not termed as alliances in our classification system) has been replaced, not by individual competitive initiatives, but by alliances. Thus, debit cards such as Switch and smart cards such as Mondex have been launched by consortia including more than one bank – a form of strategic alliance designed to share the costs and risks of a new venture and avoid a proliferation of customer-unfriendly incompatible technologies. At the same time, banks which hitherto offered their automated teller (ATM) services only to their own customers, or those of affiliated banks, have formed networks with other banks using compatible technology, allowing each bank's customers access to the others' machines. Alliances, in short, have emerged as a frequently preferred strategic response to both individual and industry-wide arrangements.

Money transmission is not the only area where banks have frequently resorted to intra-sectoral collaboration. The most important example is international banking, where the main mechanism for allowing a bank's customer's access to banking services in another country was through correspondent banking arrangements. The relationships thus forged between banks of similar complexion in different countries were not strategic alliances as such, but they frequently formed the basis for the development of alliances.

In particular, it was frequently banks with existing correspondent relationships who formed clubs and consortia in the 1970s to take advantage of the opportunities presented by the emergence of the Euromarkets – opportunities which few of them felt able to grasp in full on their own. Some of the clubs, such as ABIN, survived, but of the jointly owned consortium banks, which were such important players in the early years of the Euromarkets, not one survives. Some were wound up, others sold to individual banks, in recognition of the difficulties of developing strategies for such multi-parented institutions. Though beyond the scope of this chapter, consortium banking represents perhaps the best example of an industry's use of strategic alliances over an entire life cycle.

Currently, as this study illustrates, international alliances are back in fashion, but with an important difference. Consortium banks were established with specific purposes, which were to raise funds and extend loans on the global Euromarkets. However, current incentives to form alliances have been largely prompted by the more regionally focused but functionally diverse opportunities presented by the emergence of the Economic and Monetary Union (EMU) in the European Union. This project is principally composed of the Single European Market and EMU programmes. The challenge is largely that of anticipating how the entire gamut of financial markets and customer needs will evolve as EMU takes increasingly substantive form.

The use of strategic alliances as a positioning device in such a rapidly changing market environment appears eminently appropriate. The main alternative strategies for a bank anxious to increase its cross-border capabilities are organic development and acquisition. Each has its place in the panoply of international banking strategies, but high entry barriers, mounting evidence of structural overcapacity in the European banking industry, a dearth of obvious acquisition candidates and a reluctance by major European banks to countenance cross-border mergers all appear to have encouraged banks anxious to develop a strategy for Europe to have frequent recourse to alliances.

THE SAMPLE

The findings reported in this chapter are based on 24 thematically-based semi-structured interviews with senior managers of a varied group of banks in nine European countries between October 1995 and June 1996 at the head offices of the banks concerned. The breakdown of the interviews per country is given in Table 3.2. The number of interviews per country varied from one each in Sweden and Spain to five in Germany and seven in the United Kingdom.

The sample has been further segmented by the geographical spread of the operations of the banks and their ownership structure. Geographically, the banks can be classified into main four categories: regional (example: the German *Landesbanken*); national; international (mainstream national banks

Table 3.2 Classification of responsibility level of interviewee

Country/level	Responsibility level of interviewee				Total
	Supervisory board	Chairman	Main Board	Head Office executive	
Belgium	—	—	—	2	2
France	—	2	—	—	2
Germany	—	—	2	3	5
Holland	—	—	1	1	2
Norway	—	—	2	—	2
Spain	—	—	1	—	1
Sweden	—	—	1	—	1
Switzerland	2	—	—	—	2
United Kingdom	—	—	4	3	7
Totals	2	2	11	9	24

with a significant international presence) and global (banks with a substantial presence in most continents).

In ownership terms, a distinction has been drawn between joint stock and cooperative banks. The former are those owned by shareholders, whether public or private sector, while the latter include cooperative and mutual banks (that is, those 'owned' by their members or customers). Given the importance of the cooperative/mutual sector in banking, it was thought that differences of culture and ethos might be reflected both in their propensity to form alliances and in the purposes and conduct of those alliances. Table 3.3 provides a matrix of the sample by country, geographical spread and cooperative and joint-stock classifications.

In the sample used, all of the interviewees were drawn from their banks' community of strategic decision-makers. They ranged from members of German and Swiss banks' supervisory boards via chief executives and executive directors to corporate planning managers and similar head office officials. This is detailed in Table 3.4.

Given the coverage of the various segments of the European banks, the sample provides a fair representation of the types of banks that might enter into strategic alliances.

METHODOLOGICAL ISSUES

Within the continuum of research methodologies with a range of positivism-empiricism-realism-idealism, where idealism is at the phenomenological extreme of the spectrum (Stiles, 1995) we have adopted a realist perspective. In this approach, the understanding of individuals of the social world affects their behaviour, which may be reflected in 'partial or incomplete' knowledge (May, 1993).

Our approach has also been influenced by the work on transcendental realism (Lawson, 1997 and 1998). This approach focuses on an understanding of 'structures, powers, mechanisms and tendencies', which are the underlying causal factors of individuals' experience, impressions and perceptions (see Table 3.5). Lawson emphasises the need to distinguish the context or 'deep domain' from 'actual or empirical domain' elements without prejudging the issue by, for instance, taking an initially Marxian viewpoint.

The transcendental realist perspective necessarily involves the researcher in 'retroductive' or 'abductive' reasoning in order to move cogently from the 'surface phenomenon' to a 'deeper' causal level. In this chapter the Faulkner codes are utilised to classify the types of alliances

Table 3.3 Classification of sample

Country	Geographical spread				Total ()	Total []	Total
	Mainly regional	Mainly national	International	Global			
Belgium	–	(1) [1]	–	–	1	1	2
France	–	(1)	(1)	–	2	–	2
Germany	[1]	(1) [2]	–	(1)	2	3	5
Holland	–	–	–	[2]	–	2	2
Norway	–	(1)	–	(1)	2	–	2
Spain	–	(1)	–	–	1	–	1
Sweden	–	(1)	–	–	1	–	1
Switzerland	(1)	–	(1)	–	2	–	2
United Kingdom	(1)	(2) [1]	(1)	(2)	6	1	7
					17	7	24
Total ()	2	8	3	4			
Total []	1	4	–	2			
Total	3	12	3	6			Totals

Key: () = Joint-stock banks; [] = Cooperative banks.

Table 3.4 Categorisation of alliances by purpose type

		Faulkner codes (see Appendix 3A)							
		FJV2	FJV>2	FNJV2	FNJV>2	CJV2	CJV>2	CNJV2	CNJV>2
Categories of alliance purpose (see Table 3.5)	Global					(2) [2]	(4) [2]	(13) [6]	(19) [12]
	Infrastructure		(2) [1]				(1)	(5)	(9) [1]
	Limited-transaction	(6) [5]	(1) [3]	(10) [3]			(1)	(1)	(19) [11]
	Other								
	Total	(7) [5]	(3) [4]	(10) [3]		(2) [2]	(6) [2]	(19) [6]	(47) [23]

Key: ( ) = Joint-stock banks; [ ] = Cooperative banks.

Table 3.5   Categories of alliances

Category	Category classification
Global	Alliances which have a multi-dimensional, unbounded purpose or scope (such as the BNP/Dresdner alliance).
Infrastructure	Alliances whose primary function is to facilitate inter organisational transactions (e.g. the clearing house, Swift, fund transfer systems).
Limited transaction	Alliances whose primary function is to facilitate a specific activity (e.g. the transfer of products, specific knowledge from an insurance company to a bank). They are usually of limited duration.
Other	A subsidiary category.

Table 3.6   Attractions of alliances compared with other forms of transactional arrangement

	Market-based	*Acquisition*	*Organic development*
Bancassurance	Inhibited by laws and regulations.	Limited choice of target companies; high premia for control; regulatory issues; cultural differences.	Steep learning curve; credibility gap in eyes of market.
European expansion	Feasible for commodity banking products; less so for higher value-added services, or where contract specification is incomplete.	As above, with even more pronounced international cultural differences plus issues of institutional national identity.	Heavy sunk and fixed costs required; major incumbency advantages to overcome; would add to problem of industry overcapacity.

that the interviewees organisations have entered into (at Lawson's 'actual' domain level), while ul-Haq and Morison classifications (see Table 3.6) have been used to attempt to elicit the 'deep domain' reasons for entering into the alliance.

FINDINGS

Four classifications were used to categorise the reasons why banks enter into alliances (see Table 3.6). An analysis of the 24 interview transcripts reveals 71 alliances, 47 involving joint stock banks and 24 cooperative banks. When these alliances were classified into the above categories using the Faulkner codes, two clear clusters were identified (see Table 3.5).

The first cluster is that of a global purpose (and complex nature) where the complex non-joint venture of two partners seems the predominant form in both joint-stock and cooperative banks.

The second cluster is that of a limited-transaction purpose (and focused nature) where the focused non-joint venture of two partners (closely followed by the focused joint venture of two partners) seems the predominant form in both joint-stock and cooperative banks, with a slight leaning towards joint ventures in the case of cooperative banks.

It is therefore possible to assert that strategic alliances in the European banking sector seem to be of two dominant types. The first is an alliance of multidimensional purpose in a non-joint venture form involving two partners – what we term a global alliance. A classic case of this type, driven by the need to serve customers throughout the world in all services, is that between Banque Nationale de Paris and Dresdner Bank. The second is a limited-purpose alliance, which may or may not involve a joint venture entity, again with two partners. Typical examples are the many alliances between banks and insurance companies, driven by the need to provide bancassurance services. As previously indicated, few alliances of the third type – those designed to create common infrastructural assets for the use of groups of banks – emerged from the interviews. As, by their nature, these are often multilateral rather than bilateral arrangements, respondents may not have thought of them as strategic alliances.

The general objective of many of the identified limited alliances, and an important objective of several of the global ones too, was to enhance the range of services that the partners were able to offer to their customers. In addition to insurance services, these included arrangements such as: offering bureau de change facilities to the customers of small banks that lacked such capabilities; providing international banking services to the corporate customers of a bank which had chosen to concentrate on domestic business; allowing corporate customers of two banks access to each other's national capital markets; and extending the technical expertise of a bank in the area of agribusiness to the customers of a bank in another country where such expertise was less in evidence.

Two further important general objectives were identified. One was to facilitate risk management. This is one of the purposes of loan securitisation, mechanisms for which may or may not involve the creation of a strategic alliance. A more focused example was the alliance formed by banks in two European countries designed to allow each to share in the other's corporate loan portfolios, thus spreading the risks of both institutions. The other was to reap economies of scale, notably through the strategic outsourcing of capital-intensive processing functions. By their nature, these general objectives are not mutually exclusive.

The precise reasons for choosing to pursue these objectives by means of strategic alliances varied from case to case, but it was frequently apparent why the alternatives of market-based transactions, outright acquisition or organic development had been judged sub-optimal. Table 3.6 illustrates some of the negative considerations relevant to the alternative means of development in the two important examples of development bancassurance capabilities and increasing a bank's European outreach.

Perhaps the most interesting finding, however, was that the distinction between global and limited alliances, while almost always clear-cut at the outset, tended to become less so with the passage of time, as global alliances concentrated on some very specific areas of transactional focus while limited alliances discovered new purposes beyond those for which they had been created. An example of the former phenomenon is the very specific focus that the well-reported alliance between Royal Bank of Scotland and Banco Santander has acquired on the handling of international money transmission business. An example of the latter is the infrastructure links between Scandinavian banks leading to – ultimately abortive – attempts to set up a global alliance in the form of Scandinavian Banking Partners.

CONCLUSION

This chapter has considered some of the distinctive features of the use being made of strategic alliances by an industry which, in terms of capital employed, is the largest in the world and one which is undergoing massive change in the face of deregulation and liberalisation, new technologies, new financial markets, new competition and new patterns of customer need. These issues were considered for European banks in the context of the challenges and uncertainties created by the emergence of the Single European Market. The pattern of usage of alliances is not the same as that identified in studies in other industries, with the management of value chain linkages seemingly a much less common phenomenon in the banking sector, and the expansion of customer services much more so.

Perhaps the most interesting question, however, is one which inevitably could not be posed directly during this research. It is whether the increasing the number of strategic alliances in the banking industry is the forerunner of more radical structural change, involving cross-border mergers. The fact that similar predictions at the time of the last major round of bank alliances in the 1970s were not borne out is a reminder of the need for caution. However, if the widespread expectations of consolidation in the international business of European banking industry are borne out, then some at least of that process is likely to involve existing alliance partners.

References

CHONG, J.C. and LEE, S.H. (1997) A knowledge-based view of cooperative interorganizational relationships. In: Beamish, P.W. and Killing, J.P. (eds), *Co-operative Strategies – European Perspectives*. New Lexington Press, San Francisco, 33–58.

COASE, R.H. (1937) The nature of the firm. *Economica* (New Series), iv, 386–405.

FAULKNER, D. (1994) The Royal Bank of Scotland and Banco Santander of Spain. In: Roos, J. (ed), *European Casebook on Co-operative Strategies*. Prentice-Hall, London, 157–73.

FAULKNER, D. (1995) *International Strategic Alliances: Co-operating to Compete*. McGraw-Hill, London.

GLAISTER, K.W. and BUCKLEY, P.J. (1994) UK international joint ventures: an analysis of patterns of activity and distribution. *British Journal of Management*, 5, 33–51.

GOOLD, M. and CAMPBELL, A. (1987) *Strategies and Styles – The Role of the Centre in Managing Diversified Corporations*. Blackwell, Oxford.

GOOLD, M., CAMPBELL, A. and LUCHS, K. (1993) Strategies and styles revisited: strategic planning and financial control. *Long Range Planning*, 26 (5), 49–60.

GOOLD, M., CAMPBELL, A. and LUCHS, K. (1993) Strategies and styles revisited: 'strategic control' – is it tenable? *Long Range Planning*, 26 (6), 54–61.

HAMILTON, R., MORISON, I.C. and UL-HAQ, R. (1996) Towards a working definition of a strategic alliance. Conference Paper presented at the ESRC Management Teaching Fellows Research Colloquium, University of Leeds, 25 March.

INKPEN, A. (1995) *The Management of International Joint Ventures – An Organisational Learning Perspective*. Routledge, London and New York.

LAWSON, T. (1997) *Economics and Reality*. Routledge, London and New York.

LAWSON, T. (1998) Critical realism: an alternative approach to economics. Guest lecture, Birmingham Business School, University of Birmingham, 16 March.

LORANGE, P. and ROOS, J. (1992) *Strategic Alliances: Formation, Implementation and Evolution*. Blackwell, Oxford.

MAKINO, S. and DELIOS, A. (1997) Local knowledge transfer and performance – implications for alliance formation in Asia. In: Beamish, P.W. and Killing, J.P. (eds), *Co-operative Strategies – Asian Pacific Perspectives*. New Lexington Press, San Francisco, 375–402.

MAY, T. (1993) *Social Research: Issues, Methods and Processes*. Open University Press, Buckingham.

MOWERY, D.C., OXLEY, J.E. and SILVERMAN., B.S. (1996) Strategic alliances and interfirm knowledge transfer. *Strategic Management Journal, 17* (winter special edition, Dec.), 77–91.

RAMANATHAN, K., SETH, A. and THOMAS, H. (1997) Explaining joint ventures – alternative theoretical perspectives. In: Beamish, P.W. and Killing, J.P. (eds), *Cooperative Strategies – North American Perspectives*. New Lexington Press, San Francisco, 51–85.

STILES, J. (1995) A philosophical justification for a realist approach to strategic alliances research. Henley Management College, Working Paper Series, HWP 9526, July.

UL-HAQ, R. (1995) An introduction to strategic alliances, part 2. International Forum on Strategic Management, Henley Management College, Newsletter no.11, Jan., 4–5.

UL-HAQ, R. (1996) Strategic Alliances: Banque National de Paris and Dresdner Bank. Case Study, ECCH, Reference no. 396-078.

UL-HAQ, R. (1997) An introduction to strategic alliances, part 1. International Forum on Strategic Management. Henley Management College, Newsletter no. 10, Oct., 6–7.

WILLIAMSON, O.E. (1970) *Corporate control and business behaviour*. Prentice-Hall, New York.

WILLIAMSON, O.E. (1975) *Markets and hierarchies: analysis and anti-trust implications*. Free Press, New York.

WILLIAMSON, O.E. (1986) *Economic organisation*. Wheatsheaf, Brighton.

APPENDIX 3A

STRATEGIC ALLIANCE CLASSIFICATION SYSTEM

as expounded by Dr David Faulkner in *International Strategic Alliances – Co-operating to Compete*, McGraw-Hill, London, 1995.

Classifications

A. Scope

1. Focused [F] – A collaborative arrangement between two or more companies, set up to meet a clearly defined set of circumstances in a particular way.

2. Complex [C] – Cooperation over a wide range of areas either as whole organisations or various parts of organisations.

B. Legal Status

1. Joint venture [JV] – Requires the creation of a separate company.
2. Non-joint venture [NJV] – Flexible and fluid boundaries.

C. Number of Partners

1. Two partners [2].
2. More than two partners [>2].

This leads to 8 possible classifications of alliances:

	Name	*Code* as [ ] above
1	Focused joint venture	FJV2
2	Focused consortium	FJV > 2
3	Focused collaboration	FNJV2
4	Focused multi-partner collaboration	FNJV > 2
5	Complex joint venture	CJV2
6	Complex consortium	CJV > 2
7	Complex collaboration	CNJV2
8	Complex multi-partner collaboration	CNJV > 2

APPENDIX 3B

Analysis Template

Name of bank		
Name of alliance		
Lorange and Roos classes	Faulkner codes	
Formal cooperative	FNJV2	CNJV2
ventures	FNJV > 2	CNJV > 2
Joint venture	FJV2	CJV2
	FJV > 2	CJV > 2
Joint ownership	FNJV2	CNJV2
	FNJV > 2	CNJV > 2
Strategic investment in	FNJV2	CNJV2
partner	FNJV > 2	CNJV > 2
ul-Haq and Morrison categories		
Global		
Infrastructure		
Limited transaction		
Other		

4 Alliances in the Natural Gas Vehicle Industry: An Application of Complexity to an Environmental Issue

Frank Martin and Robin Matthews

INTRODUCTION

Not surprisingly, at times scholars from different subject disciplines find that their approaches to quite diverse problems coalesce. At the Centre for International Business Policy we have developed a model that synthesises cooperative game theory, complexity and statistical mechanics. The essential idea is that organisations structure themselves and evolve through a process of forming coalitions. This can take place at the microscopic level, through coalitions between teams and activities in the value chain between business units, divisions and functional areas, and at the macroscopic level, through alliances, mergers and various kinds of joint ventures.

This chapter represents an application of the model to the emergence of a new industry, natural gas vehicles (NGV). The goal of organisations is to optimise given the constraint of limited consciousness of the potential available to them at a point in time. The problem is akin to that of attempting to reach the highest peak in an unmapped mountain range, which is subject to shocks and transformations. Conventional optimising techniques are of little help in such circumstances. Surfaces are not smooth. They are subject to change. Knowledge is limited. A peak may represent local but not global optima. Indeed it may be a peak in the Alps, when metaphorically the firm is seeking to operate on the kind of scale found in the Himalayas. The firm in other words may be playing the wrong game, producing the wrong products and focusing on the wrong business areas from the point to view of its competencies and aspirations. The model provides a methodology for solving such problems.

In brief, the optimisation problem we were concerned with was the emergence of a new industry that potentially offers gains to the community in the form of reduced emissions of pollutants. The questions we asked were about consistency and incentives. Did satisfying this environmental aspiration which concerns the community at large, the European Union, the British and other world governments, conform with the goals of firms which seek to optimise payoffs in the form of profits, sales growth and stock values? Furthermore, did a reward system exist that would foster the growth of the NGV industry? Since the initiative came from the British government and the firms potentially concerned with the industry, we took as given the desirability of its emergence, provided that the consistency and incentive issues could be satisfied at an appropriate cost.

The application reviewed the economics and technology of natural gas vehicles in the UK (Martin, 1998) and identified the key stakeholders (Freeman, 1984; Doyle, 1994; Polonsky, 1995). A financial model was used to evaluate real, lifetime costs of different types of urban vehicle fleets running on conventional fuels, mainly diesel, and natural gas. A key finding was that there was no single economic solution (an optimal tax) that satisfied all vehicle fleets moving to environmentally friendly natural-gas vehicles. Many of the green policies were seen merely to constitute additional fiscal revenue streams for the Treasury and to have little positive environmental impact (Andersen, 1994). Organisations and government departments needed to work more cooperatively if potential environmental benefits were to be realised.

Alliances here as elsewhere (Ohmae, 1990, 1995; Porter, 1990; Murray and Mahone, 1993; Buckley and Michie, 1996; Caves, 1996) involve rivalry and cooperation. Partners learn from each other, and their relationship evolves (Doz, 1996). They focus upon their own share of payoffs, but there is usually a willingness to trade (Doyle, 1994). In the search for higher payoffs, alliances reshape firms and industry structure, evoking the image of an evolving game (Maynard Smith, 1982). Application of game theory to economic behaviour including alliances is extensive (Von Neumann and Morgenstern, 1944; Schelling, 1960; Lorange, 1988; Porter, 1990; Fudenberg and Tirole, 1993) and the importance of the distribution of payoffs is recognised (Pfeffer and Salanik, 1978; Bleek and Ernst, 1991).

The claim to originality is twofold; content and application. The first, content, is the link between alliances, complexity and cooperative games, summarised by expression (A) in the next section. The second, application, is where we consider alliances as a necessary condition for co-evolution and the emergence of a new industry and network.

THE MODEL

The model we adopted to approach this research question was based on a simple relationship; an alliance creates the potential for payoffs, but these can only be realised through effective cooperation. Potential payoffs come from joint action of partners, interactions between activities j and k. Realisation of these payoffs depends on the joint decisions by the actors or stakeholders of j and k. Call potential payoffs B_{kj} $(k>j)$ and the joint actions of decision makers S_{kj}. We initially constrained decisions to cooperation or non-cooperation and assigned the former unit value and the latter zero, S_{kj} $(1,0)$. The dependence between realising payoffs and cooperation can be summarised by the expression

$$B_{kj} \sim S_{kj}. \tag{A}$$

This expression (A) is similar to a process in which stakeholders learn to trade with one another in order to gain payoffs. As we will show, there was an array of potential payoffs necessary to achieve environmental goals and they included image, desire to influence opinion, reputation and power, as well as monetised economic rent. Payoffs can be imagined as either contours on mountainous, uneven landscapes of peaks and valleys, or random matrices. Cooperative game theory is concerned with the joint actions of groups of players whose interests may conflict, although binding arrangements might be negotiated. In this chapter we address the problems of creating joint payoffs by different stakeholder groups. Attempts at synergy, that is reaching highest peak, or realising potential payoffs, comes by forming coalitions in a cooperative game between the relevant stakeholders – a complex problem of identifying and mapping the terrain, making appropriate decisions and trying the ascent.

In formal terms (A) coincides with expressions in evolutionary biology, learning theory, neural networks and statistical mechanics (Matthews, 1996; Matthews and Korolev, 1997). In particular it is akin to the spin glass (Merzard *et al.*, 1987), the origin of current applications of statistical mechanics to complex systems. The spin glass is a confection of positive and negative feedbacks occurring, as each of the magnetic atoms in the glass tries to align its associated magnet with neighbours. Frustration occurs because of conflict and competition among the interaction of spins. For spins, read decisions. Often goals are incompatible. Some have to be renounced, and we feel frustrated. Much of management consists of designing organisational activities so that positive-sum games exist, and of generating enough trust, commitment and transparency to counteract opportunistic behaviour.

Consider for example forming a team of Green, Brown, Pink, White and Black and getting them to cooperate, when Brown and White hate one another, but Brown likes Pink, and Pink hates Black, but Green likes them all, and Black won't say. The situation becomes much more complex when there are many people. Transforming the organisation landscape into a random matrix and transforming this into a cooperative game enables us to derive an expression that relates payoffs (or payoff contours) to decisions. In the application, joint decisions were those of the stakeholders: government, owners of vehicle fleets, natural gas suppliers, the community, individuals and so on.

BACKGROUND

Environmental pollution affects local, regional and global communities, and threatens the survival of wildlife and future generations. As illustrated in Figure 4.1, it is a complex issue with a large number of interactions and interdependencies between numerous stakeholders. Urban air quality and global warming are two issues forcing governments worldwide to seek measures to reduce pollution. Emissions from road transport are one of the fastest growing concerns in these two areas. Natural gas when used as an alternative transport fuel to the traditional fuels of diesel and petrol offers

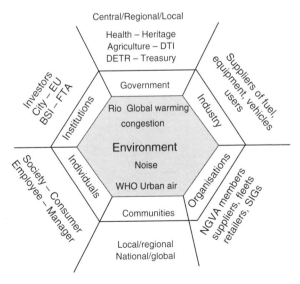

Figure 4.1 The NGV industry stakeholders.

significant reduction in most key pollutants (ETSU, 1996). The initial problem was perceived to be how to overcome the economic barriers of scale and scope associated with developing and sustaining an embryonic NGV (natural gas vehicle) industry in order to deliver the positive environmental benefits. The main problem was to set out a framework for cooperation and alliances between the relevant stakeholders.

How could a new natural gas vehicles (NGVs) industry evolve? What comes first – demand, vehicles and fuel infrastructure, or supporting industries, institutions and expertise (Porter, 1990)? Market research from the USA and the UK was consistent concerning the barriers to the development of alternative fuels industry. More importantly other research (ETSU, 1996) highlighted the need for many of the stakeholders to work actively together to realise the environmental benefits offered. In all surveys the largest barrier was the economic disincentives associated with new technologies.

The high capital costs associated with natural gas vehicles and refuelling stations meant that depot-based, centrally refuelled urban fleets were the most likely pioneers and early adapters. Apart from the extra capital costs associated with the NGVs, there were additional economic, technical and operational factors to take into consideration.

Remembering (A), we needed to address the problem of activating potential synergies (an issue summarised by a tilde, ~). To do this we needed incentives. So, for a fleet manager to commit to NGVs the net present value (total life real-cost differential) needed to be positive or zero when compared to traditional fuels. Another way to express this is the extra capital costs associated with the new vehicles must be equal or less than the cumulative savings on fuel minus any extra maintenance costs over the fleet life of the vehicle – x years. This is shown in equation (B):

$$C_e \leqslant \Sigma_x [P_d - (P_g \times E_f)] \times F_d - M_c \qquad \text{(B)}$$

where C_e = extra capital,
        P_d = price of diesel,
        P_g = price of natural gas,
        E_f = gas engine efficiency,
        F_d = annual fuel (diesel) consumption,
and M_c = extra maintenance costs.

Given the tax structure for gaseous and diesel fuels, the NPV was negative from the point of view of the fleet manager. Fuel duty accounts for over 80 per cent of UK fuel prices. The British government has declared a 'polluter pays' policy, which translates into annual fuel duty increases of inflation $+6$ per cent minimum for diesel and petrol. Even if the fuel duty on gaseous fuels moved with inflation only or was held constant, it would still take too long (that is, beyond the normal fleet life of the vehicle) for NGV investments to be economical. The current fiscal policy delays the environmental benefits and puts UK manufacturers in an unfair European competitive position with a negative impact on the UK economy. However, the UK government could speed up the economic equilibrium process between traditional and gaseous-fueled vehicles by reducing further duty on gaseous fuels as well as maintaining their declared increases on diesel and petrol.

RESEARCH APPROACH

The approach was to review the economics for natural gas vehicles in the UK and identify the key stakeholders that needed to be engaged to create the correct conditions for market uptake of NGVs (Martin, 1998). Rather than taking a conventional approach examining externalities, demand economics from a vehicle fleet owner's perspective was explored. A standard DCF financial model was constructed to evaluate the economic equilibrium of fleet lifetime costs for different types of urban vehicle running on conventional fuels, mainly diesel, and natural gas. The financial model analysed the required reduction in gaseous fuel duty to provide an $NPV = 0$ for different types of urban fleets. Table 4.1 shows the selected input data after detailed discussions with industry experts.

Table 4.1   Selected input variables by vehicle type

Vehicle type	Fuel and mpg	Gas engine efficiency (Ef) (%)	Extra capital (£) (Ce)	Life of vehicle (x) years	Ave. miles per year
Fleet car	Petrol 30	0	2 500	4	15 000
Light van	Diesel 33	−25	1 500	5	22 000
Rigid (6t)	Diesel 20	−25	12 500	6	40 000
Rigid (17t)	Diesel 11	−30	12 500	5	23 000
Artic (<28t)	Diesel 10	−25	22 500	6	55 000
Artic (32.5t)	Diesel 8.5	−20	22 500	5	75 000
Urban bus	Diesel 6	−30	25 000	10	30 000
Refuse truck	Diesel 1.4 gal/hr	−30	12 500	6	2 400 hr/yr

To explain briefly the financial analysis, we examine one vehicle type –
a 32.5-tonne articulated vehicle. Figure 4.2 shows the expected movement
in diesel and natural fuel prices over 10 years and plots the NPV achieved
over the same period. The fleet manager would eventually recover the
additional capital associated with a NGV in 2005, after 8 years. However,
the vehicle replacement norm is 5 years and there is uncertainty about the
NGV's resale value.

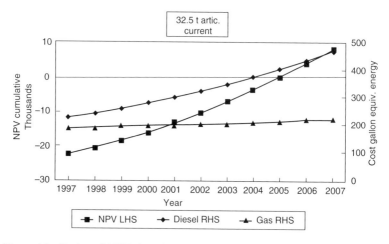

Figure 4.2   Projected NPVs based on current fiscal policy.

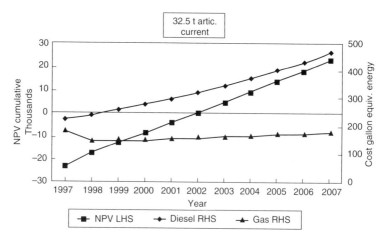

Figure 4.3   Projected NPVs based on fiscal changes.

Table 4.2   Fuel duty reductions required by vehicle type

Vehicle type	Current reduction required (%)	Future potential reduction required (%)
Fleet Car	− 105	− 19
Light Van	− 46	− 8
Rigid (6.0t)	− 162	− 98
Rigid (17t)	− 188	− 121
Artic (< 28t)	− 94	− 44
Artic (32.5t)	− 52	− 10
Urban bus	− 177	− 132
Refuse truck	− 95	− 49

Figure 4.3 shows that a further reduction in natural gas fuel duty of 52 per cent would have allowed a NPV of zero to be achieved in 2002, after 5 years, the normal replacement period.

The results achieved for each vehicle type from the financial model are listed in Table 4.2 and show that there was no single economic (optimal-tax) solution that satisfied all vehicle fleets moving to environmentally friendly natural gas vehicles. Experts expect that an emerging industry over time would enjoy economies of scale and scope and so potentially in the future the additional capital costs and fuel costs could decline by 25 per cent and 12.5 per cent respectively. Table 4.2 shows that even when these future potential reductions were used as inputs into the financial model there was still no single fiscal signal to satisfy all vehicle types.

FINDINGS

Fiscal policy alone is too blunt an instrument to achieve the desired outcomes. The research reaffirmed the need for the stakeholders to work actively together to achieve the environmental benefits offered by gaseous fuels. The findings also supported previous work (Andersen, 1994) showing that environmental pollution is neither market nor government failure but state failure. The failure is not that of government policies and instruments nor is it pure market economics but the complex interactions between these two, with the resultant perceptions of, and impact upon the institutions that govern the markets. It was also found that not only did organisations, industry and government need to work together, as demonstrated in Figure 4.4, but they had to develop a cluster of complementary, integrated,

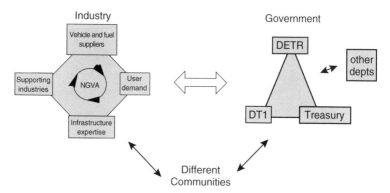

Figure 4.4   Industry and government working together for environmental benefits.

synergistic policies and strategies through a number of business and political instruments to overcome the institutional barriers that created the state failure of environmental pollution from road transport emissions.

Many of the green policies were perceived as additional fiscal revenue streams for the Treasury with little or no positive environmental impacts. Apart from this obvious Treasury benefit there was no immediate payoff for any of the other stakeholders. Yet, without the decisions and signals from the different organisations and government departments to participate and cooperate in a cohesive way, the future payoffs such as the environmental benefits, world political leadership, economic rent, reputation, image, influence and power could not be realised.

GOVERNMENT PERSPECTIVE

From a government perspective there were four broad instruments at its disposal: regulation, technology, economics and information. It was found that the many stakeholders in government departments needed to cooperate and share common goals with each other. Some recent government activities are as follows:

- *Information*   The government have announced that their car pool will be changed to operate on gaseous fuels. Some of the royal family vehicles have also been converted.
- *Economics*   The polluter-pays policy, earlier reductions in gaseous fuel duty and the Integrated Transport early initiatives all suggest a range of fiscal measures are to be introduced.

- *Technology*   Late last year the prime minister announced that a Vehicle Technology Foresight Programme was to look at a range of issues. The steering group was made up of government ministers and industry leaders, and one of the six sub-groups was specifically set up to look at the alternative fuel arena.
- *Regulation*   The EU Auto-oil II programme and joint meetings between EU transport and environment ministers have indicated that tighter emissions standards, access restrictions, and incentives for early adoption of future standards are all being considered.

INDUSTRY PERSPECTIVE

A new form of multiple alliance between numerous stakeholders was observed, with cooperation, coalition and alliances being formed at the macro and micro levels. The industry micro perspective could initially be examined by looking at the stakeholders in a typical project, as shown in Figure 4.5, namely the launch of a mini-fleet of ten articulated vehicles in London for a major retailer, Marks & Spencer (M&S). Through different phases of the project, different alliances were pre-eminent, but all stakeholders had to fulfil their appropriate obligations at each stage for the total project to be successful. The expectations and payoffs varied throughout the project and it was important that the project leaders maintained relationships with each of the stakeholders to ensure they fully understood

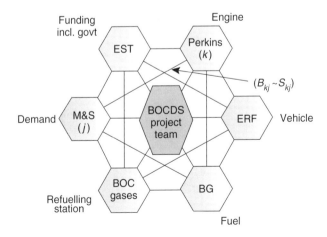

Figure 4.5   Project success through stakeholder alliances.

the total positive-sum game for the environment, the industry, their organisations and themselves. Some stakeholders formed alliances that are more permanent and partnerships transferring the learning, products, and services developed to other projects, in an attempt to leverage market share and even greater future payoffs. Figure 4.5 can be thought of as a subset of Figure 4.4.

At the macro level within the emerging industry the same pattern of temporary and more permanent alliances and partnerships were formed under the umbrella of the Natural Gas Vehicle Association (NGVA). Current and future potential competitors and suppliers decided to cooperate and develop joint policies to create a new industry niche that was as large as possible, knowing that in future they would cooperate further with some and fiercely compete with others.

Another important observation at the macro and micro levels was that open conflict and early disagreements from any of the stakeholders could prevent the new potential industry or projects emerging respectively. It was noted that the idea of cooperation (1) or non-cooperation (0) was too simple. We needed to distinguish between passive non-cooperation and open conflict with its negative impact. In fact, there was a continuum between total long-term commitment (1) and hostile competition (-1). This meant that providing a stakeholder was neutral (0) or partially positive (>0) then other stakeholders were able to complement gaps and shortcomings.

In Figure 4.5, we demonstrate the link with the decision model (A). We can think of the lines connecting the project stakeholders as potential

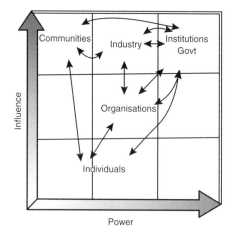

Figure 4.6   Interactions, interdependencies and alliances between stakeholders.

payoffs that need to be activated by cooperation. So each line represents $B_{kj} \sim S_{kj}$ for a particular relationship between k and j.

Within this new form of multiple alliance, activities cut across the traditional supply chain boundaries and new cooperative supply channels emerged, where the several payoffs were shared, traded and transferred between the stakeholders. The new activities, boundaries and links were established based on the best complementary and combined competencies in terms of technology, commerce, finance, knowledge, relationships, media access, influence and power.

Considering the large number of projects, discussions, interactions and interdependencies that were taking place at the micro and macro levels, and the changes over time, what emerged was a high degree of complexity. As Figure 4.6 shows, sometimes individuals through their interactions with organisations, communities and institutions could affect decisions critically, although nominally their power and influence were minimal.

STRONG INCLUSIVE LEADERSHIP WITHIN A 'HARMONY ZONE'

How did cooperation happen? How were the expectations, attitudes, behaviours and activities of the stakeholders aligned in order to affect the environmental benefits? A single policy was inadequate. This we consider a fundamental finding of the research.

Developing a cluster of integrated, complementary, joint and synergistic policies produced a larger harmony zone (Figure 4.7) where trade-offs between conflicting and often ambiguous objectives from stakeholders could be accommodated and balanced to produce cohesive, harmonious interactions and interdependencies with acceptable and potentially larger payoffs from a common goal. Strong inclusive leadership was required to attract, align, engage and build relationships with the stakeholders in order to harmonise their expectations, activities and payoffs (Global Integration, 1998). The multidimensional harmony zone changed over time and so the zone leaders or stewards of such a solution-centred approach needed to constantly check and realign stakeholders' objectives, policies and strategies accordingly. Over time, new zone leaders emerged to meet the changing needs and requirements of the markets and the stakeholders.

CONCLUSIONS

The research discovered that organisations, industry and government needed integrated and complementary policies to develop cooperation, and

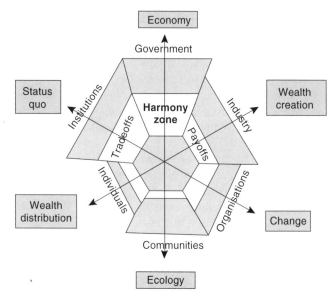

Figure 4.7   Harmony zone.

to foster the evolution of the new NGV industry, using a number of business strategies and political instruments to overcome the institutional barriers. Identifying the affected stakeholders, their objectives, requirements, influence and power allowed the detailed mapping of interdependencies of payoffs and interactions of decisions. Through socialisation it was possible to understand their own conflicts and ambiguities as well as those between the stakeholders. With strong inclusive leadership it was possible to attract, shape and influence alliances to overcome institutional, organisational and individual barriers in order to effect the necessary changes. A cluster of synergistic policies from stakeholders allowed greater freedom to leverage harmonious tradeoffs and potentially larger payoffs towards a common goal. Another feature of such complex systems was their sensitive dependence upon initial conditions and parameters. Figure 4.6 shows a web of interconnected actions by individuals that can be critical in transforming an alliance. We have also been able to expand upon existing process and decision tools in this area.

The initial view of cooperation being 'either–or' (1, 0) was extended to show that a negative position (−1) from one major stakeholder can stop a whole project or industry emerging. We therefore have a continuum of cooperation from total long-term commitment (1) through passive non-cooperation (0) to open conflict (−1). The extended model provides a way of analysing the two issues of consistency and incentives we set out in the introduction. Briefly, we find that the goals of the various stakeholders, though conflicting, are reconcilable. So, our conclusion about consistency is that the conditions for it exist. The problem is to construct the appropriate game, which generates incentives for each stakeholder to realise potential gains. Not surprisingly, no single incentive mechanism exists. Instead, a cluster of policies, strategies, and other measures needs to be instituted.

References

ANDERSEN, M.S. (1994) *Governance by Green Taxes: Making Pollution Prevention Pay*. Manchester University Press.

BLEEKE, J. and ERNST, D. (1991) The way to win in cross border alliances. *Harvard Business Review*, Nov.–Dec. 69, 127–35.

BUCKLEY, P.J. and MICHIE, J. (1996) *Firms, Organizations and Markets*. Oxford University Press.

CAVES, R.E. (1996) *Multinational Enterprise and Economic Analysis*. Cambridge University Press.

DOYLE, P. (1994) *Marketing Management and Strategy*. Prentice-Hall International, London.

DOZ, Y. (1996) The Evolution of Cooperation in Strategic Alliances: Initial Conditions for Learning Processes. *Strategic Management Journal*, 17, Special Issue, 55–84.

ETSU (Energy Technology Support Unit) (1996) *Alternative Road Transport Fuels – A Preliminary Life-Cycle Study for the UK*. HMSO, London.

FREEMAN, R.E. (1984) *Strategic Management: A Stakeholder Approach*. Pitman, Boston.

FUDENBERG, D. and TIROLE, J. (1993) *Game Theory*. MIT Press, London.

Global Integration (1998) Models, frameworks, techniques and tools from various consultancy and training programmes. London.

LORANGE, P. (1988) Cooperative Strategies: Planning and Control. In: Hood, N. and Vahine, J. (eds), *Strategies in Global Competition*. Croom Helm, London, 117–30.

MARTIN, F. (1998) Review of the economics for natural gas vehicles in UK. Dissertation, Kingston University.

MATTHEWS, R. (1996) Competition and complexity in organisations. Paper delivered at special session on organisational complexity, Informs Conference, Atlanta.

MATTHEWS, R. and KOROLEV, A. (1997) *Organisations, Cooperative Games and Statistical Mechanics*. Kingston Business School Series.

MAYNARD SMITH, J. (1982) *Evolution and the Theory of Games*. Cambridge University Press.

MERZARD, M PARISI, G. and VIRASORO, M.A. (1987) *Spin Glass Theory and Beyond*. World Scientific, New York.

MURRAY, E.A. and MAHONE, J.F. (1993) Strategic Alliances: Gateway to the New Europe. *Long Range Planning*, 26 (4), 102–11.

OHMAE, K. (1990) *The Borderless World*. Collins, London and New York.

OHMAE, K. (1995) *The Evolving Global Economy*. Harvard Business School Press, Cambridge, Mass.

PFEFFER, J. and SALANIK, J.R. (1978) *The External Control of Organisations: A Resource Dependence Perspective*. Harper & Row, New York.

POLONSKY, M.J. (1995) A stakeholder approach to designing environmental marketing strategy. *Journal of Business and Industrial Marketing*, *10*, 77–88.

PORTER, M.E. (1990) *The Competitive Advantage of Nations*. Macmillan, London.

SCHELLING, T. (1960) *The Strategy of Conflict*. Harvard University Press, Cambridge, Mass.

VON NEUMANN, J. and MORGENSTERN, O. (1944) *The Theory of Games and Economic Behaviour*. Princeton University Press.

5 The Challenges of Multisector Collaboration in Community Development

David Sink

COMMUNITY DEVELOPMENT THROUGH COLLABORATIVE ADVANTAGE

Creating and operating a neighbourhood resource centre, designed to encourage and facilitate regenerative community development in a mid-sized US city, provides a valuable case-study in which to explore key concepts of multisector collaboration based on a shared vision. Development of the centre may be possible through the sustained efforts of one of the principal stakeholders working alone. However, the opportunity for creating and capturing a vision of something greater, a centre for community development that both facilitates change and empowers the city's neighbourhoods and their residents, demands a collaboration of stakeholders working in the same problem domain.

Yet, instrumental collaboration, a process in which participating organizations seek to accomplish their individual goals by working in partnership, is still not enough truly to transform a community. What is needed is nothing less than the creation of synergistic, creative, culture-changing, transformative, multisector collaboration, which may be construed as 'collaborative advantage'. As a vision of something greater than project collaboration, collaboration advantage takes on strategic-level dimensions whose mission and ultimate achievement transcends those of individual partners. This is what Huxham envisioned when she created the term and proposed its meaning (Huxham and MacDonald, 1992; Huxham, 1993; Huxham, 1996).

Collaborative advantage seems particularly appropriate for community development because of the comprehensive, higher-value and ambitious forms that are required. An argument for conceptualising community development as inherently collaborative in nature and particularly in need

77

of achieving collaborative advantage is based on a definition of shared meta-strategy, implicitly essential to this higher form.

'Meta-strategy' as a statement of mission for the collaboration results from participants committing to ends which are outside their organisational goals and objectives (Huxham, 1993). Rather than individual organisations attempting to meet only their own strategic objectives by seeking arrangements that involve others, a meta-strategy is developed once the collaboration is formed. In this case, which comes first is quite clear. For example, in the context of community development, a housing construction firm may seek a partnership with a bank for the purpose of building houses. Or, a public health agency may form a collaboration of clinics and hospitals for the purpose of immunising all children less than three years of age. Each may succeed, but fail to consider the larger issue – the meta-strategy – of helping create safe, healthy neighbourhoods in which residents can improve their lives. The comprehensiveness needed in true community development defies an incremental approach, extends beyond a traditional problem domain and demands big-picture thinking characterised by collaborative advantage and meta-strategy.

Community Development as a Meta-Domain

For this chapter, community development is defined as a process or concerted effort to build and mobilise systemic capacity for the purpose of improving the general quality of life of residents within a target neighbourhood or community of neighbourhoods (adapted from Selsky, 1991). Within the system are community-based organisations, neighbourhood-level voluntary organisations, community-oriented government agencies, and other not-for-profit service providers such as churches, clubs and unions. With such an emphasis on capacity-building and the need for many kinds of resources – for example, human, financial, leadership – community development must crosssectoral boundaries.

Although instructive to change agents, a focus on community development may defy generalisation owing to its breadth. It may be of such complexity that it extends beyond traditional problem domains of common concern for its organisational members (Gray, 1989; Trist, 1983). In the case of the subject neighbourhood resource centre, whose staff and volunteers facilitate multi-organizational efforts in a variety of functional areas – for example, housing, job training, physical infrastructure, health, youth development and crime prevention – a more accurate conceptualisation might be a meta-domain. Combining the work of Huxham and Gray, the concept of the meta-domain is used to indicate a multi-problem domain that transcends several single-problem domains and requires a comprehensive strategic plan and well-organised, appropriate negotiated order (Gray, 1989).

The advantage of the concept of meta-domain is its comprehensiveness, where the focus is on improvements in quality of life, not merely on one functional service area. The disadvantage is vagueness and incomprehension that may frustrate erstwhile stakeholders. However, typical responses by society to this problem do not encourage such proactive behaviour. 'We continually fragment problems into pieces; yet the major challenges we face in our organizations and beyond are increasingly systemic' (Kofman and Senge, 1995: 17–18).

Overcoming this mindset, which may be a compensating approach to complexity, depends on designing a meta-strategy which not only 'throw(s) down the walls' between different functions, but also changes the 'fragmentary mental models that created the walls in the first place' (Kofman and Senge, 1995: 19).

There exists a tendency for collaborating partners involved in highly differentiated systems with contrasting values to attempt to routinise the functioning of the collaboration as a means of reducing conflict among organisations, both within and from different sectors (Alter and Hage, 1993). Trist warns of extending central power and hierarchical form throughout the domain as the wrong path to take. The opposite reaction is equally non-functional; where no attempt is made 'to weave an appropriate fabric at the domain level, the result can only be further social fragmentation' (Trist, 1983: 271). Still, reducing complexity (both task and organisational complexity) appears to be an important goal.

Finding the right functional order of the problem domain is a major challenge facing stakeholders who are attempting to structure and implement meta-strategy. Bureaucratic responses are typically heavy-handed and discourage participation by citizens. At the other end of the spectrum, the community development meta-domain is so fragmented that it defies easy coordination. This has been described as 'fractionated organizational communities' (Selsky, 1991: 95). These can become collections of dissimilar organisations that are related to one another only in a general way, that do not interact directly and are not linked by any centralised coordination or authority (Astley and Fombrun, 1983). However, they make up a system, which is characterised by some degree of unity. That unity may be the key to seeking some sort of domain structuring, especially if such interconnection is characterised by common clients, services, and/or policies. Collaboration provides a form of joint control over that interconnection by reducing environmental turbulence (Wood and Gray, 1991).

Community Development as a Multisector Collaboration

The subject of this chapter is regenerative community development, which addresses social and economic development of urban areas in a comprehensive fashion. Its target may be as broad as a metropolitan area, but more likely is focused on low-income, degenerating areas in the inner city. Implicit in the approach is the inclusion of the people who occupy these neighbourhoods, whose involvement is critical to success, and whose capacity for self-help and self-government requires nurturing (Barr and Huxham, 1996; Sink and Huxham, 1996). Increasingly, advocates for community development have sought to 'empower' or to create the conditions for empowerment of the target community and its residents by enhancing their capacity for self-determination (Himmelman, 1996).

The foundations of successful community development require consideration of five main factors:

- Successful community development must achieve collaborative advantage, which demands an unusually creative, higher-level accomplishment that no stakeholder could achieve alone.
- A collaboration of this nature must create a shared meta-strategy which is a commitment to ends which are outside the mission and objectives of the individual participants and captures the higher-level vision needed in community development.
- Comprehensive community development must attract stakeholders from all relevant domains which can contribute to complex collaboration in a meta-domain.
- The complexity and difficulty associated with accomplishing the community development meta-strategy accentuates the critical task of organising the meta-domain. A collaborative approach may facilitate that task.
- To acquire resources that are unavailable or rationed in the public and not-for-profit sectors, collaborators must reach out to private sector stakeholders. Community development requires a multisector collaboration.

To elaborate on these factors requires discussion of the characteristics of a multisector collaboration. The following section leads into the case-study of collaborative development based on a shared vision of a neighbourhood resource centre.

CHALLENGES TO MULTISECTOR COLLABORATION

'Problems in which the interests of business, government and communities intersect are now everyday occurrences' (Gray, 1996: 57). In fact, it is difficult to identify a domain that doesn't have at least the potential for multisector interest (Eden *et al.*, 1996). Social problems such as community development are of such breadth and complexity that they are inherently difficult to solve, owing to their unbounded nature, and resist quick fixes, so that there is likely a role for stakeholders from all sectors (McCann, 1983).

Advancing a shared vision through collaboration involves a number of important steps, not the least of which is identifying and coordinating 'a diverse set of stakeholders, each of whom holds some but not all of the necessary resources' (Gray, 1989: 9). Numerous researchers have laid out the benefits and obstacles or challenges to collaboration (Alter and Hage, 1993; Gray, 1989; Huxham, 1996). Many of these may be applied to multisector collaboration. The benefits are well known and are argued persuasively in these works. However, the challenges to collaboration presented by the different sectors, which may alert the local collaborative effort, are particularly stubborn ones.

The challenges can be highlighted by using four categories that are based on a review of previous research:

- varying cultural characteristics;
- differing organisational goals;
- ideological and procedural differences;
- institutional incentives and disincentives.

Varying Cultural Characteristics

Society holds culturally determined attitudes about the appropriate role of government in solving social problems (Elazar, 1972; Sink and Wilson, 1983). A population's political and social behaviour likewise can support or frustrate community-based strategies. For example, public apathy can thwart even the best-designed collaborative initiatives (Berman, 1996). A loss of civic virtue or engagement in public affairs likewise can gridlock the development of community networks and comprehensive problem-solving (Chrislip and Larson, 1994). Social ills such as racism, class separation and a dilution of community leadership can prevent assembling the critical mass necessary for community development and regeneration.

Cultural and social distance between public, private and not-for-profit organisations can also prevent effective collaboration. Applying the concept of value homophyly (resemblance due to common ancestry) to coalitional formation reveals that a high degree of value, attitude and belief incongruence can prevent a relationship from forming (Laumann and Pappi, 1976). Finding ways of creating dialogue in order to bridge cultural divisions between organisations from different backgrounds acknowledges the real threat which such cultural gaps present to long-lasting partnerships (Ritchie and Montanheiro, 1996).

Cultural change within stakeholder organisations may be required for collaboration to occur. How an organisation approaches its own work, for example, hierarchical control, division of labour, service delivery, affects willingness to try extra-organisational strategies (Gray, 1989; Sink, 1996).

Differing Organisational Goals

The roles and responsibilities of organisations in each sector may vary widely and should not be discounted (Himmelman, 1992b). Previous experiences, social context, and the varying natures of clients and joint efforts may be difficult to overcome (Dymsza, 1988; Gray, 1989). For example, private firms may desire to fulfil their public responsibility, but not when it runs counter to their private interests (Gray, 1989; Wood, 1991). Collaborative facilitators must ensure that the differing objectives of partners are reconciled (Ritchie and Montanheiro, 1996).

Ideological and Procedural Differences

Organisational belief patterns vary. For example, emphases on efficiency and economy, long present in the private sector and growing rapidly in both public and not-for-profit sectors, may restrict organisations from undertaking high-risk collaboration strategies (Himmelman, 1992b; Oliver, 1990). Stakeholders in the same domain may approach resolution of problems in diametrically opposed ways. For example, police officers and social workers espouse opposing theories about dealing with youth gangs. The cops want to bust them up; the social workers want to redirect them, contending that the kids are seeking affiliation and belonging (Sink, 1996).

Basic variations in ways of doing business may restrict cross-sectoral partnerships. Budget cycles, personnel, union policies and practices, and technological complexities vary among agencies (Gray, 1989; Sink, 1996). Within the not-for-profit sector, social service agencies adopt crisis-oriented modes of operation, artificially fragment the service delivery system, fail to communicate adequately, and show an inability to craft comprehensive solutions (Chrislip and Larson, 1994; Melaville and Blank, 1993).

Institutional Incentives and Disincentives

Even if the obstacles discussed above are overcome, potential collaborators still weigh the incentives and disincentives of participation. An organisation will question its interest in solving a social problem in the context of other competing interests before committing to joint problem-solving, and will test its perceived interdependence with other groups as necessary for the social problem to be addressed effectively (Logsdon, 1991: 25, 26). Although community development needs a meta-strategy as the product of goal-setting by collaboration members, 'they must believe that their interests will be protected and advanced throughout the process' (Gray, 1989: 263) in order to compel them into the collaboration in the first place. If conflicting interests stand in the way of joint interests, that would justify a rational decision to collaborate if it is likely that individual stakeholder organisations will not get involved (Shubik, 1982).

Varying degrees of trust and risk-taking are experienced by stakeholders (Gray, 1989; Selsky, 1991). Suspicion and lack of trust of government or of large corporations, for example, frequently are given as reasons why neighbourhood-level associations resist collaboration (Sink and Huxham, 1996). Community organisations and associations are critical to the furtherance of community development strategies, for reasons to do with both empowerment (Himmelman, 1996) and ownership (deJong, 1996).

In the context of these challenges to multisector collaboration, in the case of a neighbourhood resource centre, it is necessary to determine which of these challenges are at work.

LITTLE ROCK'S NEIGHBOURHOOD RESOURCE CENTRE: A CASE-STUDY

The Mission

In an attempt to decentralise its community outreach functions, to make local government more accessible to residents in all neighbourhoods of the city and comprehensively plan and execute a community development strategy, the Little Rock city government is renovating an old school building in the inner city to house a neighbourhood resource centre (NRC). The city government has engaged the local public university (whose campus lies one mile from the proposed centre) to coordinate the planning and operation of the centre. The primary mission of the NRC will be to study neighbourhood issues, develop problem-solving strategies, and join with others to implement community development strategies in order to improve the quality of life for Little Rock citizens. The NRC will bring together the collective talents of citizens, neighbourhood associations, the university, city government, corporate entities, and not-for-profit agencies, all working toward the goal of bringing practical problem-solving skills to community development, to test new ideas, and to make the centre a problem-solving urban laboratory.

The Implementation

To finance the renovation, city officials arranged creative funding through a US housing and urban development federal loan programme, an approach not endorsed by neighbourhood community development representatives. They expressed concern that the loan would obligate the city government to a long-term payback, which would diminish funds for refurbishment of poorer neighbourhoods. To overcome this resistance and its lingering effects and to ensure that neighbourhood residents will use the NRC, city and university officials have created a collaboration called Neighbourhood Resource Centre Development (NRCD). The intent is to be inclusive of all elements of the community.

The premise on which the collaboration is organised is that high-risk strategies, especially those whose success depends on use and participation by urban residents, must generate considerable 'buy-in' or 'ownership' by the residents. Stated another way, end-users have as much a legitimate stake in a project as providers, although examples abound in Little Rock and other cities where this common wisdom has been ignored. Additionally, there exists a great need for a coordinating function to pull together the various stakeholders who have designated space in the building or who can bring resources to the project.

Attached to the federal loan are strict regulations that only community-based-and-oriented agencies and projects, which serve primarily low-income, inner-city residents, are to be included in the centre. Although the City of Little Rock is the loan recipient, members of its governing board (11 elected directors including a mayor) have pushed for inclusion of the entire Neighbourhoods and Housing Department, which would utilise fully one-half of the renovated space. Present plans do not include that department. The Community-Oriented Police Programme (COPP), which is primarily prevention-oriented, is at present included, but the police chief has pushed for inclusion of the entire special operations division, of which COPP represents one-half. If that request were approved, police activities would fill the other half of the centre not used by Neighbourhoods and Housing. Space for community-based programmes would be minimal.

The city has hired an architect through a competitive bid process and that firm has started its work by interviewing each of the major stakeholders who will have space in the centre. The architect has developed a schematic drawing showing the assignment of rooms. Other activities at present included are a neighbourhood alert centre (housing code enforcement, policing, and substance-abuse prevention), several university activities, housing-related programmes and a technology centre for neighbourhood use.

The NRCD Collaboration

NRCD is a structured approach to collaboration, which has sought to include elements from each part of the stakeholder community. Three representatives from each of three teams (corporate, citywide and technical assistance) make up the steering committee, although corporate representatives have yet to be recruited. The power and influence of the steering committee, and hence the collaboration, is uncertain. Future negotiations with the City's board of directors and city manager will determine whether the collaboration is primarily advisory or has authority to make decisions.

Of particular concern has been neighbourhood representation. Some effort has been made to differentiate between community representatives who represent community-based organisations and those who live in the community immediately around the NRC (the 'host community'). The citywide team includes overrepresentation of the host community, but generally represents all parts of Little Rock. The citywide team has met regularly and made progress in integrating residents and neighbourhood association members from the city at large with residents from the host community.

Since the NRC is to be a citywide function to serve all neighbourhoods, any collaborative planning must include participants from many parts of the city. Stakeholders do not want the city at large to view the NRC as a service to the host community only. Overcoming that misperception and establishing a zone of safety around the NRC so that residents from other parts of town will enter the inner-city site are two critical strategies.

The host community had independently formed a committee to work on NRC issues, but now has been brought into the NRCD. The plan has been to merge the host community committee into the larger, more comprehensive end-users' team. This strategy concerns some members of the host community committee, most of who represent low- to moderate-income households. Some have felt that broadening the membership adds delegates but de-emphasises inclusion.

The exact mix of services, projects and offices to be located in the NRC is of considerable importance to the NRCD. Not only do neighbourhood stakeholders wish to guarantee themselves a role and physical space in the centre, but they also are concerned about creating and broadcasting the 'right message' about the centre. Community stakeholders warn that if the city government merely relocates offices to the NRC without a change in philosophy about the role of recipients, then the City of Little Rock will have missed a great opportunity to capitalise on a true partnership with the people it serves.

Recruitment of corporate leaders and businesses into the NRCD is beginning. City and university officials have been asked to nominate likely candidates who have been supportive of or worked in public–private partnerships in the past. Initially, corporate representatives will be asked for advice on a wide range of topics including fundraising, organisational structure and managerial strategies.

Eventually, stakeholder corporations will be asked to underwrite some of the costs of operating the centre and eventually renovate the remaining 30 per cent.

Less active at present is recruitment of not-for-profit agencies, which can bring service and volunteer recruitment expertise to the NRCD. Not-for-profit agencies are important to developing a full complement of services. In the US, many health and human services are delivered not by government but by private, not-for-profit agencies, which contract with government to provide those services. Public funding is rarely adequate and the not-for-profit agencies frequently must generate a portion of their own revenues through grant-writing and fundraising. Likewise, these agencies are encouraged to build alliances with other agencies that have a stake in a particular service or domain in order to generate other forms of support and reduce unnecessary duplication of effort.

The Planning Process

The hiring of the renovation architect by the city has provoked a renewed interest in the physical planning of the building. Representatives of the university, police department and general services department of the city represent the technical assistance team, and three neighbourhood residents represent the citywide team. Three corporate representatives will fill out the steering committee. A full-time city employee, first hired by the university and then transferred to city employment, chairs the steering committee and manages the day-to-day planning. She sits in on all steering committee meetings. The steering committee periodically briefs the city council on the development's status. The collaboration laboured under a deadline because the centre was scheduled to be opened in late 1999.

The NRCD's Future

Planning for the centre had languished after an initial flurry of activity in the first year of the collaboration. Uncertainty about funding was largely to blame, although a lack of steady leadership and vagueness about the community's role in planning the facility contributed. The pace has quickened considerably since the architect was hired, and leaders of the NRCD are rushing to catch up so that stakeholders influence decisions. Genuine involvement of the corporate sector remains a concern. Stakeholders have observed that similar efforts in other cities almost always have significant corporate involvement and financial backing.

AN ANALYSIS OF THE CHALLENGES FACING NRCD

The chaotic development of the NRCD collaboration is a textbook case of how not to organise collaboration. Numerous factors contribute to its halting maturation, some of which could and should have been anticipated, and some for which little preparation and solution were possible.

Primary among the many challenges facing the NRCD are these:

- The NRC did not start out to be a centre for addressing community development problems. Its purpose is evolving into that, but lacking a clear motive from the start has weakened the NRCD in its attempt to attract stakeholders.
- The role of the university likewise has been uncertain. Committing to financial resource support is problematic, although university leaders generally embrace the collaborative approach to community development. Regenerating poor, inner-city neighbourhoods, especially those in proximity to campus, is in the best interest of the university.
- Most of the resources are provided by the city government, making it a powerful stakeholder. City officials can choose to downplay inherent power disparities or continue to dictate the terms of collaboration. The latter likely will spell defeat for a fragile collaborative spirit.
- Basic acknowledgement of and agreement to transforming from a betterment collaboration to an empowerment collaboration (Himmelman, 1992a, 1996) which is not part of the current city psyche. Full community buy-in, ownership and control are remote at this point. Whether the NRCD will endure in any meaningful form without this transformation is doubtful.
- Several environmental limitations greatly hamper the autonomy and power of the NRCD. Regulations dictate the kind of activities that can operate at the centre (although they may be consistent with more of a community-based character to the collaboration). Uncertainty about the

city's board of directors and its intent to include a full line department, and the desire of the police chief to include an entire division, create a highly turbulent environment for the NRCD. Competing community projects may distract corporate leadership from fully supporting the NRC.

- The architect was probably hired too early in the process, before the NRCD was fully formed. Also, the city organised and dictated the terms of the selection process and the contract. Such unilateral action flies in the face of collaborative decision-making.

- No serious consideration of using a facilitator (from either inside or outside) has developed. Enlightened, independent leadership has not appeared and the NRCD is struggling with direction as a result.

- A focus on services has driven space allocation in the NRC. Instead of making decisions by consensus, key stakeholders have let external pressures such as those from the federal department and the architect drive the process.

- Not all relevant stakeholders have been brought into the process at approximately the same time. Many decisions will be made before corporate and not-for-profit partners are introduced.

We will analyse the challenges under the four categories that emanated from the review of previous research on challenges facing multisector collaboration.

An Analysis of Varying Cultural Characteristics

Cultural Attitudes of the Citizenry

Depiction of Little Rock's civic culture and its possible effects on collaboration-building far exceed the bounds of this chapter. For immediate purposes, three brief characteristics – one common to most US cities, one common to most southern US cities, and one common to council-manager-governed cities – are examined. First, many US cities, particularly the older, central cities, face severe economic and social problems (Ross and Levine, 1996). Although wealth abounds in US metropolitan areas, much of it resides in the suburban fringe or in private hands. 'The irony of urban wealth is ... the inability of cities to use what lies just beyond their reach ... ' (Lineberry and Sharkansky, 1974: 19). Although the dispersal of wealth may encourage cities to seek collaboration with entities that have it, a tendency to concentrate on core, essential services seems to cloud the central city's vision.

Second, proactive change strategies continually fight to overcome a prevailing sociopolitical culture of the US South in which citizens yield to traditional, hierarchical and centralised power structures. State and local governments in the South tend to reinforce the status quo (Elazar, 1972). Government–citizen–business partnerships are less frequent in this subculture.

Third, Little Rock's council-manager form of government traditionally has lacked strong policy leadership. Modifications of the plan, especially direct election of the mayor and district representation of the council, have lessened the leadership problem, but studies indicate that this 'reform model' has the tendency to take government out of the political give-and-take of the city and make the local political system 'more sterile and antiseptic' (Lineberry and Sharkansky, 1974). These cultural characteristics are likely to make collaboration more difficult because citizens are less inclined to facilitate or encourage community-based collaboration with local government.

Cultural Distance

Planning for the neighbourhood resource centre was largely the function of city government with some assistance from university representatives. Eighteen months passed before community representation was built into the process. Although difficult to measure in terms of social distance, interviews and observation suggest that early designers thought of the project as what Himmelman (1992a) terms a 'betterment collaboration', which begins outside the community among institutions and is later brought into the community. Most collaborations begin this way, but need to be transformed to an 'empowerment model' to ensure long-term ownership and control by the community (Himmelman, 1992a).

Early meetings of the NRCD reveal deeply held opinions and attitudes about the role of government in society and a certain 'uncomfortableness' between representatives of government, the university and neighbourhoods. The NRCD needs to develop a strategy for easing the tension caused by cultural distance and division.

Intraorganisational Culture

Local government in the US operates largely on a service delivery model, with its efficiency and economy values. Attitudes about this role tend to polarise the city and its potential partners into a 'we/them' mentality. We provide the services and they consume them. Rarely in this model are service recipients – the taxpayers – asked to participate in decision-making and co-production of services.

In an interesting parallel, the faculty and administration of the public university in Little Rock are struggling with competing role perceptions as part of their organisation's culture. Many urban and metropolitan universities in the US are redefining core missions to balance outreach and professional service with classroom teaching and academic research. Broadly tapping faculty expertise will be affected by how well the applied-mission advocates can change the culture.

An Analysis of Differing Organisational Goals

Since the NRCD has not yet included corporate stakeholders, a thorough analysis of this challenge to multisector collaboration cannot be completed. Based on observation of two other public–private partnerships between members of the Little Rock business community and city government, the profit vs. service goal disparity may challenge a close, collaborative working relationship. Risk-taking may vary as well.

The difficulty of convincing corporate leaders that they and their companies are stakeholders in community development may challenge the multisector collaboration. Following Logsdon's (1991) logic, potential private sector participants must determine if community development is relative to their overall interests and how critical it is to those interests (p. 25).

In a macroanalysis, there is little doubt that community development and regeneration are in the best interests of local corporations. Whether viewed from a market or a social responsibility perspective, they probably want to do business and live in a healthy, secure metropolitan area. In a microanalysis, whether or not corporate representatives perceive adequate interdependence with NRCD stakeholders and enough direct impact on their profit-making ability may help determine the extent of their involvement.

An Analysis of Ideological and Procedural Differences

Since the city government plays such a central role, its hierarchical, functionally organised departments tend to approach development of the NRC from that bureaucratic perspective. Coupled with resource limitations and its dependence on federal funding for renovation of the building, this means local government is unlikely to approach problem-solving from a collaborative perspective (Chrislip and Larson, 1994; Gray, 1989). For the City of Little Rock, true community-based collaboration is an unnatural state of affairs.

Size and power differentials between city officials and their prospective partners are likely to reinforce these differences (Gray, 1989). Several key city officials desire to collaborate and realise that neighbourhood representation in the NRCD is critical, but can't help dominating meetings and decision-making. The attitude of 'he who pays the piper calls the tune' unfortunately may prevent all voices from being heard.

Interviews with city government officials provided mixed opinions about sharing power with community representatives. For example, the police representative to the collaboration agrees that community representatives need to be included in the planning process, but argues that only the police have the knowledge to decide actual space allocation. Others appear genuinely to believe that community representatives are important collaborative members and seek to include them in each step of the planning and implementation process. The real test of this open approach will come when allocation decisions are made about space and resources.

An Analysis of Institutional Incentives and Disincentives

The city's government will continue providing services and solving problems in an incremental, fragmented fashion, regardless of whether or not the NRC becomes a reality. Even a fully functioning, collaborative model will not change the overall patterns of service delivery. For the public administrator who is truly committed to making a difference in the quality of life of Little Rock residents, actively reaching out to other stakeholders may be likely. However, bureaucrats, even enlightened ones, may lack incentive to participate in collaborative organisations. Because public administrators generally have little flexibility and autonomy in defining the purposes of their organisation and programmes, and because their objectives are more diverse and harder to specify, collaborative behaviour (both inside government and with external organisations) is usually subject to a more complex set of influences and is more difficult to facilitate. Reward systems are generally standardised and discourage risk-taking and going beyond the explicit tasks assigned. Unless the job description calls for actively working with elements of a shared domain, the public administrator appears unlikely to take the initiative and invest in collaborative formation (Barr and Huxham, 1996; Sink, 1996).

Neighbourhood associations must satisfy the usual 'What's in it for me?' query before they participate, as well. One citizen representative to the NRCD steering committee expressed extreme frustration with local government, accusing it and its representative of trying to smother real, citizen input. 'If government is going to make all the decisions,' he said, 'I'd just as soon be home drinking a beer.' Not-for-profit agencies, especially those that deliver services and advocate for the poor, frequently must seek resources to keep operating. Voluntary collaboration may be seen as a drain of valuable resources, but many not-for-profit agencies lack the wherewithal to go it alone. Yet, ironically, facilitators are finding fewer collaborative forms than they expected in response to crisis scarcity (Sink, 1987). That may be because the need to reduce uncertainty and enhance resources is outweighed by an unwillingness to increase an agency's dependence. A fear of lost autonomy seems to dominate the thinking. From a rational perspective, such decision-making appears absurd. And, at some point, imminent demise does tend to jump-start even those most reticent to reach out. Still, many agencies exercise a so-called 'bunker mentality', where one keeps the head down, the neck tucked in and the shelter door closed tight until the storm blows over. They lack a domain focus or an inability to conceptualise problems and organise solutions at the domain level.

What are the incentives for the University and its Faculty to participate? For those who advocate an active outreach agenda in which university staff render professional service and complete technical and applied research that directly addresses real community problems, what might be a great incentive to reach out to the NCRD may be stymied if the organisational reward system continues to focus on the traditional model of 'publish or perish'. Although the University shares some bureaucratic characteristics with city government and corporations, its decision-making model is more decentralised. Creating incentives for active participation in community development collaboration will be more difficult.

Summary of Challenges

The resources and benefits that stakeholders from each sector may bring to a collaborative effort are as follows:

Sector	Anticipated resources	Potential obstacles
Municipal government	Legitimacy, access to federal funding, services	Service delivery mindset, centralisation
Corporation	Executive leadership, in-kind and financial resources	Social distance, heavy emphasis on 'bottom line'
Not-for-profit agencies	Social service networks, organised volunteers	Narrow focus, client orientation
Neighbourhood organisations	Sense of ownership, self-help, empowerment	Limited resources, suspicion of government, resistance to change
University	Richness of technical expertise, research	Devaluation of service, heavy emphasis on research

A STRATEGIC BRIDGING PROPOSAL

Using work by Westley and Vredenburg (1991) to explore the value of strategic bridging as a form of collaborative facilitation. Although applied in a different interorganisational setting (a Canadian example of negotiations among two environmental groups and a retail grocery chain), the concept of a 'bridging organisation' may have real usefulness for the NRC in Little Rock. 'Bridging organisations "span the social gaps among organizations and constituencies to enable coordinated action"' (Westley and Vredenburg, 1991: 67). Strategic bridging may be the most appropriate form of collaborative facilitation for working with stakeholders, which have significant cultural differences, interests and values. Bridging may be most appropriate as a strategy when the problem domain is under-organised, when stakeholders are uncertain of their role in the domain, and when the stakeholders tend to be unwilling to collaborate (for any of the reasons cited above). The bridging mechanism may be most useful in the early stages of collaborative formation (Westley and Vredenburg, 1991).

The bridging organisation may be a stakeholder with an interest in forwarding its own ends. Over time, the bridging organisation engages in incremental creation of the negotiated order that may permit greater collaboration among all stakeholders. In this sense, the bridging organisation acts as both broker and agent in the problem domain.

In light of the characteristics of the stakeholders and potential stakeholders and the halting development of Little Rock's neighbourhood resource centre, we would propose the public university as an appropriate bridging organisation. We believe it has the respect as a neutral but interested stakeholder whose involvement is not seen as self-serving as much as it is facilitative. The University may be in the best place to enter into negotiations with stakeholders because it is perceived widely as a growing, integral part of the community with a strong interest in supporting community development. The University has several large projects underway in its immediate neighbourhoods (its 'footprint') to improve housing and build neighbourhood leadership capacity.

The role is not one to be taken lightly. As a bridging organisation, not only would the university engage in multiple negotiations in an attempt to 'sell' a collaboration to other stakeholders, but it also must secure a commitment from the home organisation (Westley and Vredenburg, 1991).

Given the competing goals embraced by the University Faculty and the resistance by traditionally oriented faculty to community outreach as a major mission of the institution, this is no mean feat. But the benefits, to the home institution as well as to the NRCD, may be greater. If the University can successfully step in for the city government in terms of facilitating the NRCD collaboration, some of the resistance by neighbourhood residents and their organisations to city dominance may be mitigated.

CONCLUSIONS

This study of multisector collaboration for the purpose of community development has confirmed previous research findings (see, for example, Gray, 1989; Himmelman, 1992a; Huxham, 1993; Chrislip and Larson, 1994) and proposes several new conceptualisations about the development of a comprehensive, community-wide collaboration. In brief summary, here are the major points of the chapter:

- In order to conceptualise the comprehensiveness of regenerating our decaying cities, we should approach the task from the perspective of a meta-domain, a multi-problem domain that transcends several single-problem domains and requires a comprehensive, multisector collaboration with a strategic plan that eschews routinisation, fragmentation or centralisation as means of handling complexity.
- Previous research on challenges to multisector collaboration held up well when applied to this case-study, the development of a neighbourhood resource centre. For example, varying cultural characteristics, differing organisational goals, ideological and procedural differences, and the lack of institutional incentives were useful predictors of obstacles faced by local stakeholders.
- Six particularly stubborn challenges can be concluded from this case:
  1. Community development collaboration is more likely to prosper in a supportive civic culture, which expects proactive local government behaviour and encourages interactive partnerships between established, large organisations and the citizens.
  2. Organisational cultures about mission and function, which discourage reaching out to potential partners, can be particularly difficult to overcome. Local government defines its role as one of service delivery; the university faculty called on to extend professional expertise to solving community problems regards this as low level work; and not-for-profit social service agencies define their work narrowly to serving clients.
  3. Convincing stakeholders that their interests are best served by participation in the community development collaboration and helping them

feel comfortable with other stakeholders, who have varying styles, behaviours and values, looms large.

4. The size and power of local government and corporations tend to pit neighbourhood residents against city hall or 'downtown interests', rather than providing authority and strength to a broad-based collaboration.

5. Contributing to such a large (and sometimes remote) project as community development challenges collaborators to find adequate incentives to motivate key agencies and their leaders. Reward systems may be lacking, the absence of direct and immediate payoff discourages quick gratification, and the press of agency survival distracts even the most well intended not-for-profit administrator.

6. The role of bridging organisation, as proposed by Westley and Vredenburg (1991), may fit the need for a collaborative facilitator when such an ambitious, community-wide effort is undertaken. Bridging may be most appropriate as a strategy when the meta-domain is under-organised and for working with stakeholders, who have significant cultural differences, interests and values.

Without an appropriate mind-set, all of these proposals may be meaningless. Approaching community development as a meta-domain may be another way of conceptualising communities as systems. Scholtes borrows from Deming (1994) to argue that 'true collaboration requires a systems view' (Scholtes, 1997: 53). He urges an application of the quality movement to communities. 'There are few continuous, concerted, coordinated, multiorganizational, public–private, cross jurisdictional systemic activities that view the community as a system of needs and respond to those needs with a system of efforts' (Scholtes, 1997: 50). Such is a community development collaboration trying to coordinate a meta-domain; such is a bridging organisation trying to persuade, negotiate, and broker reluctant stakeholders from each sector; and, such is a people, trying to organise itself in useful, coordinative fashion to tackle the truly tough problems facing cities of the late twentieth and early twenty-first centuries.

References

ALTER, C. and HAGE, J. (1993) *Organizations Working Together*. Sage, Newbury Park, CA.

ASTLEY, W.G. and FOMBRUN, C.J. (1983) Collective Strategy: Social Ecology of Organizational Environments. *Academy of Management Review*, 8, 576–87.

BARR, C. and HUXHAM, C. (1996) Involving the community: collaboration for community development. In Huxham, C. (ed.), *Creating Collaborative Advantage*. Sage, London, 110–25.

BERMAN, E.M. (1996) Local government and community-based strategies: evidence from a national survey of a social problem. *American Review of Public Administration*, 26, 71–91.

CHRISLIP, D. and LARSON, C.E. (1994) *Collaborative Leadership: How Citizens and Civic Leaders Can Make a Difference*. Jossey-Bass, San Francisco.

DEJONG, A. (1996) Inter-organizational collaboration in the policy preparation process. In Huxham, C. (ed.), *Creating Collaborative Advantage*. Sage, London, 165–75.

DEMING, W.E. (1994) *The New Economics for Industry, Government, Education*, 2nd edn. MIT Center for Advanced Engineering Study, Cambridge, MA.

DYMSZA, W.A. (1988) Successes and failures in joint ventures in developing countries: lessons from experience. In Contractor, F. and Lorange, P. (eds), *Cooperative Strategies in International Business: Joint Ventures and Technology Partnerships between Firms*. D.C. Heath, Lexington, MA, 61–81.

EDEN, C., HUXHAM, C. and S. VANGEN (1996) *The Dynamics of Purpose in Multi-Organizational Collaborative Groups: Achieving Collaborative Advantage for Social Development*. University of Strathclyde, Glasgow, Management Science Working Paper 96/3.

ELAZAR, D. (1972) *American federalism: A view from the states*. Crowell, New York.

GRAY, B. (1989) *Collaborating: Finding Common Ground for Multiparty Problems*. Jossey-Bass, San Francisco.

GRAY, B. (1996) Cross-sectoral partners: Collaborative alliances among business, government and communities. In Huxham, C. (ed.), *Creating Collaborative Advantage*. Sage, London, 57–79.

HIMMELMAN, A.T. (1992a) *Communities Working Collaborating for a Change*. Himmelman Consulting Group, Minneapolis, MN.

HIMMELMAN, A.T. (1992b) *Local Government and Collaborative Change*. National League of Cities, Washington, DC.

HIMMELMAN, A.T. (1996) On the theory and practice of transformational collaboration: From social service to social justice. In Huxham, C. (ed.), *Creating Collaborative Advantage*. Sage, London, 19–43.

HUXHAM, C. (1993) Pursuing collaborative advantage. *Journal of the Operational Research Society*, 44, 599–611.

HUXHAM, C. (1996) Collaboration and collaborative advantage. In Huxham, C. (ed.), *Creating Collaborative Advantage*. Sage, London, 1–18.

HUXHAM, C. and MacDONALD, D. (1992) Introducing collaborative advantage: achieving inter-organizational effectiveness through meta-strategy. *Management Decision*, 30 (3), 50–6.

KOFMAN, F. and SENGE, P. (1995) Communities of commitment: the heart of learning organizations. In Chawla, S. and Renesch, J. (eds), *Learning Organizations: Developing Cultures for Tomorrow's Workplace*. Productivity Press, Portland, OR, 1–21.

LAUMANN, E.O. and PAPPI, F.U. (1976) *Networks of Collective Action: A perspective on community influence systems*. Academic Press, New York.

LINEBERRY, R.L. and SHARKANSKY, I. (1974) *Urban Politics and Public Policy*, 2nd edn. Harper & Row, New York.

LOGSDON, J.M. (1991) Interests and interdependence in the formation of social problem-solving collaborations. *Journal of Applied Behavioral Science*, 27 (1), 23–7.

McCANN, J.E. (1983) Design guidelines for social problem-solving interventions. *Journal of Applied Behavioral Science*, 18, 177–92.

MELAVILLE, A. and BLANK, M. (1993) *Together We Can*. US Government Printing Office, Washington, DC.

OLIVER, C. (1990) Determinants of interorganizational relationships: integration and future directions. *Academy of Management Review*, 15, 241–65.

RITCHIE, L. and MONTANHEIRO, L. (1996) Forging public and private sector alliances in Britain: the South Yorkshire experience. Paper presented at the Third International Workshop on Multi-Organisational Partnerships, Glasgow, Scotland.

ROSS, B. and LEVINE, M. (1996) *Urban Politics: Power in Metropolitan America*, 5th edn. Peacock, Itasca, IL.

SCHOLTES, P.R. (1997) Communities as systems. *Quality Progress*, July, 35, 49–53.

SELSKY, J.W. (1991) Lessons in community development: an activist approach to stimulating interorganizational collaboration. *Journal of Applied Behavioral Science*, 27 (1), 91–115.

SHUBIK, M. (1982) *Game Theory in the Social Sciences*. MIT Press, Cambridge, MA.

SINK, D. (1987) Success and failure in voluntary community networks. *New England Journal of Human Services*, 5, 25–30.

SINK, D. (1996) Five obstacles to community-based collaboration and some thoughts about overcoming them. In Huxham, C. (ed.), *Creating Collaborative Advantage*, Sage, London, 101–09.

SINK, D. and HUXHAM, C. (1996) Collaborative advantage as a strategy for inclusive urban policymaking: the cases of Glasgow and Little Rock. Paper presented at the Urban Affairs Association conference, New York.

SINK, D. and WILSON, M. (1983) The intersection of political culture and fiscal federalism: state block grants in Alabama. *Journal of Sociology and Social Welfare*, 29, 230–9.

TRIST, E.L. (1983) Referent organizations and the development of interorganizational domains. *Human Relations*, 36, 247–68.

WESTLEY, F. and VREDENBURG, H. (1991) Strategic bridging: the collaboration between environmentalists and business in the marketing of green products. *Journal of Applied Behavioral Science*, 27 (1), 65–90.

WOOD, D.J. (1991) Corporate social performance revisited. *Academy of Management Review*, 16, 691–718.

WOOD, D.J. and GRAY, B. (1991) Towards a comprehensive theory of collaboration. *Journal of Applied Behavioral Science*, 27 (2), 139–62.

6 Leveraging Professional Knowledge in Healthcare Networks through Integrated IT: The V-NBS Approach

Graham Winch and François Sauer

INTRODUCTION

Technological advances such as the convergence of communication and information technology play a significant role in the perceived disorder in health systems (Butters and Eom, 1992). The paradox is that to re-establish order in these systems requires an innovative use of the same technology. Technology has to be used differently; more of the same, or, for that matter, further simple automation of current processes, will not be sufficient. A keyword that is frequently used is 'enabling' change processes and agents through the intelligent and innovative implementation of technology to leverage human thinking, action and learning. Another paradox of this evolution is, on the one hand, a trend towards globalisation and yet, concurrently, a trend towards differentiation at the level of smaller, interdependent entities. 'Downsizing', 'outsourcing' and 'partnerships' are but a few keywords. What will count ultimately is arriving at satisfactory outcomes from the many factors that result from the myriad of interacting stakeholders, more than simply taking into account individual stakeholders or their local relationships. This state will depend on the mutuality of objectives or goals of the stakeholder groups, which include the goals of the network or collaborative venture, those of the partnering organisations, and those of the individuals within them (see Vangen and Huxham, 1998). This mutuality will come not just from each stakeholder having a clear vision of the collaboration from their own viewpoint, but also because they are able to take a perspective from the reference points of their partnering organisations.

Healthcare delivery is a particularly vivid example of how restructuring, political rethinking and modern management paradigms conspire to produce complex, network-type organisations. At the same time, their social and political importance in conjunction with the high costs involved – typically of the order of 4 to 8 per cent of GDP for major developed countries – make it crucially important that stakeholder benefit is maximised. Given the disparate stakeholders in the sector, healthcare delivery is thus coming under serious scrutiny from many quarters – administrative, financial, management and clinical. However, the very complexity and interrelatedness brings problems. Examination of healthcare provision using a strategic information modelling in various different contexts highlights the difficulties of arriving at effective systems (Bytheway, 1996). This problem reflects on the role and position of a UK healthcare trust that is at the same time the principal client and a major shareholder of the privatised company that provides its information system services. Further, dissatisfaction with many computer-based information systems has been attributed by Butters and Eom (1992) to a design perspective based on misunderstood and/or outmoded views of the healthcare environment. Specifically, the current focus on procedure and/or service renders useless decision support systems based on departmental or day-to-day operational activities. This emphasises the need for integrated solutions with single data architectures, through which both clinical and managerial challenges can be simultaneously addressed. This too enables a switch in management focus from an event perspective, which responds to discrete errors that impact on individuals – patients and clinicians – to a clinical delivery process perspective, which takes a systemic view.

The potential of a 'virtual-neural business system' (V-NBS) was originally described in Winch *et al.* (1997), and its specific role in network-form organisations and extended enterprises was considered in Winch (1997). This chapter examines the role and benefits in integrating the disparate member organisations of a healthcare system by focusing on their position as stakeholders within the networked system. The value added of the 'virtual-neural business system' is the leveraging of the human creative thinking process and the infrastructure for communication, collaboration and coordination. This is achieved through the integration of data, information and knowledge, and the provision of the relevant monitoring, simulation, change management and learning tools, under a single, coherent platform for all of the system stakeholders and at the appropriate level of recursion for each participant.

The chapter considers the specific managerial needs of network-form organisations, and the reasons that these place particular demands on an integrating IT system. A review of the components and structure of typical healthcare systems in developed countries from a stakeholder perspective is also provided. The conceptual framework of the V-NBS is then briefly described together with its features which enables a 'professional partnership' relationship between the network members. The focus here is on administrative, financial and managerial integration, and on the importance of such a partnership relationship for the sharing and leveraging of professional knowledge in the preventative and clinical domains. Pointers are also given to the scope for exploiting this approach in the medical-related domains.

COORDINATION AND INTELLIGENCE IN NETWORK-FORM ORGANISATIONS

One important manifestation of the trends in managerial, political and social thinking has been the increasing importance of intra- and inter-firm networking, which has been consistent, and supported by well-argued cases. The terms network-form organisation and extended enterprise have been coined for these new structures that have emerged from internal reorganisation through demergers and devolutions into autonomous but linked operational units, or from the sealing of long-term strategic alliances between firms in complex supply chain structures, shared R&D programmes or other commercialisation ventures. Many of these network-form systems, of which healthcare delivery is a prime example, operate across the public–private sector divide.

Grandoni and Soda (1995) argue that the benefits derive from the organisations' ability to regulate complex transactional interdependence as well cooperative transformational interdependence. In other words, these new operating units are offered the opportunities of working closely and jointly with key business partners, developing competitive advantage collectively through supply chain efficiencies, coordination of research and product and/or process development activities. The important distinctiveness with such networks is in the interdependence between firms achieved through cooperative endeavour. This is quite different from the aggregation of these units within a single firm and from coordination between them though market signals and processes (prices, strategic moves, tacit collusion, and so on).

Some other recent writings have focused on the importance of certain corporate and leadership traits, which have traditionally been associated with head-office functions in large organisations. These may potentially conflict with, and deflate, the expected benefits of the newer organisational structures if they are still needed but not exhibited. This chapter briefly reviews some of this thinking on control and coordination needs, reconciling it with the particular demands of these new organisational structures. It then considers how network-wide IT systems, an operational necessity, may be developed to provide a 'shared visioning' facility (Stewart, 1993). This may offer coordination and intelligence functionality to the network through providing independent but coherent at-the-desk support to all network partners.

Simons (1995) has described the issue of how to exercise adequate control in organisations that demand flexibility, innovation and creativity as a fundamental problem. He points specifically to the dangers that the pursuit of some opportunities may lead to excessive risk or invite behaviour that could damage integrity. This specifies a key requirement on such organisations that they be able to operate in the present, while creating the future and managing transitions. This represents what Harari describes as 'bifocal vision' – the ability to continually perfect existing processes, while, at the same time, developing new products and processes (Harari, 1994). In supporting these needs, the corporate centre or 'parent' in traditional organisations may be seen as having served a key role in terms of holding, then drawing on the mental maps that it possesses – what Campbell *et al.* (1995) identify as 'the values, aspirations, rules of thumb, biases, and success formulas that guide managers as they deal with the (subordinate) businesses'.

Hout and Carter (1995) argue further that evolving management structures if anything demand more, not less, top-down management. They point to a continuing hands-on role for senior managers, even after organisations have been re-engineered, because they can use their authority to get to the heart of a problem and therefore provide superior solutions. They also argue that by linking process improvement to strategy, senior executives are uniquely positioned to create competitive advantages. Managers in newer organisational types will have to be supported in their task of evaluating decisions in the context of the whole network given that, unlike their head-office predecessors, they may have had very limited experience of working within partnerships. They must also have well-developed communication systems to appreciate impacts throughout the network. Ghoshal *et al.* (1994) demonstrated the importance of lateral communications within multinational corporations, but these conclusions could apply equally to the network-form organisation.

Ironically, while rapid advancement in information technology has been a significant driver of the turbulence in the business environment, it is also proving to be a major facilitator of the multi-organisational strategic alliance. The basic function of IT support systems in such alliances is to coordinate the operations of the various partner enterprises through electronic procurement processes, financial transactioning, computer-aided design (CAD) and even distributed CIM (computer-integrated manufacturing), and electronic data interchange (EDI). However, the potential for IT to support more fundamental strategic processes in network organisations is less developed and understood. Dynamic system models and 'enterprise models' have already been recognised as facilitators in the building of consensus in management teams (Winch, 1993) and in the development of a shared view of a business and its environment. Robert Curtice is quoted in his support of 'enterprise modelling' (see Aranow, 1991):

> The enterprise model is important as a communication tool and as a vehicle for assessing the impact of change on business ... the enterprise model helps you map changes to the various parts of your business to understand how the business will be affected.

The critical feature of any such modelling approach is that it must contend with the structural and dynamic complexity that the many interrelationships within network-based organisational structures bring.

THE CHALLENGES AND STAKEHOLDERS IN HEALTHCARE DELIVERY

As a result of economic uncertainties and sociopolitical rethinking, many industrialised countries are witnessing turbulence and tension in their health-care systems. The stakeholders can no longer afford the (financial) means to satisfy the needs and expectations of the population or their own require-ments, or to fulfil the promises made to maintain and enhance healthcare services. The healthcare system's nature as a mixed private/public industry with traditionally different rhythms (short/long), different purposes (profit/social well-being) and different operating modes (business management/administration) increases the challenge to consolidate positions in order to reach a new order and harmony.

Each type of stakeholder in the healthcare system faces a number of issues and preoccupations. Some of these problems are documented in Table 6.1.

When commerce in western societies recently traversed a downturn, Winch *et al.* (1997) identified a number of structural transitions or phe-nomena, which are reproduced in Table 6.2. Similar trends to these have already begun to be established in the healthcare sector and will continue to shape the coming years. The effects of the overall phenomenon will be:

- a growing number of small and interdependent organisational units;
- shorter organisational cycles, that is, at the same time a greater capacity to change but also a greater need to adapt as the interdependency of the various players evolves and increases;
- a shift in the demand for process automation to an ever-greater coordi-nation-and-integration capability at all levels, in all organisations.

Table 6.1   The disparate stakeholders in healthcare delivery

Stakeholder	Description	Problems/preoccupations
Population	Citizens	• Continued/increased need for direct participation • Access to quality service at • Lower prices • Expanded coverage
Government	Legislation	• Social malaise • Social well-being • Human rights
	Social security (operations)	• Maintain/improve service quality and coverage • Reduce operating costs • Create awareness on preventive actions and trends • Manage social well-being
Healthcare providers	Hospitals, primary providers (GP practices), MDs, nurses, other medical and paramedical institutions	• Access to comprehensive information for professional and management decisions • Maintain/increase quality of service • Understand and reduce the cost of service • Keep employees satisfied
Healthcare suppliers	Suppliers of technology, products and services	• Increase revenues, profits and market share • Identify new market trends • Maintain/increase customer satisfaction
Healthcare education/ research	Teaching hospitals, nursing schools, paramedical trainers, universities	• Relevance/value of training and research • Funding • Demand for graduates
Insurance companies	Complementary policies (sickness, accident, life)	• Contain healthcare costs • Maintain/increase customer satisfaction, margins and market share
NGO's	WHO, etc.	• Capture, store and disseminate complete, correct and up to date information • Create co-ordinated plans and actions

Table 6.1   Continued

Stakeholder	Description	Problems/preoccupations
V-NBS	Provision of IT solutions	• Achieve the committed benefits of the new IT solution to stakeholder benefit and satisfaction • Support economical and effective delivery • Leveraging professional knowledge throughout the system

As a result, the analysis and selection of alternatives for resource allocation will be more essential than ever. Managers will be faced with the challenges to:

• proactively absorb and use far greater amounts of information;
• understand the dynamic of the global healthcare system (stakeholders' needs, wants and priorities, and their interactions);
• make decisions that are globally sound for them and their community;
• implement the decisions effectively (*speed* and *quality*).

Unfortunately, different stakeholders within such systems are unlikely to have a shared view of the system in which they operate, or be in consensus on what are the key drivers for the system. It has long been postulated that clinicians and managers in health service systems are typical in showing this lack of a shared 'world-view'. Work by Cavanna *et al.* (1999) using various group mental mapping techniques has highlighted just such a diversity of view among examples of these groupings in the New Zealand Ministry of Health; the resulting cognitive maps demonstrating the quite different perspectives that they had of the same health and disability system.

INTEGRATING INFORMATION AND SHARED VISIONING THROUGH THE V-NBS

The analysis of structural transitions and phenomena outlined above led to the development of a framework of support required by network-form organisations within the concept of a V-NBS (Winch *et al.*, 1997). The envisaged structure of the V-NBS is given in Figure 6.1.

Table 6.2 Dimensions of change driving organisational rethinking.

Phenomenon	From	To
Identity	Barriers to protect physical resources	Relationships to thrive and leverage Intellectual assets
Business focus	Inside-out product approach	Outside-in customer-driven approach
Privatisation	Public/government organisations	Private,commercial organisations
Decision-making	Centralised, sequential, hierarchically structured	Decentralised, concurrent, networked organisations
Partnerships	Commercial/economic transactions, independence, control, volatile	Long-term evolving interdependence, achievement of mutual goals and interests
Interaction	Transactional	Transformational
Integration	Large, monolithic, vertically integrated organisations – managed through hierarchy	Many smaller business structures, profit/loss centres, integrated through projects
Outsourcing	Self-sufficient	Concentration on core-competence/purpose with outsourcing of non-core activities/competencies
Customisation	Standardised mass products and services, target of single product/service	Individually customised products and services, run volume of 1
Cost imperative	Economies of scale	Economies of scope
Information	Limited access to information	Information overload (with a need for navigation and decision support tools)
Process	Mass production, sub-optimisation, automation	End-to-end (all players, from suppliers to end-users), process innovation
Technology	Support and automation, accounting	enabling, assistance, decision support
Competence	Resource-based	Competence-oriented
Team-based	Monodisciplinary departments	Multi-disciplinary teams

The primary functionalities of each component of the system are:

- *Facilitating architectures and infrastructures*   Beneath the above functions are the basic hardware, software and network structures of the system along with various office and application programmes.

- *The operations repository*   The operations repository comprises the databases, or access mechanisms to the databases, of the various process (administration) and content (professional) applications.
- *The knowledge repository*   The knowledge repository includes structured descriptions of the business model for each organisation stakeholder in the overall context. These mental maps reflect the values, aspirations, rules of thumb, biases and success described by Campbell *et al.* (1995), referred to above.
- *The monitoring and simulation functions*   The monitoring and simulation functions proactively assist the organisation's stakeholders to manage and evolve their enterprises. The monitoring function updates the perceived state of each stakeholder, generates warning signals and proposes proactive or corrective actions. The simulation function enables the evaluation of the potential impacts of their decisions before they take them, in a virtual environment. This, along with the visualisation function (see next item), provides the 'visioning' facility that is the focus of this chapter.
- *The visualisation function*   The visualisation function allows each stakeholder in the organisation to access and represent all information available in the operations and the knowledge repositories according to their access privileges, to enable them to *observe*, *incorporate* and *integrate*.

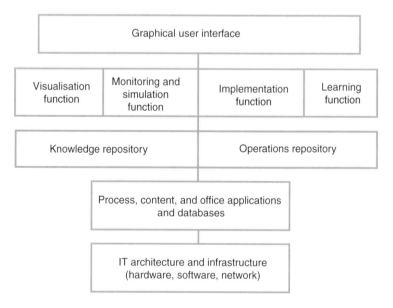

Figure 6.1   Components of the virtual-neural business system.

- *The implementation function* This function supports the organisation's stakeholders in turning decisions into actions and results. It consists of the formal documentation of requests and commitments, expected deliverables, resource allocations and progress monitoring.
- *The learning function* The learning functionality develops from elucidation and analysis of gaps between expected results and achieved results. It is argued (Sauer *et al.*, 1995) that learning happens as a result of the 'connectivity' that enables collective behaviour and not as the result of a central processor or controller.
- *The graphical user interface* The GUI brings and presents the different components of the system together in a single, coherent user environment to provide an intuitive access mechanism to multiple views of data, information and knowledge, tailored to the specific needs of each stakeholder.

THE PARTICULAR ATTRIBUTES OF THE V-NBS APPROACH

If the V-NBS is to mimic its medical analogue – the neural system (of, or relating to, or affecting a nerve or the nervous system) – in any meaningful way, it has to include a number of features. These are to be found particularly in the knowledge repository, the visualisation function and the learning function.

The knowledge repository includes structured descriptions of the business model for each healthcare system stakeholder in the overall context. It includes the following:

1. *Belief System* The inner motivation of the enterprise's participants – that is, the purpose, culture, norms and values; as such, the 'compass' or model according to which the enterprise 'behaves' in the market.
2. *Resources and intangible assets* The capacity of the organisation to make decisions and transform them, through actions into results – for example, processes, policies, competencies, knowledge, products, and so on.
3. *Decisions and actions* Outstanding requests as well as commitments made and received.
4. *Vital signs, expectations and gaps* Vital signs are those qualitative and quantitative factors that describe the viability of the enterprise. Gaps are the delta between expectations and actual results.
5. *New events* Combinations of new events that create the circumstances in which gaps will be or have been generated.
6. *Context* Information about partners, competitors, suppliers, government policies and so on.

The visualisation function allows each stakeholder in the healthcare system to access and represent all information available in the operations and the knowledge repositories. Stokke *et al.* (1991) emphasised the importance, in any analysis of the future, of there being a focus on the specific trends and issues that are important to the decision being made. They also cited the old adage, 'Forewarned means forearmed.' Godet and Roubelet (1996) identified the development of an ability to recognise and respond to early signs of change or unanticipated benefits as critical to the process of enabling organisations to prepare for necessary transformation. Winch (1999) has highlighted the particular importance of using dynamic rather than static-model-based scenarios, whether stimulated by qualitative structural mapping or by computer-modelling approaches, in appraising strategic moves in highly dynamic environments. Included in the V-NBS are a number of predefined views for each system stakeholder; these maps represent the state of the healthcare system from different perspectives, and at different levels of detail. Four examples of the type of views are:

- an epidemiological view about trends in morbi-mortality;
- a financial view about trends in the health costs from a community, enterprise or individual perspective;
- a geo-political view about patterns in the demand/offer ratio for healthcare services;
- a systemic view about warning signals and the impact of specific healthcare programmes at the community or enterprise level.

Other combinations of information objects display, for example, the business model, the basic organisational structure, processes and resources. The system also provides a capability for building personalised views or accessing information objects of occasional interest while guaranteeing security, confidentiality and authentication. Through these multiple views, stakeholders are better equipped to discover new ways to improve globally the operations of their enterprise, while maintaining the integrity, harmony and shared objectives of the whole system.

The learning function comprises the elucidation of gaps between expected results and achieved results. Because it is linked with all other components of the V-NBS, it constitutes a powerful tool to explore the consequences of changes in the healthcare context and business structures or processes in the pursuit of continuous improvement. It further identifies trends in healthcare service requirements and their fulfilment, as well as patterns of present and potential business maladies. The result is a leveraging of the individual learning and the organisational knowledge assets through the systematic documentation of assumptions and decisions, as well as expected and achieved results and the gap or difference between them.

CONCLUSIONS

The primary features of the V-NBS for the healthcare system stakeholders are the capabilities to:

- organise, associate and present data;
- interlink the 'virtual world' and the 'real world';
- compress and expand the time and space dimensions;
- test alternatives in a safe environment;
- actively support the capacity to learn, at the level of the individual and the organisation.

In organising, associating and presenting data, information and knowledge from various perspectives at the same time the system offers a concurrent and multi-dimensional view of the delivery system. For example, a process view of how a patient requests and obtains services from a healthcare system reflects a financial view of the system rather than to plan for a specific enterprise, and, simultaneously, to deliver the desired volume of services to a specific community with the associated system costs.

The process of interlinking the 'virtual world' and the 'real world' is achieved using OO-technology (object oriented – a computing approach based on structuring of programs around 'objects' reflecting real-world structures). This linkage guarantees the cohesion between the past and the future and thus allows V-NBS users to test alternatives and make realistic decisions that leverage the overall system. Using the same 'business model' as an execution engine not only provides a higher level of automation – it also ensures that operations are actually performed in accordance with the business model. Further, and importantly, the time and space dimensions can be compressed or expanded as required for the users to perceive trends. Such trends might typically relate to morbi-mortality, or, at an enterprise level, the patterns of and potential business sicknesses, such as stagnation or decrease in market share, erosion of profits or relative attractiveness, decrease in employee moral or decrease in the rate of innovation.

By offering the facility to test alternatives in a safe environment, users are able to choose decisions knowing that, based on the current understanding, they are the best to leverage the overall system. The system consequently actively supports, at the level of the individual and the organisation, the capacity to learn by reviewing the gaps identified through the systematic documentation of assumptions, decisions, expected results and achieved results. The V-NBS approach delivers quality improvement that addresses the problems in the design of the systems, not in the behaviours of individuals. This creates an environment in which key players in health-care delivery can identify how their professional positions can be undermined by poorly designed processes.

The purpose and goal of any V-NBS is therefore to impact positively all stakeholders of the healthcare system. Patients benefit directly through improved healthcare, participation in the change process and an enhanced awareness through direct interactions, such as viewing their own health record on the system. Providers have access to comprehensive health information on which to base decisions and treatments, while eliminating many non-value-added administrative processes. Government has improved healthcare for its citizens while concurrently benefiting from cost savings. In addition, more comprehensive information is available for decision-making purposes.

References

ARANOW, E. (1991) Modelling exercises shake up enterprises. *Software Magazine*, 5, January, 36–41

BUTTERS, S. and EOM, S. (1992) Decision support systems in the healthcare industry. *Journal of Systems Management*, June, 26, 28–31.

BYTHEWAY, A. (1996) Strategic information modelling: some experiences with a new framework. *Journal of Applied Management Studies*, 5 (1), 17–46.

CAMPBELL, A., GOOLD, M. and ALEXANDER, M. (1995) Corporate strategy: the quest for parenting advantage. *Harvard Business Review*, Mar.–Apr., 73, 120–32.

CAVANNA, R.Y., DAVIES, P.K., ROBSON, R.M. and WILSON, K.J. (1999) Drivers of quality in health services: different worldviews of clinicians and policy managers revealed. *System Dynamics Review*, 15 (3), 331–40.

GHOSHAL, S., KORINE, H. and SZULANSKI, G. (1994) Inter-unit Communications in Multinational Corporations, *Management Science*, 40 (1), 96–110.

GODET, M. and ROUBELET, F. (1996) Creating the future: the use and misuse of scenarios. *Long Range Planning*, 29, 164–71.

GRANDONI, A., and SODA, G. (1995) Inter-firm networks: antecedents, mechanisms and forms. *Organisational Studies*, 16 (2), 183–214.

HARARI, O. (1994) Beyond the 'vision thing': management's new way of looking at strategic planning. *Management Review*, 83 (11), 29–32.

HOUT, T. M. and CARTER, J.C. (1995) Getting it done: new roles for senior executives. *Harvard Business Review*, Nov.–Dec., 73, 133–45.

SAUER, F., GYLLSTROM, H. and WINCH, G.W. (1995) Towards a Global Health Network. *Current Issues in Public Health*, 1, 160–4.

SIMONS, R. (1995) Control in an age of empowerment. *Harvard Business Review*, Mar.–Apr., 73, 80–8.

STEWART, T.A. (1993) Welcome to the revolution. *Fortune*, 13 December, 32–8.

STOKKE, P.R., RALSTON, W.K., BOYCE, T.A. and WILSON, I.H. (1991) Visioning and preparing for the future. *Technological and Social Change*, *40*, 73–86.

VANGEN, S. and HUXHAM, C. (1998) Creating a TIP: issues in the design of a process for transferring theoretical insight about inter-organisational collaboration into practice. *International Journal of Public–Private Partnering*, *1* (1), 19–42.

WINCH, G.W. (1993) Consensus building in the planning process: benefits from a 'hard' modelling approach. *System Dynamics Review*, *9* (3), 287–300.

WINCH, G.W. (1997) Computer-aided visioning in the 'network-form' organisation. Paper presented at the Fourth International Conference on Multi-Organisational Partnerships and Co-operative Strategy, Oxford University, July.

WINCH, G.W. (1999) Dynamic Visioning for Dynamic Environments. *Journal of The Operational Research Society*, *50* (4), 354–61.

WINCH, G.W., GYLLSTROM, H., SAUER, F. and SEROR-MARKLIN, S. (1997) 'The virtual-neural business system: a vision for IT support in the net-work form organisation. *Management Decision*, *35* (1), 40–8.

7 Knowledge and Trust in Partnership Formation

Richard Butler and Jas Gill

INTRODUCTION

As organisations have faced increased competition, and changes in technological developments and institutional rules, partnerships and other types of cooperative arrangements between organisations have become increasingly common (Freeman and Hagedoorn, 1994; Harbison and Pekar, 1998; Tyler and Steemsa, 1995). However, such partnerships have not been without problems. For example, joint ventures are regarded as being difficult to manage and Franko (1971) found that one-third of joint ventures were eventually dissolved, while Beamish (1984) reported that the performance of nearly two-thirds of joint ventures in industrialising economies were considered unsatisfactory by managers of multinationals. Problems are considered to arise through choosing the wrong partner, the inherent instability of joint ventures and so on (Killing, 1988).

Previous work on alliances has focused on strategic motives for collaboration (Glaister and Buckley, 1996), the choice between different forms of equity investment (Hennart and Reddy, 1997; Woodcock *et al.*, 1994), between equity and non-equity forms of collaboration (Das and Teng, 1996) and the importance of partner selection in the viability of international joint ventures (Farr and Fischer, 1992; Geringer, 1991; Luo, 1997; Zahra and Elhagrasey, 1994). These analyses are derived largely from the perspective of neo-classical economics, which assumes that decision-makers are rational and have perfect knowledge. This is problematic given the problems of bounded rationality (Cyert and March, 1992; Simon, 1947) and the importance of intangible factors, such as trust and commitment, in the formation and evolution of joint ventures (Parkhe, 1993). The focus here is on how organisations ensure that they can have confidence in knowledge about a potential partner and the processes by which this occurs.

This chapter has two related aims. The first is to examine the ways in which organisations build up knowledge about a potential partner in practice, which is done by analysing the process of partner selection in a joint venture between a UK water company and an Australasian waste disposal company. The second is to develop a framework for investigating the process of partner selection and for understanding the factors that led to the formation of partnerships. A case-study is used to illustrate these issues. Discussion of why organisations form partnerships, and the nature of knowledge-based relationships is viewed from the rational positivist, institutional theory and collectivist approaches, by using the evidence found in the case-study.

This study focused on the processes underlying partner selection in a service-based joint venture (WACL) operating in the waste disposal industry. Regulations are constantly becoming more stringent in this fast-growing niche market. WACL was formed in the early 1990s between WASO (a UK-based water company), which had a 55 per cent share of the equity, and TEWA (an Australasian-based waste treatment company), with a 45 per cent stake. The core technology was designed and supplied by TEWA.

The research design was based on the case-study approach. A single case-study methodology is the appropriate method for examining a process that is not well understood or for addressing the 'how' and 'why' questions in research, and can use single or multiple cases and involve multiple levels (Yin, 1984). Case-studies can also be use to describe events or generate theory (Gersick, 1988) but are not generally suitable for testing theory except possibly by falsifying an existing theory (Pinfield, 1986).

THE CONCEPT OF TRUST

Considerable work has been done on trust as a general concept in the social sciences (see for example Fukuyama, 1995), leading to a variety of meanings (Furlong, 1996; Gambetta, 1988; Shapiro, 1986). In this chapter, trust is conceptualised as having procedural, personal and institutional dimensions.

Types of Trust

Procedural trust is about confidence in the routines used by an organisation. It reflects knowledge, which accurately predicts outcomes and is closely connected to the workings of bureaucratic organisation. A bureaucracy can have a memory apparently independent of the people that built those procedures, making it possible to slot different people into roles to carry out tasks (Weber, 1968).

Personal trust is based on confidence that a particular person or persons will act in a predictable way in order to fulfil expectations. This is trust linked to people rather than to roles and procedures. If the individuals directly involved in the setting up of a partnership between organisations change, trust in that partnership can decline. With personal trust, knowledge is associated with an individual located within a social context. For example, a person who is trusted as an expert in a particular area is an expert only within the 'technical community' that comprises that subject (Nelson, 1993).

Institutional trust is the confidence that can be placed in a particular organisation or other established body to fulfil expectations simply by virtue of being that institution. Institutional trust involves symbolic factors such as reputation, and reliable knowledge derives from the presence of a symbol, for example, brand name or International Standards Organisation certification (Shapiro, 1986).

The Dynamics of Trust

Building trust may involve a cycle that starts from a low level of trust but where there are attempts to gather additional information to build trust (Lewicki and Bunker, 1996). Experiences likely to lead to personal trust are demonstrated by goodwill, as shown for example in one person not taking advantage of an opportunity to exploit another person, or forbearance in times of difficulty, as shown by the willingness of one person to support another in times of difficulty. Conversely, an act of betrayal can destroy trust. Search may also involve a more calculative process of trying to work out the motives of a potential partner. Hence, the process of trust-building between potential partners can also include making each other's motives visible. Overall, then, knowledge of the other party can be considered in terms of goodwill (Ring and Van de Ven, 1994) and competence-based trust (Sako, 1992).

DATA COLLECTION

Data collection was primarily through in-depth interviews lasting between one and a half and three hours with senior management of the joint venture and parents using a semi-structured questionnaire, supplemented by information from annual reports of the UK parent. Interviews were carried out with the joint venture general manager (April 1995 and July 1996), the managing director of the Australasian firm (July 1996), and both the technical director (March 1997) and commercial director (August 1995) of the UK parent.

Two types of data were collected. The first, structured data using a number of Likert-type scales, covered six main factors: interdependence, competition, ambiguity, trust, autonomy and performance. Interdependence between parties is required of potential partners. This can be divided into pooled, sequential and reciprocal (Thompson, 1967), while ambiguity in the means to achieve organisational goals affects trust relations between organisations (Perrow, 1970). The aim was to categorise data to enable comparison, to plot changes over time, and to allow comparison across cases. The second kind of data gathered was much more open-ended and was obtained by means of prompts and discussion. The interviews were tape-recorded in addition to taking notes. The emphasis was to capture the interviewee's interpretation of the situation and to explore the quality of key concepts such as trust.

The balance between the two types of data collected varied considerably over the six factors. Given the centrality of trust in collaborative ventures and lack of agreement in the literature on the nature and dynamics of trust, an inductive approach was used to explore how the informants perceived interorganisational trust. It was in this area that the greatest amount of qualitative data was collected. This was done in two main ways: first, through a series of open-ended questions about trust, and second, by asking the informants to draw graphs of how their 'trust' (vertical axis) in each of the other organisations had changed over time (horizontal axis). Each graph was used to probe their conception of trust by, for example, asking them to explain its form and critical events underlying changes in trust or points of inflection.

Structured data was collected covering the type of interdependence in the joint venture arrangement, which was categorised by asking each informant how their organisation was dependent upon the others, and vice versa, as well as how dependencies had changed over time.

The level of competition between the parents or with the joint venture was rated on a five-point, Likert-type scale, ranging from 1 for 'not at all' to 5 for 'across a very wide range of activities'. These questions were also designed to elicit more qualitative data, thus stimulating discussion as to the degree and nature of these activities and competition within and outside the joint venture, and how this had changed over time.

The degree of goal ambiguity for the joint venture as perceived by each parent was assessed using a five-point, Likert-type scale, ranging from 1 for 'clearly defined in all major areas' to 5 for 'a great many areas of ambiguity'. Again, these structured questions were used as a stimulus for discussion in order to elicit more detail about the nature of such ambiguity.

Validation of qualitative data involved triangulation of responses from the various informants, and, where possible, against relatively objective anchorage points which could be checked by consulting written records.

THE PARTNERS OF THE JOINT VENTURE

TEWA is a small but rapidly growing, technologically based, entrepreneurial Australasian-based company providing specialist waste management services. TEWA had three directors (engineering, marketing and transport) and relied on a small number of directly employed staff. Its operations are highly dependent upon outside organisations and individuals who are contracted for their services. In effect, it has many characteristics of the 'networked' firm or 'lean production' and was positioned at the centre of a network of relationships. These relationships were not restricted by national boundaries. For example, design work for its plant was carried out in the US. This system of operations allowed flexible and rapid responses to changes in the environment as well as shifting risks and costs outside the boundary of the organisation. Like such organic companies, it was characterised by rapid decision-making, a willingness to take risks and high growth rates. Thus, its turnover in 1995 was seven times that in 1990. Its managing director described the culture of his company as 'small is beautiful'.

The strategic advantage of TEWA lay in its domestic market, which was based on the high technical performance of its waste disposal plants and the networked organisational structure. The former ensured that its plants met strict technical emission standards and so it was able charge premium rates, while the latter reduced direct costs in waste disposal service provision and allowed a flexible response to changes in demand. Consequently, TEWA had a good reputation in its home base. The policy of TEWA was to supply, own and operate plants using proprietary technology. The technology was not sold in order to maintain control of know-how. Technology sales on the open market would have provided a more immediate income stream, but at the cost of losing control of the technology.

WASO is one of a group of water companies formed in the late 1980s when the then Conservative government in the UK privatised the publicly owned regional water authorities and set up a regulatory body (OFWAT) to oversee this sector. In 1995, less than 15 per cent of WASO's income was from non-regulated activities.

Organisational Strategy of the Parents

In the early 1980s, TEWA was largely dependent upon revenue and profits from its operations in its home base. However, by the late 1980s, its technological superiority and organisational capabilities in supplying services to this niche market led to a near monopoly position. Entry to this sector was restricted by stringent technical environmental emission standards established by regulatory agencies. Over time, these standards became stricter, thereby increasing entry barriers. Restricted entry created the opportunity for supernormal profits. However, the combination of a small domestic market dominated by TEWA with little scope for further growth and expansion, and the eventual technological catching up by potential and actual competitors, could potentially undermine its market position. Overseas expansion was therefore a logical organisational strategy enabling further growth and reducing dependence on its domestic market (Table 7.1).

WASO has to meet regulatory requirements imposed by OFWAT under the conditions of its licence to operate in this sector. OFWAT can set technical standards, limit price increases for water supply and sewage treatment services and compel capital expenditure. Price controls by OFWAT effectively limit the scope for profits from the local monopoly power of the water companies in the regulated sector. Moreover, annual data on technical and financial performance of water companies is published by OFWAT, allowing stock market comparison and scrutiny by investors, speculators and market analysts. Like any other public limited company (plc), water companies are vulnerable to a takeover. The possibility of a takeover increases as demand for their shares falls. As profit levels and growth in the regulated sector are constrained by OFWAT, water companies have been actively seeking to diversify into unregulated sectors.

TEWA's Entry and Expansion into the UK

The UK was an attractive market for TEWA since it was familiar with the culture, used the same language and had lower emission standards than its domestic market which its existing plant could meet, but which were expected to be raised, thereby increasing entry barriers and the potential for high profits. Officials had approached TEWA from a UK regulatory body regarding emission data and cleaner technologies in order to draft change to increase environmental standards. The managing director of TEWA believed very few UK-based operators would to be able to meet the higher standards that were due to implemented within a few years. Existing technology was capable of meeting most of these standards by retrofitted components from plants in the US. In effect, the UK market offered significant growth potential in a near monopoly situation, thereby allowing supernormal profits and in the longer term, a base for expansion into other European markets.

Table 7.1   Context, strategic choice, search and trust in the formation of WACL

WASO	TEWA
Potential partner contexts	
Reduce dependence upon highly regulated income.	Find alternatives to existing small regional markets.
Lack of knowledge about waste disposal.	Lack of knowledge about UK and European markets.
Public sector, British, and bureaucratic.	'Small is beautiful' and entrepreneurial.
Potential partner strategic choices	
Diversification from basic water industry operations.	Prospector strategy.
Cannot 'home grow' technology but could buy in.	Home-grown technology but wished to retain control.
Some existing joint ventures.	Previous experience of joint ventures.
Water companies operate in quasi-monopolies market, but highly regulated.	Competitive international.
High concentration, scarcity of customers.	
Search	
Initial contact with TEWA through visit to home base and to US plant.	Came to UK and set up a plant in public sector organisation.
Expectations	
Growth in non-regulated income.	High sales from joint venture.
TEWA to provide competence.	WASO to provide capital.
Learn new about waste technology.	Learn about UK.
No difficulties over compatibility.	Worries about compatibility.
No internal competition.	
Trust	
Institutional trust, backgrounds of managers.	Reliable but staid.
Personal trust in ability of TEWA to effectively operate plant.	Reputation of WASO by customers was good.
Due diligence exercised.	
Procedural trust based on observation of plant and tests.	

The Need for a Partner

Expansion into the UK by TEWA required knowledge about the market – for example, labour law, customs, regulatory approval and so on – and substantial capital. TEWA had formed a joint venture in another Australasian country, but this had not been successful because of the unwillingness of the partner to commit the level of expenditure to maintain technical standards. This partnering experience added to TEWA's knowledge about managing joint ventures.

TEWA had three options regarding capital: generate the funding itself, share capital funding requirements with the public sector organisation with which it had set up a waste disposal facility in 1991, or select a new organisation with which to form a partnership. The first two options were not possible because TEWA as an Australasian company found it would be very difficult to raise the finance in the UK. It also would have been difficult to expand and acquire the necessary managerial input over a longer time as this would involve some managers from the parent company living in the UK. Moreover, its existing UK customer was unable or unwilling to enter a market unrelated to its core activities on a large scale. Consequently, a search for a new partner was instigated.

WASO's historical origin in the public service provision means that its norms were characteristically bureaucratic and relied heavily on rule-based procedures. It was also a cautious organisation owing to the influence of its chairman and its finance director. Thus, its diversification strategy was based on 'organic growth', by entering closely related activities to its core business in which it already had some degree of competence and knowledge rather than establishing or acquiring firms in totally new and unrelated sectors.

A strategy was introduced by WASO to reduce dependence on its regulated businesses by entering related sectors, which had high earnings and profits growth potential. Specialist waste disposal was not an area it had targeted for entry. However, it did so after being approached by TEWA. Entry into this sector was opportunistic, but undertaken because it fitted in with WASO's strategy of diversification, because of the scope for high earnings and profits growth and because this business was closely related to WASO's existing competencies and knowledge.

WASO could have entered the specialist waste disposal market without using a joint venture arrangement with TEWA. This could have been done by purchasing a company providing the specialist waste disposal services or by acquiring and unpackaging the technology to build a waste-processing plant. Neither was possible, because in the first case there were virtually no stand-alone businesses operating in this sector, and the one that was had recently been bought up by another company. The latter strategy was problematical for four inter-related reasons. First, while WASO had considerable expertise in domestic water waste management, its technological knowledge in this area of specialist waste was limited. Second, buying the main component parts and integrating them was not a straightforward task because industrial plant often never performs as expected, thus requiring fine tuning and post-installation modification, and so takes time before reaching design levels of performance – a phenomenon referred to in the nuclear industry as the 'shakedown period'. Third, performance guarantees by suppliers of the major components were unlikely to be honoured. Consequently, WASO considered that each supplier would state that problems had arisen due to the other major technology component suppliers. Fourth, capital costs in going it alone would have been high.

These reasons meant that both WASO and TEWA had a rationale for selecting a strategy based on a seeking a partnership. WASO wished to diversify out of a traditional regulated market into a new venture which was closely related to its core business but which allowed it to learn about new technology, operate almost as a monopoly supplier thereby generating supernormal profits and potentially grow the business at a high rate. An alternative strategy would have been to buy the technology outright, but this would require a search process for which it did not have the expertise and also a greater capital commitment. A key aspect of TEWA's strategy was to sell know-how, which, once it was transferred, would mean losing its competitive advantage. Selling know-how is central to Miles and Snow's (1978) prospector strategy. The dilemma is that a prospector company always has to run to keep ahead of the competition. The joint venture gave TEWA an opportunity to enter the large (by the standards of a small company) UK market, and learn about a new market, and provided an alternative to a joint venture it had established in another country in the mid 1980s. TEWA aimed to sell the plant to the joint venture at lower cost than other suppliers would, in order to improve the operating finances.

The Process of Partner Selection

Search

In 1991, TEWA initiated a search for a partner in the UK by placing an advert in a newspaper asking for expressions of interest. Eight responses were obtained, nearly all from water companies. One inquiry was from a general waste company that was considered by TEWA to be in competition with them and so was not followed up. As it became apparent that water companies were interested in the venture, the managing director of TEWA directly contacted ones which had not responded, such as WASO. Overall, eight companies were visited and a ten-minute videotape of the waste disposal technology was shown to each. TEWA thus played a proactive and strategic role in seeking a partner in contrast with the reactive approach of the water companies.

Partner Assessment

The problem for the potential partners is how to assess whether their expectations would be met by forming a partnership. For TEWA, all three directors of TEWA were directly involved in visiting the various interested parties and assessing their suitability, while for WASO the technical director was given this responsibility.

Trust is generally acknowledged to be a vital component in a partnership. However, the issue is not whether there is perfect trust but if there is enough trust to start out on a joint venture. According the WASO's group technical director, trust between partners was 'vital' to the success of a joint venture, and was seen in terms of 'a belief that both sides are acting in the interests of the joint venture'.

The question arises as to how is it possible to know whether the other organisation can be trusted. WASO's technical director's response was, 'I suppose the word some people would use is instinct.'

Similarly, the managing director of TEWA clearly expressed the importance of feelings in assessing the other water companies and reasons for rejecting them. Thus, the management of one of the water companies was 'too insecure', while another was described as

> too aggressive; they didn't want us except our technology. Another said 'no' at the outset of discussions but changed their minds when they saw the test results of the technology. We did not like two other water companies because they were shallow, although their technical competence was OK. Overall, though, we did not like them. You walk into a room, four of us, and we all came to the same conclusion. They seemed too much like the people in our failed joint venture we had finished dealing with a few years before.

The last part referred to TEWA's experience in a joint venture it had formed in another part of Australasia. TEWA had exited the joint venture once the other parent had shown it was unwilling to build plants capable of meeting statutory levels of emission standards in order to reduce costs and increase profitability. Operating plants, which did not meet emission standards, would have damaged TEWA's reputation and thus it sold its equity share to its partner. Subsequently, there was a considerable loss of business and TEWA was invited back by its partner, which it previously declined.

Although terms like 'feel' come into trust-building, there is also rational searching (calculation) combined with trial and error (experience). For example, according to WASO's technical director,

> what we tried to establish was the reality of what they told us they could do. I went to America where they produced part of the kit and to their home country where they were operating their plants and met several of the people they worked with over the years.

When two partners previously unknown to each other come together, symbolism can play an important role in triggering a more systematic search of the calculative or experiential type. TEWA's directors came to Britain with certain general assumptions – for example, an obvious cultural and language affinity.

Another form of symbolic information is reputation. TEWA's interpretation of UK water companies involved a degree of reputational information whereby knowledge about the 'thing' (in this case two organisations) was replaced by knowledge about the person giving a view on the 'thing'. This was also true of WASO's interpretation of TEWA. However, being separated by geographical, social and technological distance, such symbolic knowledge was quite limited. For WASO to assess a small company on the other side of the globe dealing in an unfamiliar technology was difficult. There were no industry recipes – a potential source of symbolic knowledge – to draw upon.

This clearly brought out the need to see and talk to people, to use the implicit personal and symbolic knowledge that are not easily captured by technical calculations. This cannot be done entirely by e-mail, fax, letter or even telephone; rather, personal meetings are required. This is the personal and institutional side of trust-building. However, WASO also needed to see a working plant. WASO's Technical Director went to TEWA's home base to observe its plants and to conduct a 'due diligence' process, that is, a systematic and routine accounting procedure used when considering the purchase of a company or merger.

In effect, the calculative and experiential elements of knowledge become intertwined – they went to see and touch and evaluate the technology. Consequently, 'instinct' and 'feel' became translated into definite actions that were symbolic, calculative and experiential. Thus, the meeting of people who made and ran the technology, environmental experts and customers became important.

The visit to the US was to see where part of the plant was made and visits to sites where the equipment was being used. Substantial technical evaluation took place, mainly trust-building by use of calculation. Since the emission levels of the plants operating in TEWA's home base were slightly below the new UK standards, observing US-based plants, which incorporated an additional process to achieve the higher standards, permitted comparisons to be made.

This type of experiential and calculative knowledge-gathering builds competence based trust in the technical sense (Sako, 1992). The competence of someone or an organisation to carry out a task can also be transferred by symbolic means such as by qualifications and other means of accreditation.

TEWA had less calculative technical knowledge to go on. There were no appropriate plants being built or in operation by water companies to visit. Though there were, in principle, records of financial performance of the various water companies, these told TEWA little about the competence of the water companies to perform in a joint venture of this nature. Nevertheless, TEWA's existing UK plant provided useful information on how it operated in the UK.

The most easily measured information available to TEWA concerned the willingness of a potential partner to put in capital. This was a critical issue for TEWA. The ownership between partners in a partnership is also symbolic and becomes a matter for negotiations at the contract-writing stage. However, TEWA was also positively inclined towards WASO because of its stated concern for environmental policies in its annual reports and since it was operating in an area of the UK with which TEWA had some familiarity.

Overall, then, the processes of building knowledge on the trustworthiness of potential partners was by calculation, experience and symbolism, with a particular focus on goodwill and competence-based trust.

DISCUSSION

Cooperation as Strategic Choice

The basis of the analysis as to why organisations form partnerships can be considered as an open system making exchanges with supporters in its environment. The overall problem is that of gaining power over critical points of dependence in the environment (Thompson, 1967). This can be done through cooperation, such as in partnerships. However, the propensity to form partnerships and the expectations what they bring for potential partners needs to be considered in relation to alternative strategies. One possibility is a replacement of a strategy of using the market, which is based on systems that ensure that critical suppliers or customers can be substituted. Another is to follow a hierarchical strategy whereby a more powerful larger organisation takes over or merges with weaker organisation.

For a market strategy to be effective there must be many potential buyers and many sellers, because market efficiency, for buyers, breaks down when markets become concentrated. For example, an organisation can find itself highly dependent upon a single or small number of vital supporters. Under these conditions, it would be rational for an organisation to follow either a hierarchical or a cooperative strategy. However, the hierarchical strategy requires the financial resources to purchase another organisation and the power to impose a managerial system, and assumes an asymmetry of finance and knowledge. For WASO this was not possible, because there were no suitable companies it could purchase, while unpackaging the technology and building its own operations were constrained by its lack of technical and market knowledge. TEWA was constrained by its capacity to raise capital to fund large-scale operations.

The partnership provides a strategy whereby power is gained over the external environment by means of an exchange of mutual obligations (Thompson, 1967). A differentiating feature of the partnership, compared with the other strategies, is the role of non-monetary exchanges as opposed to the high reliance upon money-based exchanges in a marketplace and upon formal authority and command in a hierarchy.

Trust and Confidence about Potential Partners

Organisations need to have confidence in their knowledge in order to use it as a basis for action, which in the case of joint venture formation was about the trustworthiness of potential partners. Knowledge is a problematical concept with little agreement on a common definition leading to interchangeability with other similar concepts, and therefore unsurprisingly it is not clearly defined by many authors (Aadne *et al.*, 1996). Here the nature of knowledge will be considered from the perspectives of rational positivism, institutional theory and social constructivism (also termed collectivism) and will show that confidence in the knowledge about potential partners was based on methods drawn from all three approaches.

Rational Positivism

The rational positivist paradigm assumes the existence of an objective and universal set of causal laws, which operate across time and space. These laws can be determined by using the scientific method based on the principles of reproducibility, repeatability, verifiability and falsifiability (Popper, 1959). Testing of knowledge is carried out by comparing predictions about outcomes with actual outcomes. There may be confidence in knowledge generated in this method if it accurately predicts outcomes of action or where there is confidence in the processes for producing such knowledge (Table 7.2).

The rational positivist paradigm is embodied in classical and neo-classical economics, as for example in the assumption of perfect information by economic agents. This approach has often been used to examine organisational behaviour and interorganisational partnerships. For example, Contractor and Lorange (1988) present a cost–benefit analysis to explain why firms cooperate rather than go it alone. Thus, cooperation is considered appropriate if the potential advantages of the partnership outweigh possible disadvantages. This perspective assumes that it is possible to use calculative or computational algorithms to determine the correct course of action. Such calculation-based knowledge was used by both WASO and TEWA in their assessment of each other as suitable partners. Thus, WASO carried out an accountancy-based process of due diligence to determine the 'objective facts' about TEWA and examined technical data on its waste disposal plants.

Computational methods may be appropriate in situations such as stock markets but are not universally applicable. Evaluating alternatives and partner selection is a highly uncertain process, characterised by incomplete information, a changing external environment and evolving preferences by leaders of organisations in response to new information. Problems also arise, for example, in situations characterised by ambiguity where for example there is lack of agreement on goals or the means to be used.

The inadequacy of the rational paradigm for organisational action suggests a need to complement the perspective with one that is based on an open systems approach and recognises that, in practice, knowledge is incomplete and therefore rationality is bounded (March and Simon, 1993).

Table 7.2   Perspectives on Knowledge

Perspective	Confidence in knowledge when ...
Rational	accurately predicts *outcomes* of action or when there is confidence in the *processes* for producing such knowledge.
Institutional	conforms to rules (that is, cultural norms and regulations).
Collectivist	conforms to collective agreement.

Bounded Rationality

The bounded rational paradigm is based on an open systems perspective where knowledge is incomplete. The focus here is on strategic choices (Child, 1972) for organisations in a situation of ambiguity (Thompson, 1967) and examines the decision-making processes by which those choices are made (Cyert and March, 1992; Hickson *et al.*, 1986). In a bounded rational model of organisations, knowledge is essentially indeterminate and action predicated upon 'limiting factors' (Commons, 1951) or 'strategic factors' (Barnard, 1938). Limiting factors set boundaries on knowledge in so far as they define critical areas of attention.

Bounded rationality is linked to the concept of 'realism' in social science methodology. Realism accepts the empirically based epistemology of positivism but rejects the notion of an absolute foundation of knowledge and instead advocates a 'common-sense' approach (Sayer, 1992). Rather than searching for absolute causal laws, the concept of 'practical adequacy' is considered more useful. According to this principle, knowledge must 'generate expectations about the world and about the results of our actions, which are actually realized' (Sayer, 1992: 69). In these circumstances what is regarded as adequate knowledge will vary with the context in which decisions are made. Two interconnected bounded rational approaches are institutional theory and the collectivist perspective.

Institutional Theory

Institutional theory is represented in a broad set of literature. However, this chapter draws principally on Scott (1995). In this theory, 'rules' provide constraints on action and define appropriate behaviour (March, 1988). Rules are a major source of the 'limiting factors' referred to by Commons (1951) and have both regulatory and normative components (Scott, 1995: 49–61). Norms are derived mainly from implicit structures, cultures and socialisation, while regulations derive from governance systems and formal laws.

To understand the origins of limiting factors in partnerships requires examination of the regulations and norms affecting individual partners within their own industrial sectors and, for international partnerships, those specific to national business systems that provide frameworks for looking at how rules affecting business organisations may very across nation states (Whitley, 1994). At the industry level, 'recipes' provide another level of analysis (Spender, 1989). At the firm level, organisational structures provide decision rules about what is most important to attend to at any given time (March and Simon, 1993).

From the viewpoint of system survival, there are minimum performance standards to be met, but the approach to these standards is by 'satisficing', a process whereby action is taken on an acceptable rather than a maximum level of performance. Under this rule-bound institutional paradigm, knowledge in which one can have confidence is derived from cultural norms or regulations that are tested according to conformity to those rules. According to this view, whether potential clients will have confidence in a hospital as an organisation would be judged, for example, by the extent to which the administration of the hospital conforms to a broad spectrum of regulations covering working practices. A hospital that does not adopt certain practices during the admission of a patient would be deemed to be breaking the bounds of appropriate behaviour. Similar boundaries of behaviour might also be suggested by cultural factors, such as the manner of speech, and the dress and demeanour of staff. In effect, confidence in knowledge about an organisation is viewed in terms of symbols regarding features considered important.

Thus, TEWA needed a partner, which would be able to provide sufficient capital to fund waste disposal plant. For TEWA, WASO's status as a public limited company symbolised its financial credibility.

Collectivist Perspective

The collectivist paradigm is derived from the social construction of knowledge (Berger and Luckman, 1966), also referred to as relativist constructivism (Knorr-Cetina, 1981). In this paradigm, cognition and meaning are socially constructed and vary with the observer(s). Thus, knowledge is not a universal constant, and shared meanings emerge through social interaction. Methods of generating such knowledge are based on such factors as discussion, discourse and debate, involving professional expertise and judgements about what is right and wrong. Consequently, knowledge in which there can be confidence is produced through a collective process involving argument and criticism (von Krogh and Roos, 1996). In effect, such knowledge is relative to a particular collective or social group rather than absolute and is similar to Nelson's (1993) conception of 'technical communities'. Some consequences follow from this paradigm on the treatment of errors. This paradigm accepts that errors will occur and is concerned particularly with the processes of how learning takes place. Knowledge from this perspective is derived from experience and discourse.

The management teams of TEWA and WASO highlighted the importance of experience and discussions in their assessment of partners. Thus, WASO's technical director went to see TEWA's plants, met customers and visited other plants in the US. The manner in which directors of TEWA interacted with the managers from the various water companies influenced their assessment of their suitability as partners.

According to the rational paradigm, procedural trust arises from a calculative form of search. In the institutional model, trust results from searching for symbols. In the collectivist paradigm, personal trust is based on experiential search.

Organisational partnerships and knowledge management are increasingly recognised as important mechanisms for creating competitive advantage and to successfully deal with turbulent environments. However, the dynamics of such partnerships and the creation and management of knowledge in which there is confidence are not well understood. The conventional wisdom in these areas is based on the rational positivist paradigm, which limits understanding of the processes underlying partnerships and knowledge management in practice. This paradigm needs to be complemented by insights from two approaches based on the bounded rational paradigm: constructivism and institutional theory. How knowledge is generated has been examined from the perspective of each of these three approaches in relation to partnership formation. The rational approach assumes an absolute reality based on universal causal laws. Knowledge that can be relied upon as a basis for action is determined by testing predictions with actual outcomes. According to institutional theory, knowledge in which there is confidence is that which conforms to (sociocultural and regulatory) rules, while for collectivism it varies with a particular collective or social group. In practice, generating reliable knowledge in which there is confidence involves an interaction between these three approaches and involves search and trust in partner selection, and observing performance after a joint venture has been formed.

Knowledge formation involves comparing actual performance with expectations, which if not sufficiently satisfactory will lead to further search for potential partners. These expectations are about economic performance, rules and learning and based on the rational, institutional and collectivist approaches, respectively. Search can be categorised into calculation, experience or symbolism and interact with personal, procedural and institutional trust.

CONCLUSION

The formation of the joint venture (WACL), providing specialist waste services, between a UK water company (WASO) and small entrepreneurial

Australasian waste-processing firm (TEWA) illustrates the difficulties of establishing criteria for partner selection. The search for a joint venture partner was triggered by the desire of TEWA to capture potentially supernormal profits in a large overseas market where it expected to have a near monopoly position due to the capability of its technology in meeting strict emission standards. Nearly all the companies responding came from the water services sector. These firms were attracted by the opportunity to reduce dependence on their regulated activities and enter this potentially highly profitable niche market, thereby positively affecting their share price.

Partner selection took place through a process of assessing the trustworthiness of potential partners. This involved gathering knowledge about the other party using calculative, experiential and symbolic methods. TEWA rejected nearly all the water companies on the basis of its initial contact with them. This would be categorised primarily as 'feeling' but was complemented by calculative methods. One company was rejected because it was considered only to be interested in its technology, not TEWA, and was therefore untrustworthy. In another case, the company lacked what TEWA considered the appropriate level of technical competence. WASO was regarded favourably because of its declared environmental concerns, its financially secure status and the fact that it was operating in a part of the UK with which TEWA directors were already familiar.

WASO was positively inclined towards a joint venture with TEWA because of its potential for diversification into a related sector. Building confidence in the knowledge about TEWA involved instinct-based observation of the technology in operation, talking to customers and suppliers and trying to determine issues such as track record and reputation. These processes do not however stop once the joint venture was formed but continue through its operation.

References

AADNE, J., Von KROGH, G. and ROOS, J. (1996) Representation: the traditional approach to co-operative strategies. In von Krogh, G. and Roos, J. (eds), *Managing Knowledge: Perspectives on Cooperation and Competition*. Sage, London, 9–31.

BARNARD, C.I. (1938) *The Functions of the Executive*. Harvard University Press, Cambridge, MA.

BEAMISH, J. (1984) Joint venture performance in developing countries. Unpublished PhD dissertation, University of Western Ontario, London, Ont.

BERGER, P. and LUCKMAN, T. (1966) *The Social Construction of Reality*. Penguin, New York.

CHILD, J. (1972) Organisation structure, environment and performance: the role of strategic choice. *Sociology*, 6, 1–22.

COMMONS, J.R. (1951) *The Economics of Collective Action*. Macmillan, New York.

CONTRACTOR, F.J. and LORANGE, P. (1988) A theory of cooperation in international business. In Contractor, F.J. and Lorange, P. (eds), *Cooperative Strategies in International Business: Joint Ventures and Technology Partnerships between Firms*. D.C. Heath, Lexington, MA, ch. 31.

CYERT, R. and MARCH J.G. (1992) *A Behavioural Theory of the Firm*, 2nd edn. Blackwell, Oxford.

DAS, T. and TENG, B.-S. (1996) Risk types and inter-firm alliance structures. *Journal of Management Studies*, 33 (6), 827–43.

FARR, C. and FISCHER, W. (1992) Managing international high technology cooperative projects. *R and D Management*, 22 (1), 55–67.

FRANKO, L. (1971) *Joint Venture Survival in Multinational Corporations*. Praeger, New York.

FREEMAN, C. and HAGEDOORN, J. (1994) Catching up or falling behind: patterns in international interfirm technology partnering. *World Development*, 22 (5), 771–80.

FUKUYAMA, F. (1995) *Trust: The Social Virtues and the Creation of Prosperity*. Free Press, New York.

FURLONG, D. (1996) The conceptualisation of 'trust' in economic thought. IDS Working Paper no. 35, Institute of Development Studies, University of Sussex.

GAMBETTA, D. (1988) *Trust: Making and Breaking Cooperative Relations*. Blackwell, Oxford.

GERINGER, J. (1991) Strategic determinants of partner selection criteria in international joint ventures. *Journal of International Business Studies*, 22 (1), 41–62.

GERSICK, C. (1988) Time and transition work teams: toward a new model of group development. *Academy of Management Journal*, 31 (1), 9–31.

GLAISTER, K. and BUCKLEY, P. (1996) Strategic motives for international alliance formation. *Journal of Management Studies*, 33 (3), 301–32.

HARBISON, J. and PEKAR, P. (1998) Institutionalising alliance skills: secrets of repeatable success. *Strategy and Business*, 11 (2), 3–15.

HENNART, J. and REDDY, S. (1997) The choice between mergers/acquisitions and joint ventures: the case of Japanese investors in the United States. *Strategic Management Journal*, 18 (1), 1–12.

HICKSON, D.J., BUTLER, R.J., GRAY, D., MALLORY, G. and WILSON, D.C. (1986) *Top Decisions: Strategic Decision Making in Organizations*. Blackwell, Oxford.

KILLING, J. (1988) Understanding alliances: the role of task and organizational complexity. In Contractor, F. and Lorange, P. (eds), *Co-operative Strategies in International Business: Joint Ventures and Technology Partnerships between Firms*. D.C. Heath, Lexington, MA.

KNORR-CETINA, K. (1981) *The Manufacture of Knowledge: An Essay on the Constructivist and Contextual Nature of Science*. Pergamon, Oxford.

LEWICKI, R. and BUNKER, B. (1996) Developing and maintaining trust in work relationships. In Kramer, R. and Tyler, T. (eds), *Trust in Organizations: Frontiers of Theory and Research*. Sage, London.

LUO, Y. (1997) Partner success and venturing success: the case of joint ventures with firms in the People's Republic of China. *Organisational Science*, 7 (6), 648–62.

MARCH, J. (1988) *Decisions and Organizations*. Blackwell, Oxford.

MARCH, J.G. and SIMON, H.A. (1993) *Organizations*, 2nd edn. Basil Blackwell, Oxford.

MILES, R. and SNOW, C. (1978) *Organizational Strategy, Structure and Process*. McGraw-Hill, New York.

NELSON, R.R. (1993) Technical change as cultural evolution. In Thomson, R. (ed), *Learning and Technological Change*. Macmillan, London.

PARKHE, A. (1993) 'Messy' research, methodological predispositions, and theory development in international joint ventures. *Academy of Management Journal, 36* (2), 227–68.

PERROW, C. (1970) *Organisational Analysis*. Tavistock, London.

PINFIELD, L. (1986) A field evaluation of perspectives on organizational decision making. *Administrative Science Quarterly, 31* (2), 365–88.

POPPER, K. (1959) *The Logic of Scientific Discovery*. Hutchinson/Routledge, London.

RING, P. and VAN DE VEN, A. (1994) Development processes of cooperative interorganizational relationships. *Academy of Management Review, 19* (1), 90–118.

SAKO, M. (1992) *Prices, Quality and Trust*. Cambridge University Press.

SAYER, A. (1992) *Method in Social Science: A Realist Approach*. Routledge, London.

SCOTT, W.R. (1995) *Institutions and Organizations*. Sage, London.

SHAPIRO, S. (1986) The social control of impersonal trust. *American Journal of Sociology, 3* (Nov.), 623–58.

SIMON, H. (1947) *Administrative Behaviour: A Study of Decision Making in Administrative Organizations*. Free Press, New York.

SPENDER, J.-C. (1989) *Industry Recipes: An Enquiry into the Nature and Sources of Managerial Judgement*. Blackwell, Oxford.

THOMPSON, J.D. (1967) *Organizations in Action*. McGraw-Hill, New York.

TYLER, B. and STEEMSA, H. (1995) Evaluating technological collaborative opportunities: a cognitive modelling perspective. *Strategic Management Journal, 16* (3), 43–70.

VON KROGH, G. and ROOS, J. (1996) Introduction. In von Krogh, G. and Roos, J. (eds), *Managing Knowledge: Perspectives on Cooperation and Competition*. Sage, London.

WEBER, M. (1968) *Economy and Society: An Outline of Interpretive Sociology*. Roth, G. and Wittick, G. (eds), University of California Press, Berkeley.

WHITLEY, R. (1994) Dominant forms of economic organization in market economies. *Organization Studies, 15* (2), 153–82.

WOODCOCK, C., BEAMISH, P., and MAKINO, S. (1994) Ownership based entry mode strategies and international performance. *Journal of International Business Studies, 25* (2), 253–73.

YIN, R. (1984). *Case Study Research: Design and Methods*. Sage, Beverly Hills, CA.

ZAHRA, S. and ELHAGRASEY, G. (1994) Strategic management of international joint ventures. *European Management Journal, 12* (1), 83–93.

8 International Staffing Patterns and Transaction Costs: Implications for Alliance Readiness and Firm Performance

Carolyn Erdener and Ingemar Torbiorn

INTRODUCTION

In the new global economy, the ability to manage complex strategic alliances is becoming crucial to success in international competition. However, for companies that lack relevant experience, the initial strategic alliance experience can be frustrating and disappointing. For these firms, it is important to establish alliance readiness as an important precursor to strategic alliance participation:

> a company whose managers are oriented toward the creation of competitive advantage in emerging arenas, who think in terms of core competencies rather than discrete businesses, who aim to deliver superior value to customers … is 'alliance ready' in one or more important respects. (Doz and Hamel, 1998: 255–6)

International staffing decisions have major consequences for the attainment of strategic alliance readiness. The strategic implications of international staffing decisions for competitive advantage and core competence must be clearly recognised and understood by managers before they can be adequately addressed. However, the management literature does not yet provide much information on these critical issues.

This chapter presents an analysis of some of the more important implications of international staffing decisions for alliance readiness and firm performance. Strategic management is linked to the management of human resources (HR), focusing on competence-based HR strategy and competitive advantage. A recent conceptual model of the relationship between culture, transaction costs and international staffing patterns (Erdener and Torbiorn, 1998) is extended in this chapter to emphasise the differential impact of strategy context on the way that these variables affect firm performance. We proceed by identifying certain risks and benefits associated with international staffing decisions, defining these risks in relation to the strategy of the firm, and evaluating them in terms of strategic priorities and objectives (Hill and Jones, 1995). The chapter builds on conceptual foundations that, with few exceptions have not been previously integrated in the management literature (Erdener and Torbiorn, 1997, 1999).

OVERVIEW

Alliance readiness requires the reconciliation of pressures for local responsiveness and customisation with pressures for global centralisation and coordination. International human resource management (IHRM) is particularly sensitive to the central-versus-local dilemma:

> The most difficult challenge management faces is administrative: the structuring of the company's internal decision-making process to allow the organization to sense, interpret and respond to tensions and the resolution of the often contradictory demands for global competitiveness and national responsiveness. (Doz *et al.*, 1981)

Finding the right balance between competing interests – corporate versus business unit, headquarters versus field, strategic versus operational – can be problematic for any firm and all the more so for international firms (Torbiorn, 1997).

The ability of the firm to meet these challenges resides largely in its resources. Building a sustainable competitive advantage through the coordination of resources (Henderson and Cockburn, 1994; Marino, 1996) logically includes among the firm's capabilities its human resources, which can be combined in unique ways to enhance overall competence and performance. Competence-based HR strategy places HRM issues within this larger context. In essence, the competence-based approach requires that HR objectives and strategies be derived from the firm's corporate- and business-level strategies and goals, and also that they support the strategies of its other internal functions and operations. This approach provides a conceptual framework that is broad enough to encompass the full range of the firm's activities, such as core competences and strategic objectives on the one hand and its HR practices and concerns on the other. Thus, HR strategy is analysed and evaluated in terms of its relevance to the competitive advantages and competitive strategy of the firm (Torbiorn, 1997). Whether competence resides in persons or in systems, the focus is on competence (rather than on staff) and on the procurement of competence as needed by the firm. Both the procurement and, ultimately, the use of competence may be hindered in so far as the goals of finding, keeping, developing and moving competence do not harmonise, and in so far as the HR parameters of staffing, appraisal, rewards and development efforts are inconsistent or inadequate when applied in international contexts (Torbiorn, 1997).

Internal and external tensions can be generated in the process, thereby undermining competitive advantage and adversely affecting performance. The explanation for these effects can be found in the analysis of transaction costs. In the following discussion, transaction cost economic theory (Williamson, 1975) provides a framework for relating specific patterns of international staffing decisions to competitive advantage and long-term firm performance. This is largely uncharted territory in the literatures of IHRM and strategic management (Erdener and Torbiorn, 1998, 1999; Festing, 1997).

TRANSACTION COST ECONOMICS

Transaction cost theory links the study of organisations and economics, to explain the origins of economic organisations as alternative governance mechanisms for managing the costs (broadly defined) of carrying out repeated economic exchanges, or transactions. The organisational implications of managing these costs of transacting through one ownership structure versus another are a major focus of the theory. In the classic model (Williamson, 1975), transaction costs provide an explanation for decisions on which activities to internalise within the organisational parameters of the firm, and which to carry out or procure on the market. The choice is complicated when markets do not follow the laws of perfect competition and become increasingly risky, inefficient and unreliable. By bringing critical exchanges under direct managerial control, certain risks and the costs of managing or controlling these risks are lowered, with the result that overall costs decline.

When an organisation is under threat, it tends to respond with measures to reduce the threat. However, these measures generate additional costs to the organisation in terms of time, energy and resources. One way to reduce these costs is to remove the underlying risks that caused the firm to incur them, for example, by reorganising economic activities and exchange relations. In the classic transaction costs model, the firm is portrayed as facing a choice between two alternatives: to *internalise* risky activities, thereby bringing them under managerial control; or to *externalise* risky activities, thereby placing them under market control. Whether managerial control or market control is more efficient for any given activity is often unclear at the outset, but is revealed retrospectively over time. Details of this process have been articulated in depth and supported empirically in the literature of transaction cost economics (Menard, 1997; Williamson, 1975, 1985).

In addition to these two alternatives – the integrated firm (direct ownership or internalisation) and the market – which are posited in the classic transaction costs model (Williamson, 1975), the theory also applies to hybrid governance arrangements that fall between these two extremes (Williamson, 1985). Research on alliances, joint ventures, licensing and long-term contract relations has made extensive use of transaction cost theory (Parkhe, 1993).

The Transaction Cost Economics Model

Transaction cost theory posits that structural arrangements for organising economic transactions gravitate over time towards those that minimise the costs of controlling the firm's exposure to certain kinds of risks. These risks are associated with *opportunism*, or self-interest-seeking with guile, and to *bounded rationality*, resulting from information processing limitations. They are more serious in areas where the firm has made significant, transaction-specific investment in assets, including human resources.

The transaction cost model combines the human factors of *bounded rationality* and *opportunism* with the environmental factors of *uncertainty/ complexity* and *small numbers*. Thus, for example, the impact of *bounded rationality* and *opportunism* is increasingly important in increasingly uncertain and complex environments. The model also includes *information impactedness*, which derives from the interaction of an *uncertainty/complexity* with *opportunism* (Williamson, 1975). See Figure 8.1.

Bounded rationality refers to physiological and linguistic limitations on the capability to handle information. 'The physical limits take the form of rate and storage limits on the powers of individuals to receive, store, retrieve, and process information without error' (Williamson, 1975: 21). In the international firm, this has a direct parallel in the ability of individuals to function effectively and to perform equally well in different cultural environments (Torbiorn, 1994a).

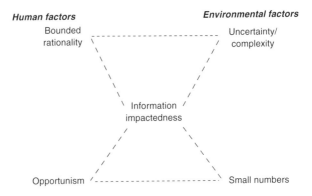

Figure 8.1   The transactions cost model.

Opportunism in the transaction costs paradigm refers to a lack of candour or honesty in transactions, and the pursuit of self-interest with guile. Political behaviour including 'selective or distorted information disclosure ... self-disbelieved promises regarding future conduct ... misrepresentation of intention ... and so forth is encompassed in the opportunism construct (Williamson, 1975: 26–8).

Information impactedness can also arise in the international firm from the interplay between *bounded rationality* and *uncertainty/complexity*. This is due to the additional information-processing requirements of managing across different cognitive frameworks when crossing national and cultural borders. Asymmetries in the complexity of various cultural systems and the associated skill level needed to function effectively across cultural systems also contribute to the problem (Torbiorn, 1994a).

Remediable Frictions

An additional underlying concept in transaction cost theory that is particularly relevant to the implications of staffing patterns in international operations, for firm performance involves *remediable frictions* (Williamson, 1975: 20). These encompass all varieties of frictions and tensions associated with the manner in which activities are organised. In the transaction costs paradigm, frictions are considered remediable if it is possible to reduce or control them by various specific means. Transaction costs originate in the firm's efforts to reduce frictions by such means. If they can be lowered, through internal reorganisation, the resulting improvements in organisational efficiency and overall reduction of costs may improve competitive advantage and performance.

CULTURAL ENVIRONMENT

The basic framework of the environment for international business contains the same elements in each country, yet each is unique in the details of its political-legal, economic, sociocultural, demographic geographic and technological characteristics, as well as in the ways in which these elements interact with one another. Successful international strategic alliances go beyond adjusting to a new culture; they must develop the ability to interact reciprocally across cultures that may be fundamentally at variance in critical regards. Furthermore, for any given cultural environment, the specific set of characteristics that are salient to cross-cultural interaction can vary widely for different cultural combinations.

Adapting to foreign environments is also complicated by the scarcity of reliable information in the public domain, without which the firm cannot adapt to environmental differences. Foreign environments change in ways that are sometimes difficult for outsiders to foresee, as leading indicators of change escape notice, and potential interaction effects are not apparent. Individuals with expertise in the local culture are often better able to monitor and interpret these changes than outsiders. A firm that does not possess such localised expertise within its own staff thus encounters a certain amount of cultural risk due to uncertainty.

Cultural Distance and Cultural Barriers

Cultural risk is a potential source of transaction costs for any firm operating in an international environment, particularly one that is also unfamiliar. Cultural distance and cultural barriers are two related components of the problem of cultural risk.

Cultural distance refers to both the nature and the degree of difference between the norms of two cultures. Cultural distance in those aspects of culture that are objectively relevant to company success can generate transaction costs. The greater the cultural distance between the firm and its international environment, the more risk and uncertainty the firm will face. Just as cultural distance exists independently of individual perceptions of cultural differences, this cultural risk and uncertainty exist independently of whether or not they are recognised by the organisation.

Individual perceptions of risks and uncertainty due to cultural distance are mediated through cultural barriers. These barriers, which arise in the culture but operate at the level of the individual, increase in height with cultural distance. They correspond to patterns of culture-specific limitations in the ability of members of one culture to understand, accept and adapt to certain norms of a given foreign culture, particularly those which differ or conflict with the norms of these persons' own culture (Torbiorn, 1988). Transaction costs may be affected by cultural barriers through individual perceptions of risk (both at operational levels in the local foreign environment, and at corporate headquarters in the parent country) and through individual misperceptions or failures to recognise risk and to take necessary precautions. Thus, for example, the harmonisation of conditions for operating within the European Union (EU) may actually expose firms within the EU that operate internationally to greater risks, if cultural barriers prevent them from correcting internal weaknesses, for example, through ignorance of subtle unresolved differences or deficiencies which, in the new environment, are increasingly relevant to competitiveness.

In addition to affecting reciprocal interactions in company operations across particular cultures, cultural distance and cultural barriers also affect non-reciprocal relations, separately in each direction (Torbiorn, 1988). Accordingly, the distance and barriers between cultures A and B (from the vantage point of culture A) may not be the same as those between B and A (from the vantage point of culture B). This is because of cultural differences in what is regarded as central, relevant, acceptable and understandable with respect to the specific interaction at hand.

Cultural Friction and Cultural Risk

Cultural distance – mediated through cultural barriers – can create tensions or frictions that contribute to risk (Doz and Hamel, 1998). The term *cultural friction* was recently coined (Erdener and Torbiorn, 1998) to link this phenomenon conceptually to Williamson's concept of *remediable frictions*, discussed above.

Cultural friction is a useful concept for explaining various findings in international management – for example, the determination that cultural distance is inversely correlated with long-term reciprocity in international cooperative alliances. One major category of frictions is associated with tendencies to use the wrong norms in judgements, decisions and actions as a result of applying one's own norms inappropriately (ethnocentrism), or refraining from using one's own norms when they actually would have been appropriate. Another major category of frictions is associated with the multiple distortions in perception and interpretation that can occur when information generated in one culture is received and applied in another culture.

Cultural risk accompanies the opportunity costs of failing to recognise and act on opportunities present in the local environment, because of the effects of cultural distance and cultural barriers on managerial perceptions and cognitions. Opportunities to develop the alliance relationship in positive directions may be overlooked. The consequences of this deficiency can be serious, as in interactions within a non-market economy where political and social relationships are paramount.

Another major type of cultural risk arises when decisions taken at (mono-cultural) headquarters are transformed in transmission to international operations. This can occur because of the mediating effects of past experience. Unique elements of corporate culture that have evolved in a particular foreign context through the cumulative effects of idiosyncratic chains of consequences and experiences may affect the transmission of information from headquarters, shaping and colouring the message in unforeseen ways. If the internalisation of foreign operations introduces these distortions back into the parent culture, other unanticipated risks may be introduced into the system.

Some of the risk which cultural distance presents for the firm may diminish with the passage of time, owing to an increase in the ability of individual organisational members to scale cultural barriers. This can occur on the part of key individuals from the parent organisation, as increasing familiarity and experience improve their understanding of the foreign culture; and on the part of key individuals among the local staff, as they gain a deeper understanding of the corporate culture of the firm. It can also occur as local consumers come to know and accept the foreign product or service.

Intercultural Trust

Problems of bounded rationality and information impactedness increase with cultural distance. Cultural barriers can be greater for those individuals who are moving in one direction between cultures than for those who are moving in the opposite direction. Both the occurrence and the perception of opportunism are influenced to some extent by culture.

International interaction involves aspects not only of understanding and technical communication but also of trust. This encompasses trust between organisational units, for example, partner firms in international joint ventures; trust between or among groups, be they partner country nationals (PCNs), home country nationals (HCNs), or third-country nationals (TCNs); trust between individuals; and trust across organisational units, groups and individuals, such as between headquarters and HCNs or TCNs. In alliances, mergers and joint ventures, problems of trust may reflect fear of opportunism, or being taken advantage of by members of the other culture.

A certain element of mistrust, independent of cultural stereotypes, is always present between partners from different cultures. However, when it is not present from the outset, trust can develop between specific partners over the course of participation in the alliance (Parkhe, 1993). For example, development of interpersonal relationships across the alliance encourages cooperative relationships to supplant the negative reciprocity associated with relationships among strangers. The gradual dismantling of negative reciprocity corresponds in terms of transaction costs theory to the replacement of opportunism with trust.

The formation of trust in intercultural relations may generally be seen as a process that, bilaterally or multilaterally, takes place at psychological levels of the actors involved. Here cognitive levels (understanding, or absence thereof) interact with evaluative levels (acceptance, or absence thereof) and, in turn, with identity levels (security/faith, or absence thereof) until trust evolves (Torbiorn, 1994b). Such processes require considerable time. Once established, however, they can result in a set of characteristics or assets that are indispensable to successful cross-cultural cooperation.

INTERNATIONAL STAFFING PATTERNS

Staffing forms one branch of a general concept of HRM along with three other branches, which are rewards, appraisal, and development (Fombrun *et al.*, 1984). International HRM strategies can be viewed in terms of their contribution to overall transaction costs.

Since managerial and organisational systems are not directly transferable from one country to another, international strategy implementation inevitably generates a certain amount of tension and friction. This can have potentially adverse effects on various aspects of operations. If frictions arise in areas that are critical to core competency and competitive advantage, the consequences can be serious.

Therefore, as pressures build up, there is often an effort to reduce them by modifying the parameters of activities experiencing stress. This may entail externalising an activity that was previously carried out within the firm, internalising an activity previously conducted outside the firm, changing certain aspects of the firm's internal organisation or modifying its relations with external organisations. Staffing decisions concerning the selection and mix of PCNs, HCNs and TCNs are integral to such measures.

International Staffing and Transaction Costs

Although the aspect of costs is often neglected in HRM research, a transaction cost perspective can be usefully applied to a wide range of IHRM issues (Festing, 1997). Like other HRM measures, staffing may be viewed as a means of organising exchange relations and therefore as a potential source of transaction costs. In the short term, it is not always clear which staffing combinations may produce the lowest net risks and costs of transaction. In the long run, however, transaction cost economic theory suggests that firms whose staffing patterns minimise overall transaction costs will gain competitive advantages over others.

There is often a tradeoff in international management between transaction costs associated with the risk of *uncertainty* and transaction costs associated with the risks of *asset specificity* and *opportunism*. The first are related to, firstly, organisational problems of *coordination* and secondly, transaction cost limitations of *uncertainty, bounded rationality* and *information-processing* (which in the international context are a function of cultural barriers and cultural distance). The second are related to organisational problems of *control* (which are influenced by cultural and individual variables) and transaction costs of *opportunism* and *asset specificity*.

Bounded rationality is a significant source of transaction costs in IHRM strategy implementation. Increasing cultural distance between the firm and its foreign country environment exacerbates the problems. The particular elements of cultural distance that contribute to transaction costs are specific to particular combinations of cultures.

Interaction between the transaction costs factors of *uncertainty/complexity* and *bounded rationality* can intensify the impact of cultural barriers. These influences are specific to each individual person operating in a given foreign culture – that is, one that is foreign to him or her (Torbiorn, 1994b).

Remediable frictions – in this case cultural frictions that can be reduced by organisational measures – affect the appropriate balance of cultural accommodation in an international alliance. Cultural frictions can arise in two ways. First, since each individual represents a distinct combination of behavioural norms, judgements and so on that reflect the norms of his or her own culture, internal friction can be generated among staff members as a result of staff composition. Second, the actions of these persons as representatives of their own cultures can generate external frictions in interacting

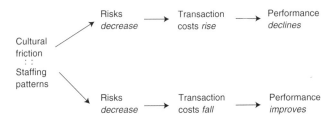

Figure 8.2   Cultural friction and staffing patterns.

with the local environment. Selective changes in the mix and ratio of PCNs, HCNs and TCNs can lower the transaction cost effects of these frictions and thus potentially enhance competitive advantage. See Figure 8.2.

The primary motives for using PCNs involve coordination, control, and knowledge transfer, whereas the primary motive for using HCNs involves mastery of the external environment. Although a company's needs with respect to these motives may vary according to its phase and scope of internationalisation, type of activity and products, type of organisation, strategic importance of markets and so on, experience shows that staffing patterns among European firms largely correspond to this profile (Torbiorn, 1997).

In general, use of PCNs reduces the risks and costs of transactions between the parent firm and overseas operations, owing to the PCN's superior understanding of the national culture of the parent firm and its culture. PCNs can also reduce risk by virtue of their mastery of the application of certain kinds of knowledge, in so far as such knowledge is firm-specific, cannot be embedded in organisational systems and is not held by HCNs. Finally, PCN staff may contribute to risk reduction by performing on-site supervisory or control functions, which cannot be embedded in organisational systems, such as in financial or administrative measures. On the other hand, PCNs may add to risks and costs of transacting with external environments, including the local culture. Ethnocentric decisions in favour of using PCN staff may raise net transaction costs, for example by limiting the foreign operation's ability to handle the local environment or by triggering internal communication frictions with local staff.

In general, use of HCNs reduces certain (though not all) risks, which the firm faces in the foreign external environment. This may explain current trends to staff locally by using HCNs, reflecting the increasing importance of mastery of foreign external environments, because of greater competition from the globalisation of markets. On the other hand, however, use of

HCNs tends to increase some of the risks and costs of intra-firm transactions. The use of HCNs can also raise internal risks, while reducing external risks posed by the unfamiliar foreign environment. Thus, a firm may forsake advantages in internal transactions, if HCNs do not understand, accept or agree with the corporate culture. The theoretically best solution would be an HCN who has mastered the firm's national culture and corporate culture, or conversely a PCN who has mastered the local foreign culture. Currently, the first of these choices seems to be gaining ground. A trend to reduce the use of PCNs and instead to bring local talent to headquarters for thorough training and familiarisation with the corporate culture of the parent is evident (Torbiorn, 1997). This may represent a recalculation of the perceived risks associated with not mastering local environments, as these environments are subjected to increasing global competition.

Within these general patterns, there is room for considerable variation in the risks and transactions costs of using PCNs, HCNs and TCNs in specific situations. To understand their potential impact on performance, these staffing alternatives must be evaluated in the context of strategic objectives and priorities.

INTERNATIONAL STAFFING AND STRATEGY

In order to manage its international activities, the firm develops arrangements for organisational structure and control that support its overall strategy. Each type of strategy has its own objectives, issues, and priorities, as well as its own preferred organisational structure, reflecting differences in the need to coordinate and integrate global task activities. Structure and controls for managing internationally depend on three considerations: how responsibility and authority are divided between domestic and foreign managers in order to maintain effective control over a company's foreign operations; how foreign operational tasks are grouped with domestic operations in order to use resources and serve foreign customers; and how the organisation functions in terms of its mechanisms and culture (Hill and Jones, 1995).

In practice, however, the selection of PCNs, HCNs and TCNs is often not based on business level or competitive strategy – as the competence-based approach to HRM requires, but on operational considerations. The resulting gradual realisation of an emergent competitive strategy (Mintzberg, 1987) based on accumulated ad-hoc responses to operational problems and opportunities may not be optimal from a competence-based view (Torbiorn, 1997). In this situation, transaction cost reductions at the operational level would not necessarily contribute to overall transaction cost minimisation, and might even have the opposite effect of increasing overall transaction costs. A competence-based approach to IHRM – focusing on the procurement and allocation of competence and enhancement of competitive advantage – ensures that operational level reductions in transaction costs associated with staffing patterns will contribute directly to competitive advantage and firm performance.

Staffing Implications of Centralised Control

One set of issues focuses on the centralisation of control. Retaining tight control at corporate headquarters over operational strategies in the marketing and manufacturing functions that are centred abroad requires that managers in the foreign country report to and are under the direct control of PCN managers in the parent company (Hill and Jones, 1995). The critical staffing decision involves the choice between PCNs and HCNs to manage the foreign operation.

In this situation, the relative advantages and disadvantages of PCNs versus HCNs are defined according to the priority of maintaining centralised control. The relative advantage of using HCN managers depends on whether or not they are amenable to strict centralised control by the parent firm. The relative advantage of using PCN managers in the foreign subsidiary depends on whether or not they can extend parent firm control over local operations. In turn, both of these advantages depend on the combined effects of cultural distance and individual cultural barriers in specific situations, on the extent to which frictions at the interface between specific cultures affect company operations, and on the significance of those effects for strategy implementation.

The choice between PCNs and HCNs also depends on what type of control is needed with respect to technology. If the firm's production technology is difficult, proprietary or central to product quality, then the need for parent firm control over local country operations implies a use of PCN managers in the foreign subsidiary. However, the transaction costs in these three situations differ considerably. Problems of bounded rationality underlie the need for control over difficult production technologies; problems of asset specificity and opportunism underlie the need for control over proprietary technologies; and problems of bounded rationality, opportunism and information impactedness underlie the need for control over technologies that are central to product image and quality. The trade-offs in choosing between PCNs and HCNs are quite different for each of these problems.

The availability of local managerial talent is another important consideration. If talent is not available in the local workforce, then using HCN managers will tend to increase transaction costs, owing to the need for training, supervision and control of HCNs by the parent firm. However, assigning PCNs to the foreign country can also incur training costs to enable them to function effectively in the new environment.

Staffing Implications of Local Market Responsiveness

The particular sources of a firm's competitive advantage also shape the implications of strategy for HRM. For a strategy characterised by local responsiveness and customisation, the difference between customisation of product, customisation of process and customisation of marketing can be significant (Hill and Jones, 1995). Heavy emphasis on local responsiveness as the basis for competitive advantage means that foreign country managers must be very knowledgeable about their own local operating environments. This has a number of important implications for HR strategy and practice. In general, it will be more advantageous for the firm to use HCNs or very experienced PCNs as local country managers. However, this varies according to the situation. Critical variables within the firm include the specific sources of the firm's competitive advantage, the nature of its production technology and the characteristics of its managerial employees. Critical variables outside the firm include the characteristics of the workforce, government regulations and the state of the infrastructure in the local country environment. For example, if a competitive strategy of local responsiveness is based largely on customisation of advertising to local customer preferences, then there is little advantage in internalising this into the foreign division by hiring HCNs. Assuming availability of local talent, it may be easier to contract with a local advertising agency.

When competitive strategy is based on customisation of product characteristics to local customer preferences, but when these preferences are unknown because it is a new market, then the firm may wish to extend managerial control over the market research effort. This is to prevent or at least inhibit the information from leaking to potential rivals. To the extent that organisational and managerial controls can be exercised more effectively than market controls in this situation, the transaction costs of externalisation are higher than for internalisation, and it will be advantageous for the firm to develop its own in-house market research capability. Since this requires managers and staff who have intimate knowledge and understanding of the local environment, it tends to favour the employment of HCNs. However, the need for control suggests possible advantages to placing them under the supervision of PCNs (or perhaps TCNs) who have assimilated corporate priorities and concerns.

Since local market responsiveness does not require centralised coordination and integration of international activities, it does not require a common corporate culture across national boundaries. Linking mechanisms are minimal. Managerial functions can be increasingly assigned to HCNs with time. However, centralised monitoring of financial, manufacturing and marketing performance by corporate headquarters requires standardisation and accuracy of reporting. This can be addressed by temporary assignment of PCNs from corporate headquarters in a control capacity.

Staffing Implications of Global Integration

Global coordination and integration require managers who can function effectively across multiple cultures (Hill and Jones, 1995). Transaction cost issues arise from the need for control, because of asset specificity and opportunism and also the presence of uncertainty, necessitating better communication and information exchange. Managers who can lower the firm's transaction costs of coordinating across cultural barriers and cultural distance represent a potential source of competitive advantage. Conversely, managers who cannot function effectively across cultures not only miss this opportunity but also may even increase transaction costs, potentially undermining competitive advantage and long-term performance.

Recruiting and developing this managerial capability is a major task for HRM. Expatriate assignments can enhance the individual managers' cross-cultural knowledge and skills with respect to a particular country. Rotating assignments in different countries facilitates the development of multicultural knowledge and skills. However, if multicultural managerial capability can be acquired by recruitment, without sacrificing organisational effectiveness or managerial control, that is a more efficient alternative for the firm.

Some strategies require a strong organisational culture across national boundaries. One way to develop this is by sending HCNs to corporate headquarters for training. While there, HCNs are exposed to the corporate culture and can be assimilated into it. This should be followed up with other opportunities to maintain personal contact with headquarters managers and staff, after the HCN has returned to his or her home country. Another way to support and extend the corporate culture in foreign divisions and units is through extensive use of TCNs rather than HCNs. Increased use of TCNs would also follow from the expansion of scope in recruitment and staffing attributed to transnational organisations

(Adler and Bartholomew, 1992). Thus, there would be a move away from vertical staffing from headquarters to subsidiaries (or the reverse) into lateral rotation across markets and cultures. Practical obstacles to such a handling of matters may, however, come from ethnocentric views at headquarters, that is, bounded rationality, and from the apprehension of opportunism due to limitations in trust from headquarters vis-à-vis TCNs (Zeira and Harari, 1977).

Staffing Implications of Local Responsiveness Plus Global Integration

The simultaneous maximisation of cost efficiencies, global learning and local responsiveness requires a high level of managerial competence (Hill and Jones, 1995). Managers must have excellent professional qualifications, international experience and cross-cultural skills including relevant linguistic and cultural proficiency. The choice among PCNs, HCNs and TCNs will depend largely on the availability of staff in each category that possesses the full range of requisite skills. Strategies that require extensive cooperation across different organisational cultures in different countries can be particularly difficult to implement. Most or all organisational members would need to have some understanding of both societal cultures. In addition, a new synthesis of organisational cultures would have to be formed (de Rond and Faulkner, 1997).

Norms or modes of operation of the internationalising firm may be said to consist of its own national culture's norms in addition to norms that are company-specific, as these two sets of norms together make up the corporate culture of any firm. In addition, norms of the acquired firm are likewise made up of local national culture norms plus local company specific norms. Efficient cross-cultural interaction may require mutual adjustment based on understanding, acceptance and trust on both sides as a precondition for gains from reduction of transaction costs. Among other things, this requires time, adaptation of leadership styles and empathetic staffing – for example, not signalling to HCNs that careers are blocked because PCNs may be installed in key positions – all in order to establish a balance between 'central and local' that economises on costs of transaction (see Doz and Prahalad, 1984).

Firms incur certain costs in developing or acquiring managers who combine good teamwork skills, cross-cultural interaction and communication skills, and professional skills, all of which can significantly lower the transaction costs of combining global integration with local responsiveness. Those firms that can best economise on these costs will have an advantage over their competitors.

Staffing Implications of International Joint Ventures

The main HRM implication of an international joint venture is that representatives of one parent company or the other must be able to function within the cultural context of the joint venture partner. The complexity and difficulty of managing the interface across cultures increases with the cultural distance between partners who, in the daily operations of local international joint ventures (IJVs), have to work together efficiently in close coordination. However, the problem is less critical if individuals who can function at a high level of competence in both contexts are available. Without such cultural integrators (Doz and Hamel, 1998), who can be PCNs, HCNS or TCNs, the effectiveness of IJVs may be seriously constrained. This can undermine the role of the IJV unit, which is weakened in terms of integrity and authority vis-à-vis strong role-senders (partners), who sometimes have limited understanding, or unresolved differences in mutual expectations. This in turn undermines the roles of IJV staff (be they PCNs, HCNs or TCNs), as partners tend to go over their heads in making decisions, or as conflicting interest between partners foster loyalty conflicts, impair decision-making, promote the withholding of information and so on among the staff of IJV units (cf. Geringer and Frayne, 1990; Zeira and Shenkar, 1990).

As cultural distance implies cultural barriers such as problems in understanding or accepting norms of the partners in IJVs, this may ultimately mean a bilateral lack of trust between them, one of the most common reasons why IJVs fail (see Killing, 1988; Kogut, 1988). Such lack of trust, which in TCE (transaction cost economics) terms corresponds to fear of opportunism, may also produce incentives of the parties to staff key positions by their own people – for example, PCNs on the part of the internationalising firm, and HCNs on the part of the local stakeholder. Such motives may actually be irrelevant for the efficiency of ongoing operations, in areas such as intended synergies or transfer of knowledge (Lei and Slocum, 1992). This will raise transaction costs, as will parallel staffing of key positions by PCNs and HCNs that is sometimes used (Koot, 1988).

CONCLUSION

Firms can reduce the managerial costs attributable to cultural distance and cognitive limitations in a variety of ways. One means of reducing the costs of managing human resources across cultural systems is to vary the mix and ratio of economic to organisational incentives. Another is to guard against ethnocentric fallacies of perception and lack of trust through systematic

expo⁣ s (and elsewhere in the firm) to
inter⁣ the effectiveness of individual
mana⁣ y paying careful attention to the
prop⁣

A ⁣ ⁣ ⁣ ⁣ ⁣ ⁣)cusing on the acquisition and
devel⁣ indicates that certain frictions
and ⁣ strategies. In terms of staffing
inter⁣ cant costs are not necessarily
those⁣ significant costs may instead
resul⁣ ise of the HRM parameters of
rewa⁣)ment, which impedes the goals
of building competence (for example, ...ng, developing and maintaining
talent) and moving competent staff to where it is needed (Torbiorn, 1997).
If IHRM measures have the effect of disadvantaging certain categories of
staff by blocking career paths, narrow or obscure perspectives in talent-
tracking, discriminatory use of rewards or criteria for appraisal, this will
generally cause frictions and raise costs of transaction, with potentially
negative implications for firm performance.

A transaction cost analysis of international staffing strategies suggests
that in the long run, firms gravitate towards staffing patterns that represent
the lowest risk and costs of transaction. Theoretically, elimination of transaction costs associated with international partnerships would require that
cultural differences and cultural distance present no obstacle to intercultural
transactions. Then there would be no risk or friction due to cultural factors,
and the decision to internalise or externalise specific activities would depend
solely on the technical functioning of the external local market. However, as
noted above, every person within or outside the firm who is involved in
making and carrying out decisions on matters relevant to company success –
whether at headquarters or in foreign markets – is a representative of his or
her own culture, and thus a potential source of friction in intercultural
exchanges. In selecting among categories of staff – PCNs, HCNs and TCNs –
one important yet often neglected consideration is the minimisation of
potential risk associated with intercultural frictions. This can be a source of
competitive advantage in operational areas that are critical to strategy implementation, thereby contributing to firm performance and alliance success.

References

ADLER, N.J. and BARTHOLOMEW, S. (1992) Managing globally competent
people. *Academy of Management Executive*, 6 (3), 52–65.

DE ROND, M. and D. FAULKNER (1997) The evolution of cooperation in non-joint venture strategic alliances: insights from the Royal Bank of Scotland and Banco Santander Alliance. Fourth International Conference on Multi-Organisational Partnerships and Co-operative Strategy, Balliol College, Oxford 8–10, July.

DOZ, Y.L., BARTLETT, C.A. and PRAHALAD, C.K.(1981) Global Competitive Pressures and Host Country Demands. *California Management Review, 23* (3), 63–74.

DOZ, Y. and HAMEL, G. (1998) *Alliance advantage: the art of creating value through partnering*, Harvard Business School Press, Boston, Ma.

DOZ, Y.L. and PRAHALAD, C.K. (1984) Patterns of strategic control within multinational corporations. *Journal of International Business Studies, 14* (2), 55–72.

ERDENER, C.B. and TORBIORN, I. (1997) Managing across economic and cultural systems: a transaction cost analysis and recommendations for the strategic management of international human resources. Fourth International Conference on Multi-Organizational Partnerships and Cooperative Strategy, Balliol College, Oxford, 8–10 July.

ERDENER, C.B. and I. TORBIORN (1998) Staffing and training practice in international firms: implications of risk effects for firm performance. Proceedings, Sixth Conference on International Human Resource for Management, University of Paderborn, Germany, 22–5 June.

FESTING, M. (1997) International human resource management strategies in multinational corporations: theoretical assumptions and empirical evidence from german firms. *Management International Review, 37*, 43–63.

FOMBRUN, C.J., TICHY, N.M. and DEVANNA, M.D. (eds)(1984) *Strategic Human Resource Management*. Wiley, New York.

GERINGER, M. and FRAYNE, C. (1990) Human resource management and international joint venture control: a parent company perspective *Management International Review*, special issue, *30*, 103–120.

HENDERSON, R. and COCKBURN, I. (1994) Measuring competence? Exploring firm effects in pharmaceutical research. *Strategic Management Journal*, special issue, *15*, 63–84.

HILL, C.W. and JONES, G.R. (1995) *Strategic Management: An Integrated Approach*, 3rd edn. – Houghton Mifflin, Boston, MA.

KILLING, J. (1988) Understanding alliances: the role of task and organizational complexity. In Contractor, F., Lorange, P. (eds), *Cooperative Strategies in International Business: Joint ventures and Technology Partnerships between Firms*. D.C. Heath, Lexington, MA.

KOGUT, B. (1988) A study of the life cycle of joint ventures. In Contractor, F. and Lorange, P. (eds), *Cooperative Strategies in International Business: Joint ventures and Technology Partnerships between Firms*. D.C. Heath, Lexington, MA.

KOOT, W. (1988) Underlying dilemmas in the management of joint ventures. In Contractor, F. and Lorange, P. (eds), *Cooperative Strategies in International Business: Joint ventures and Technology Partnerships between Firms*. D.C. Heath, Lexington, MA.

LEI, D. and SLOCUM, J. (1992) Global strategy, competence building and strategic alliances. *California Management Review*, Fall, *34*, 81–97.

MARINO, K.E. (1996) Developing consensus on firm competencies and capabilities. *Academy of Management Executive, 10*, 40–51.

MENARD, C. (1997) *Transaction Cost Economics: Recent Developments.* Cheltenham, Edward Elgar.

MINTZBERG, H. (1987) The strategy concept: five Ps for strategy. *California Management Review, 3/1*, 27, 11–24.

PARKHE, A. (1993) Strategic alliances structuring: a game theoretic and transaction cost examination of inter form cooperation. *Academy of Management Journal, 36*, 794–829.

SELMER, J.O., TORBIORN I. and DE LEON, C.T. (1988) Sequential cross-cultural training for expatriate business managers: pre-departure and post-arrival. *International Journal of Human Resource Management, 9*, 831–40.

TORBIORN, I. (1997) Staffing for International Operations. *Human Resource Management Journal, 7*, 42–52.

TORBIORN, I. (1988) Cultural barriers as a social psychological construct: an empirical validation. In W. Gudykunst and Y. Kim (eds), *Cross-Cultural Adaptation: Current Theory and Research*. Sage, Beverly Hills, CA.

TORBIORN, I. (1994a) Dynamics of cross-cultural management. In Althen, G. (ed.), *Learning Across Cultures*. NAFSA Publications, Washington, DC. 31–55.

TORBIORN, I. (1994b) *Strategisk Internationell PA*. Studentlitteratur, Lund.

WILLIAMSON, O.E. (1975) *Markets and Hierarchies*. Free Press, New York.

WILLIAMSON, O.E. (1985) *The Economic Institutions of Capitalism: Firms, Markets and Relational Contracting*. Macmillan: London.

ZEIRA, Y. and HARARI, E. (1977) Third country managers in multinational corporations. *Personnel Review, 6/1*, 32–7.

ZEIRA, Y. and SHENKAR, O. (1990) Interactive and specific parent characteristics: implications for management and human resources in international joint ventures. *Management International Review*, Special Issue, *30*, 7–22.

9 The Role of Power Relationships in Partnership Agreements between Small Suppliers and Large Buyers

Frank McDonald

INTRODUCTION

The use of partnerships in supply chains as a means of creating competitive advantage has received strong support from the work of academics (for example, Carlisle and Parker, 1989; Womack *et al.,* 1990; Macbeth and Ferguson, 1994; Saunders, 1994). Many government agencies have also supported the development of partnership agreements (European Commission, 1991; Partnership Sourcing, 1993, 1994, 1995). Empirical evidence supporting the adoption of partnership agreements has been inferred from the ability of Japanese car manufacturers successfully to penetrate Western markets. This success has been partly attributed to the adoption of partnership agreements (Burt and Doyle, 1993; Dyer and Ouchi, 1993; Dyer, 1996). These factors have contributed to a momentum to create and develop partnerships in supply chains as a means to improve competitiveness.

There has been criticism of the gallop towards the adoption of partnerships, and questions have been raised about the efficacy of partnerships including the effects on the competitive environment, industrial structure and practical issues connected to efficiently administering partnerships (A.T. Kearney, 1994, 1995; Van Weele, 1994; New and Ramsay, 1997). Furthermore, empirical evidence suggests that only a small number of buyer–supplier relationships appear to conform to the ideals of true partnerships (Helper, 1991; Royal Society of Arts, 1995; Sinclair *et al.*, 1996; Boddy *et al.*, 1998). Notwithstanding these criticisms, resolving the problems that arise in partnerships is normally regarded as one of ironing out the teething problems of establishing effective relationships between buyers and sellers. Solutions to these problems are sought by encouraging greater integration between buyers and sellers and by fostering changes in the attitudes and practices of managers and workers. In effect, the orthodoxy recommends that organisations need to learn how to manage partnership relations effectively (Hines *et al.*, 1996; Rich, 1996; Ali *et al.*, 1997).

This chapter highlights the importance of asymmetric power structures as an important limitation to the effectiveness of partnerships in supply operations. The analysis suggests that asymmetric power may undermine the ability of partnerships to deliver and maintain competitive advantage and thereby questions the validity of the orthodox view.

TRANSACTION COST THEORY

The theoretical case for partnerships rests on the transaction cost advantages of obtaining supplies by use of collaborative relationships as opposed to the use of vertically integrated company structures or competitive, market-based tendering systems. Transaction cost theory suggests that power structures within organisational arrangements such as partnerships do not affect their effectiveness. Williamson has argued that the economic benefits of implementing effective organisational structures will overcome opposition from powerful groups that consider organisational change to be against their interests.

> The power approach to vertical integration appears to assume that everything that feasibly can be integrated will be ... The efficiency hypothesis, by contrast, is that vertical integration will occur selectively rather than comprehensively, that mistaken vertical integration can rarely be sustained, and that more efficient modes will eventually supplant less efficient modes – though entrenched power interests can sometimes delay the displacement. (Williamson, 1985: 236)

Therefore, the pursuit of efficiency that lies at the heart of the transaction cost theory is considered to overrule power structures that might prevent organisational changes that can improve effectiveness. Transaction cost theory tends to regard power structures (or vested interests) as a minor irritant in the finding of organisational arrangements that promote efficiency. This emphasis on efficiency has led to the relative neglect of the importance of power for the design and development of organisations.

However, the ability to exercise power within organisations is considered to be important in transaction cost theory because the use of power is thought to reduce uncertainty and thereby to help in the effective operation of cooperative organisational arrangements (Williamson, 1975, 1985;

Schonberger, 1990). Transaction cost theory assumes that agreements are reached by rational agents who act in a self-interested manner. In these conditions, parties to agreements will not voluntarily enter into arrangements that make them worse off. Consequently, in organisational structures where asymmetric power exists, the benefits may be skewed towards powerful partners, but this should not lead to some parties to the agreement being worse off as compared with other possible organisational arrangements.

The distribution of benefits from organisational arrangements is important in transaction cost theory because of the incentive problem. This problem is related to the share-out of benefits within organisational arrangements. Incentive systems provide inducements that encourage the parties to the arrangement to deliver desired outcomes. These inducements come from the transfer, to the members of the organisation, of the benefits of cooperating within an organisational arrangement. Power structures within organisations influence the level of such transfers. However, this is primarily a struggle over the share of the benefits that arise from cooperation. Asymmetric power structures within partnerships could lead to problems for effective organisational design were incentive systems to emerge that allowed powerful parties to acquire too many of the benefits of collaboration. The possibility that power structures may lead to incentive systems that undermine the creation of efficient organisational arrangements is not considered to be serious because the impetus to create efficient organisations to deliver competitive advantage is thought to overcome such vested interests. However, the possibility that the development of organisations maybe hampered by inappropriate incentive systems is acknowledge in the transaction cost literature (Groenewegen, 1996; Menard, 1997). Nevertheless, these problems are normally considered to be connected to learning how to make the organisational arrangement work effectively. The possibility that asymmetric power structures could fundamentally undermine cooperative organisational arrangements is not considered in the transaction cost literature.

EFFICIENT SOLUTIONS

Transaction cost theory focuses on organisational structures that provide an *efficient solution*, that is, an outcome that maximises the total value of operations by minimising the costs of engaging in the activities necessary to complete operations. The concept of an *efficient solution* is based on the seminal work of Coase, in which he provided a theoretical rationale for the role of organisations (firms) as providers of solutions to the problem of efficiently allocating resources (Coase, 1937). Coase's theorem assumes that individuals seek to maximise their wealth, and that property rights over resources are clearly identifiable and can be protected by the legal system. Moreover, changes in wealth that result from agreements are assumed not to lead to a reordering of the preferences of the parties to the agreement. In these conditions, the theorem predicts that the outcome of the bargaining process is not affected by power relations. Therefore, in a system where agents seek voluntarily to maximise their wealth, bargaining will determine an *efficient solution*, and this is not affected by factors such a power, ownership or the method of distributing net benefits.

Various types of organisational forms can provide *efficient solutions* – ranging from markets for simple and infrequent transactions to hierarchical organisations (vertically integrated companies) for complex and frequent transactions. Participatory arrangements (divisional or subsidiary organisational structures) and cooperative agreements (alliances and partnership relationships) occupy the middle ground in this continuum between the market and centralised hierarchical organisational forms (Williamson, 1975, 1985, 1991).

Other approaches advocate the use of cooperative organisational arrangements based on management theories such as strategic supply chain management systems, concentration on core competencies and lean production systems (see for example, Prahalad and Hamel, 1990; Womack and Jones, 1994; Lamming and Cox, 1995). Concepts such as game theory have also been used to justify cooperative organisational arrangements (see for example, Lorange and Roos, 1992; Kay, 1993). All of these approaches assume, either explicitly or implicitly, that the transaction costs associated with cooperative organisational arrangements are smaller than alternatives such as vertically integrated companies or the use of markets; in effect, these approaches are related to the central tenet of transaction cost theory, that is, they involve a search for an *efficient solution*.

THE ROLE OF ASSET SPECIFICITY IN PARTNERSHIPS

Investment in specific assets to meet the requirements of effective supply chain management reduces the production and logistic costs of operations and enables improved performance in meeting desired quality targets (Dyer, 1994). However, high asset specificity increases transaction costs because the quantity and quality of information exchanged between buyers and sellers increases. High asset specificity can also lead to a dependence situation that can be exploited by powerful partners. Arm's-length, market-based relationships are normally too short-term to safeguard against the potentially harmful effects of developing high levels of asset specificity, especially as the transaction cost of finding new suppliers or buyers are high if contracts are not renewed. Vertically integrated companies can provide an organisational solution to these problems, but they are normally associated with high transaction costs connected to the complex control and monitoring systems that are required to manage such companies.

Partnership relationships based on trust, can, in principle, provide an alternative organisational solution to these problems. Partnerships allow the necessary investment in specific assets that will lead to reductions in production and logistics costs and quality advantages while avoiding the high transaction costs that are connected with market-based relationships and vertically integrated companies. The development of trust can be seen as a rational and self-interested method of maximising the total value of transactions because of 'mutual dependency' (Buchanan, 1992) or 'mutual hostage' situations (Buckley and Casson, 1988). Analysis of the use of 'tit-for-tat' strategy in repeated games suggests that adoption of a cooperative solution such as partnerships provide an optimal solution to these trust problems (Parkhe, 1993).

There are two factors that limit investment in specific assets. First, in some cases only low levels of asset specificity will be required to meet price and quality targets, for example, mundane products such as nuts and bolts. In these circumstances an arm's-length, market-based relationship is likely to secure the required outcomes. However, securing appropriate targets for price and quality for more complex products will necessitate a higher level of asset specificity, requiring a deeper relationship than would the monitoring approach. Second, asset specificity may restrict the ability of companies to supply more than a few buyers. In such cases, high levels of investment in specific assets can limit economies of scale and scope and thereby lead to loss of production efficiency. However, if the gains from enhanced quality of product or service from the specific investments outweigh the costs in terms of lost production efficiency then these investments will be worthwhile.

Three possible reasons can be put forward to explain the low number of partnerships that have been found in empirical studies:

- High levels of asset specificity are not required in large parts of the supply chain.
- Economies of scale and scope are widespread and require many companies to avoid large-scale investments in specific assets.

- Management systems are failing to design and develop effective partnership agreements that can provide an *efficient solution* to the problem of asset specificity.

However, finding *efficient solutions* may be very difficult when asymmetric power structures exist within partnerships. Therefore, problems connected to asymmetric power provide a fourth possible explanation for the low number of partnerships that have been observed in supply chains.

POWER IN SUPPLIER RELATIONSHIPS

The ability to exercise power in supplier relationships stems from four main sources:

- control of information,
- control of strategically important technology,
- a high share of the total sales revenue of suppliers,
- market power.

Control of information can lead to loss of intellectual property and dependency on partners for strategically important knowledge. These problems have led to termination or downgrading of many collaborative relationships such as joint ventures and strategic alliances (Inkpen and Beamish, 1997). Companies that control access to strategically important information in areas such as technology, product and labour market conditions and the activities of regulators and governmental agencies can use the power that this gives them to secure higher benefits for themselves. The use of such power is evident in the relationship between manufacturers of branded products and supermarket chains. The power that supermarkets acquire from their information on consumer behaviour has allowed them to gain very beneficial terms in their dealings with the manufacturers of branded products (Ogbanna and Wilkinson, 1996).

Dependence on partners in important areas of technology can also lead to problems with asymmetric power. Suppliers or buyers can lose the ability to understand and employ the technology used in strategically important areas of their business. In these circumstances, the partner that possesses technological expertise can exercise power over the other one (Lincoln *et al.*, 1998).

Buyers who represent a large share of the total sales revenue of suppliers are able to exercise power because of the costs associated with finding new outlets for sales if the buyer limits purchases (Ramsey, 1995). The power of supermarkets over manufacturers of branded products is partly attributable to the large share of total sales revenue of manufacturers that stems from a small number of supermarkets.

The ability of agents in partnerships to exercise power in the final market-place is also important. Suppliers of well-known or high-specification products can command high prices for their products, whereas suppliers of mundane parts for such goods lack such market power. The possession of asymmetric market power in partnerships will lead to unequal bargaining power over the division of the spoils that arise from collaboration (Cox, 1997).

The exercise of power in supply relationships does not necessarily depend upon the size of partners. Asymmetric power structures can exist in partnerships that are composed of large companies or of small companies or with a combination of small and large. However, the capability to wield power is often related to size because large companies tend to have good access to information, advanced technological knowledge, a large share of the total sales revenue of their suppliers and also significant levels of market power.

The literature on supplier relationships places heavy emphasis on trust between partners as a safeguard against the dangers of asymmetric power (Womack *et al.*, 1990; Sako, 1992; Macbeth and Ferguson, 1994). Nevertheless, cooperative solutions, supposedly based on trust, may embody extensive use of the exercise of power. The Japanese Keiretsu supplier system, for example, depends on the existence of the power of large manufacturers of final products. The use of such power is deemed to be necessary to reduce uncertainty about supplier performance and thereby to minimise transaction costs (Schonberger, 1990). Others have argued that close collaboration within supply chains can be part of a process to create or defend market power. This is done by creating a connected set of assets (a value chain) that cannot be easily replicated by competitors. This allows companies to exercise monopoly power in their markets. Companies use control over supply chains to prevent replication by competitors and to secure the bulk of the benefits that arise from their value chain. In these cases, maximum value is extracted not only from the final sale of products but also from the value-adding operations in the supply chain (Cox, 1997).

Nevertheless, supplier relationships that are voluntarily entered into should be mutually beneficial. Asymmetric power within relationships will probably lead to the lion's share of the benefits going to the powerful partner, but all parties should benefit. Moreover, institutional frameworks may limit the ability of powerful partners to exploit weaker partners. Mistakes may be made because of deficient management and poor information, but it is most unlikely that large numbers of companies voluntarily enter into supplier relationships that result in harmful outcomes. However, collaborative relationships may begin on a mutually beneficial basis, but as they develop it is possible that powerful partners can erode the position of weaker partners to the point where they can become worse off, or at least, no better off than in the pre-collaborative position.

A MODEL OF PARTNERSHIP AGREEMENTS

The superiority of partnerships, for the parties involved in the supply chain, can be illustrated by use of simple stylised model. In Figure 9.1, the relationship between two companies (X and Y) is considered. Point A refers to the initial distribution of net benefits between the two companies. Initial distributions such as this may arise from existing relationships – for example, a short-term, market-based relationship. Alternatively, point A could refer to the net benefits that the parties receive if they are not in any relationship with each other, for example, where the buyer and supplier has relationships

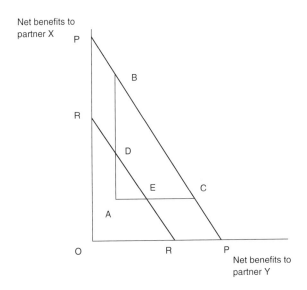

Figure 9.1   Benefits of partnership agreements.

with other companies. The line PP is the locus of the possible distribution of net benefits between the companies if they establish a partnership. The line RR traces the potential net benefits from developing an alternative to a partnership relationship, for example, an arm's-length market relationship. In this case, the partnership provides an *efficient solution* because this organisational structure leads to the maximisation of total value.

Assuming that agreements are voluntarily entered into, it is possible to arrive at satisfactory outcomes by an appropriate redistribution of the net benefits that ensures that all parties benefit from the agreement, or do not suffer from it. The Pareto criterion fulfils this condition. Using this criterion will require a post-agreement outcome within the area ABC. Anywhere in the area, ABC is preferable to the current situation. Outcomes in the area ADE fulfil the Pareto criteria, but they are available from a lower-level relationship. Furthermore, outcomes within the area ABC do not confer the full potential benefits of the relationship. Therefore, such outcomes will give rise to disappointment and are likely to stimulate substantial efforts to make the partnership work more effectively (that is, to reach an outcome on the section BC).

Transaction cost theory may explain why disappointing outcomes can arise from partnership agreements. There may be problems of asymmetric information such as adverse selection or moral hazard that require special arrangements in order to minimise the transaction costs of operating the partnership (Dow, 1993). It is also possible that the institutional structures within which the partnership must operate may not be of the type that would allow an *efficient solution* to be obtained by use of partnerships that are based on those that prevail in different institutional systems. If failure to reach a feasible *efficient solution* lies at the heart of the problems with partnership agreements, then the orthodox view that learning effectively to manage partnership relations will provide a good guide to the steps necessary to make such agreements effective.

However, a more fundamental problem may arise with regard to maintaining effective partnerships in cases where there are asymmetric power structures in the relationship. In these circumstances, the distribution of the net gains can lead to serious problems in sustaining a mutually beneficial outcome.

EROSION OF THE GAINS FROM PARTNERSHIPS

Transactions cost theory suggest that the *efficient solution* is not affected by the distribution of power between the parties to the agreement.

Therefore, power relationships are not considered to have any effect on the problem of finding optimal organisational structures.

The benefits of greater integration of organisational structures in supply chains stem from replacing market-based relations by control systems based on hierarchy (Williamson, 1975). In such hierarchical systems, the distribution of net benefits is likely to be affected by the location of such power. For example, in partnerships between a large buyer (for example, an assembler of a final product) and a number of small and medium enterprises (SMEs) supplying components, the assembler is normally at the apex of the hierarchical power system. These power relationships arise from the size of the assembler relative to the suppliers and the control over the details of the supply chain that the assembler possesses. Furthermore, partnerships tend to make suppliers reliant on the assembler because these agreements tend to develop specific assets and skills in the supplying SMEs. Therefore, buyers may be able to skew the net benefits of the agreement in favour of themselves. In such circumstances, powerful partners will be able to skew the net benefits of the relationships towards themselves.

In terms of Figure 9.1 (if Y is the powerful partner), an outcome near to point C would arise. An outcome such as this is in accordance with Coase's theorem – it is an *efficient solution*, providing that the outcome is on the line PP. Points close to C that are not on PP are not efficient, but are more favourable to Y than to X.

In the longer term, the ability to exercise power over the distribution of the net benefits may lead to outcomes that result in net losses to weaker parties to the agreement. The dynamics of such partnership agreements can be highlighted by use of two concepts developed by a public choice theorist (Holcombe, 1980). These concepts are the locking-in and erosion effects. The locking-in effect arises from the alteration to relationships that follow from an agreement to collaborate. These alterations lock the parties together and result in significant disruption costs if attempts are made to dissolve an agreement. Disruption costs would arise from the need to adjust assets and skills that had been developed to meet the needs of the buyer. The disruption costs to the buyer result from the need to find alternative suppliers who can deliver the same quality of supplies. The erosion effect is the ability of the powerful partner to capture most of the net benefits from the collaboration – to the extent that the weaker partner ends up at an inferior outcome than the pre-agreement position.

The effects of erosion are illustrated in Figure 9.2. Starting from the initial position at A, the companies X and Y agree to a partnership and the distribution of the net benefits is at a point close to C. If this agreement is

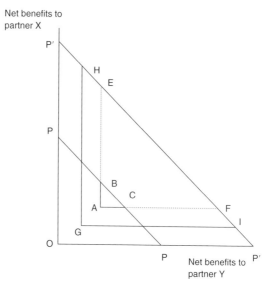

Figure 9.2   Erosion of net benefits – I.

effective then the potential net benefits will be enhanced as the partnership develops – shown by a shift to the right of the line PP to P'P'. The enhancement of potential net benefits could arise from learning effects and/or from the evolution of better techniques of supply chain management. If there were no locking-in effects, this would not lead to any problems. A new outcome would arise, probably close to point F. Such an outcome would be mutually beneficial. However, if locking-in effects lead to significant disruption costs the distribution of net benefits would move to a point such as G if the agreement were to be terminated. The closer collaboration between the parties that allows the potential net benefits line to shift outwards requires the development of specific assets and, therefore, leads to locking-in effects. In these circumstances, the area of mutually beneficial outcomes would become GHI. If Y is able to exercise power it will obtain a distribution of the net benefits close to the point I. This outcome is worse (for X) than the pre-agreement distribution (that is, at point A). The net benefits to X have been eroded by Y.

Therefore, it is possible for partnerships to start well but to end badly. The heart of this problem is that there are asymmetric power relationships in the agreement and that partnerships are able to evolve and thereby boost the potential net benefits from the cooperation. Ironically, this problem results from the pursuit of effective supply chain management.

THE LIMITS TO THE EROSION PROCESS

If erosion leads to problems for maintaining effective partnerships, questions arise as to why buyers would exercise their power to erode the position of their suppliers. An obvious answer is that buyers who operate in competitive markets will be disadvantaged if they do not obtain the same level of net benefits from their partnerships as their competitors. The adoption of 'best-practice' techniques will further reinforce the tendency for buyers to obtain the best possible deal for themselves from their partnerships. Furthermore, in cases where partnerships are 'benchmarked' to 'best-practice' arrangements the expectations of what is regarded as an effective partnership may be high. In these circumstances, buyers will gravitate towards the optimal level of erosion: that is, at a level that is just above that outcome that will induce the partner to withdraw from the agreement. In Figure 9.2 this is shown by a point very close to I. Buyers are constrained from eroding beyond this point because they will face significant disruption costs if partnerships are terminated.

Another limit to the exercise of the power to erode stems from the danger of reducing the potential net benefits of the partners to the extent that it becomes impossible to prevent a breakdown of the partnership. In Figure 9.3, the net benefits to X have been reduced from OPX to OPX1 because of the pressure from the powerful partner to meet tough conditions on price and quality. Partner Y secures an increase in the maximum possible benefits from OPY to OPY1. If the locking-in effect leads to a no-agreement distribution shown by the point G, then partner Y could erode the benefits to partner X to the point I. This point corresponds to the maximum level of erosion that does not result in X becoming worse off after the impact of the locking-in effect. At point I, partner Y receives the same benefits as were available before the change to the net benefits curve. However, if X experiences further erosion of the possible benefits then the powerful partner will exercise their power to the extent that it becomes impossible to maintain the partnership.

Attempts to practise optimal erosion require careful assessment and monitoring of the magnitude of the locking-in effect and of the potential net benefits position. Consequently, as partnerships evolve, and as deeper and more effective agreements are sought, buyers will find that the transaction cost of this type of organisational arrangement will grow. However,

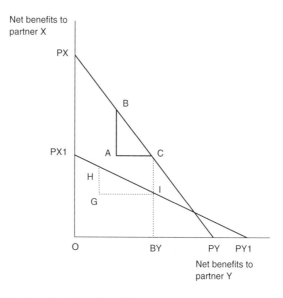

Figure 9.3   Erosion of net benefits – II.

the incentives to practise optimal erosion are strong. In these circumstances, a fine balancing act is necessary by the buyer to secure maximum benefits without destroying the partnership. It is possible that practising optimal erosion could so increase transaction costs that it would become preferable to replace partnership agreements with some other kind of organisational structure. Alternatively, the buyer may have to limit attempts to improve the benefits that are available from the partnership in order to prevent unacceptable increases in transaction costs.

POSSIBLE SOLUTIONS TO PROBLEMS WITH PARTNERSHIPS

The above analysis provides a set of reasons as to why effective partnerships have proved to be difficult to establish and maintain. Three major problems can be identified:

1. Partnerships are not *efficient solutions*, but the orthodoxy exerts pressure for the adoption of unsuitable supplier relationships.
2. Partnerships are *efficient solutions*, but the detailed arrangements of agreements do not deal adequately with problems connected to institutional frameworks and the motivations of the parties to the agreement.

3. Partnerships are *efficient solutions*, but the net benefits from agreements are liable to be eroded by powerful partners.

The first two problems are, in principle, capable of resolution. In the first case partnerships should not be sought; rather, alternative solutions should be developed (Parker and Hartley, 1997). In the second case, the partners need to learn how to manage partnerships effectively. This may require significant changes to the arrangements of the agreement in order to allow it to operate effectively. The first two problems can be solved if the transaction and production costs connected to the agreement are correctly identified and measured and if appropriate policies are adopted to find the minimum total costs (Hines *et al.*, 1996).

The third problem is more intractable. Moreover, it may affect many partnerships that initially achieve an *efficient solution*. The incentive to practise optimal erosion may be very strong, leading to tensions that may result in the breakup of the partnership because of the decline in the net benefits to junior partners as the agreement seeks to develop by focusing on ever increasing benefits to powerful partners.

If potential partners are aware of the problem of erosion before they enter into partnerships, it may be possible to constrain arrangements such that it is not possible to practise erosion. If transparent and enforceable rules about the distribution of net benefits can be established it may be possible to construct contracts that prevent, or limit, the practice of erosion. Alternatively, the partners may acquire a financial stake in the other company and thereby limit the incentive to practise erosion. In these circumstances, the transaction cost advantages of partnerships may be lost because finding and implementing solutions to the problem of erosion is likely to increase transaction costs.

In such cases, market-based contractual relationships or vertically integrated organisational structures may deliver lower transaction costs. Appropriately constructed, short-term, market-based contractual relationships may be capable of providing incentives for suppliers to develop asset-specific investments if this leads to strong learning effects. Such outcomes have been found in high-technology industries. This learning from securing contracts from high-specification buyers is prominent in the strategy of the supplying firms. These learning effects helped supplying companies to secure repeat contracts or to win contracts from other companies by developing abilities to supply high-quality output (Nordberg *et al.*, 1996).

Limited-life, product-specific consortiums that are constructed for the purpose of creating a supply chain for the life of a product may also provide a type of cooperative buyer–supplier relationship that permits the acquisition of appropriate specific assets (Hall, 1999). Such limited-life consortiums minimise the risks of erosion because the acquisition of specific assets is constrained to a particular product that has a given life span. This type of arrangement may restrict the ability of powerful partners to erode the position of weaker partners because assets are not committed on the basis of a long-term relationship, but only to a particular product for the life of that product. However, this solution forgoes the benefits of the reduction in production and transaction costs that arise from the acquisition of specific assets that are devoted to long-term partnerships. In cases where acceptable cooperative solutions cannot be found, market-based relationships or vertically integrated organisational structures may deliver lower transaction costs. It is likely that there are other solutions to the problems of asset specificity than partnerships, and some of these solutions may be better options.

CONCLUSIONS

Partnerships are unlikely to be a panacea for delivering competitive advantage. Nevertheless, partnerships may provide an *efficient solution* in some cases, but delivering such solutions may require careful analysis of the conditions that affect transaction and production costs and the development of a set of suitable policies to allow such a solution to emerge. Furthermore, if erosion is a serious problem then an *efficient solution* will not be easily maintained. It is possible that new organisational structures, or modified ones, could deliver *efficient solutions* that are preferable to partnerships, particularly if such organisational structures can avoid the problems associated with erosion.

References

ALI, F., SMITH, G. and SAKR, J. (1997) Developing buyer–supplier relationships in the automobile industry. A study of Jaguar and Nippondenso. *European Journal of Purchasing and Supply*, *3*, 33–42.
A.T. KEARNEY (1994) *Partnership or Powerplay*. A.T. Kearney Ltd, London.
A.T. KEARNEY (1995) *Profiting from Partnership: Maximising the Benefits from Supply Chain Collaboration*. A.T. Kearney Ltd, London.
BODDY, D., CAHILL, C., CHARLES, M., FRASER-KRAUS., H. and MACBETH, D. (1998) Success and failure in implementing supply chain partnership: an empirical study. *European Journal of Purchasing and Supply*, *4*, 143–51.

BUCHANAN, L. (1992) Vertical trade relationships: the role of dependence and symmetry in attaining organisational goals. *Journal of Marketing Research*, 29, 65–75.

BUCKLEY, P. and CASSON, M. (1988) A theory of co-operation in joint-ventures. In F. Contractor, F. and Lorange, P. (eds), *Cooperative strategies in international business: Joint Ventures and Technology Partnerships between Firms*. D.C. Heath Lexington, MA.

BURT, D. and DOYLE, M. (1993) *The American Keiretsu: A Strategic Weapon for Global Competitiveness*. Irwin, Homewood, CA.

CARLISLE, J. and PARKER, R. (1989) *Beyond Negotiation: Redeeming Customer-supplier Relations*. Wiley, London.

COASE, R. (1937) The nature of the firm, *Economica*, 4, 386–405.

COX, A. (1997) *Business Success*. Earlsgate Press, Boston, Lincs.

DOW, G. (1993) The appropriability critique of transaction cost economics. In Pitelis, C. (ed), *Transaction Costs, Markets and Hierarchies*. Blackwell, Oxford.

DYER, J. (1994) Dedicated assets: Japan's manufacturing edge. *Harvard Business Review*, 64, 174–78.

DYER, J. (1996) Does governance matter? Keiretsu alliances and asset specificity as sources of Japanese competitive advantage. *Organisational Science*, 7, 649–66.

DYER, J. and OUCHI, W. (1993) Japanese style business partnerships. Giving companies a competitive edge. *Sloan Management Review*, 35, 51–63.

European Commission (1991) *Pan-European Forum on Subcontracting*. SEC(91)1286. final Brussels.

GRONENEWEGEN, J. (1996) *Transaction Cost Economics and Beyond*. Kluwer Academic, London.

HALL, R. (1999) Rearranging Risks and Rewards in a Supply Chain. *Journal of General Management*, 24, 22–33.

HELPER, S. (1991) How much has changed between US automakers and their suppliers? *Sloan Management Review*, 32, 15–28.

HINES, P., JAMES, R. and JONES, O. (1996) A cost benefit model for decision making in supplier development activities. In Cox, A. (ed.), *Innovations in Procurement Management*. Earlsgate Press, Boston, Lincs.

HOLCOMBE, R. (1980) A contracterian model of the decline in classical liberalism. *Public Choice*, 35, 277–86.

INKPEN, A. and BEAMISH, P. (1997) Knowledge, bargaining power, and the instability of international joint ventures. *Academy of Management Review*, 40, 177–202.

KAY, J. (1993) *Foundations of Corporate Success*. Oxford University Press.

LAMMING, R. and COX. A. (1995) *Strategic Procurement Management in the 1990s: Concepts and Cases*. Earlsgate Press, Boston, Lincs.

LINCOLN, J., AHMADJIAN, C. and MASON, E. (1998) Organisational learning and purchase supply relationships in Japan: Hitachi, Matsushita and Toyota compared. *California Management Review*, 40, 241–64.

LORANGE, P. and ROOS, J. (1992) *Strategic Alliances: Formation, Implementation and Evolution*. Blackwell, Oxford.

MACBETH, D. and FERGUSON, N. (1994) *Partnership Sourcing: An Integrated Supply Chain Approach*. Pitman, London.

MENARD, C. (1997) *Transaction Cost Economics: Recent Developments*. Elgar, Cheltenham.

NEW, S. and RAMSAY, J. (1997) A Critical Appraisal of Aspects of the Lean Chain Approach. *European Journal of Purchasing and Supply Management, 3*, 93–102.

NORDBERG, M., CAMPBELL, A. and VERBEKE, A. (1996) Can market-based contracts substitute for alliances in high technology markets? *Journal of International Business Studies, 27*, 963–79.

OGBONNA, E. and WILKINSON, B. (1996) Information technology and power in the UK grocery distribution chain. *Journal of General Management, 22*, 20–35.

PARKER, D., and HARTLEY, K. (1997) The economics of partnership sourcing versus adversarial competition: a critique. *European Journal of Purchasing and Supply Management, 3*, 115–25.

PARKHE, A. (1993) Strategic alliances structuring: a game theoretic and transaction cost examination of interform cooperation. *Academy of Management Journal, 36*, 794–829.

Partnership Sourcing Ltd (1993) *Partnership Sourcing.* Department of Trade and Industry/Confederation of British Industry, London.

Partnership Sourcing Ltd (1994) *4th Annual Survey.* Department of Trade and Industry/Confederation of British Industry, London.

Partnership Sourcing Ltd (1995) *Partnership Sourcing and British Industry.* Department of Trade and Industry/Confederation of British Industry, London.

PRAHALAD, C. and HAMEL, G. (1990) The core competencies of the corporation. *Harvard Business Review, 60*, 79–91.

RAMSEY, J. (1995) Purchasing Power. *European Journal of Purchasing and Supply Management, 1*, 125–38.

RICH, N. (1996) The use of quality function development for relational assessment: adversary or partner In A. Cox, (ed.), *Innovations in Procurement Management.* Earlsgate Press, Boston, Lincs.

Royal Society of Arts (1995) *Tomorrow's Company.* London.

SAKO, M. (1992) *Prices, Qualities and Trust.* Cambridge University Press.

SAUNDERS, M. (1994) *Strategic Purchasing and Supply Chain Management.* Pitman, London.

SCHONBERGER, R. (1990) *Japanese Manufacturing Techniques.* Macmillan, London.

SINCLAIR, D., HUNTER, L. and BEAUMONT, P. (1996) Models of customer–supplier relations. *Journal of General Management, 22*, 56–75.

VAN WEELE, A.J. (1994) *Purchasing Management: Analysis Planning and Practice.* Chapman & Hall, London.

WILLIAMSON, O. (1975) *Markets and Hierarchies: Analysis and Anti-Trust Implications. A Study in the Economics of Internal Organisations.* Free Press, New York.

WILLIAMSON, O. (1985) *The Economic Institutions of Capitalism: Firms, Markets, Relational Contracting.* Macmillan, London.

WILLIAMSON, O. (1991) The logic of economic organisation. In O. Williamson and S. Nelson, (eds), *The Nature of the Firm.* Oxford University Press.

WOMACK, J. and JONES, D. (1994) From lean production to lean enterprise. *Harvard Business Review, 64*, 34–47.

WOMACK, J., JONES, D. and ROOS, D. (1990) *The Machine That Changed the World.* Rawson Associates, New York.

10 Joining Two Organisational Units: Managing Cultural Threats and Possibilities

Jens Genefke

INTRODUCTION

In the wake of coalitions, mergers and joint ventures we often find organisations encountering severe problems of internal cooperation. Internal reorganisations demanding a joining of hitherto independent units face the same kinds of problems. There are many reasons for such problems, but one particular explanation keeps coming up – cooperative problems are caused by difficulties encountered in the clash between two different organisational cultures.

When organisations form partnerships we know that there is often trouble brewing, but our concepts of culture are so diffuse and may be so overly academic that we cannot use them to predict the particular kinds of trouble. When we cannot make predictions, we are unprepared when the storm breaks out.

This chapter addresses the problem of pre-diagnosing the organisational state after the joining of previously separate units – whether they be whole organisations, departments inside a single organisation or an interface between two organisations.

In my experience many firms have problems in establishing the distinction between 'cultural assumptions' and 'cultural values'. The problem seems to be that these two concepts are often presented as being so closely connected that this makes it hard to see the difference. Contemporary books for students and managers are not very helpful – although a great many of them offer definitions such as: 'assumptions are beliefs about the factors that influence the firm' and 'values are guiding criteria for what is good or bad for the organisation'. Hence, when managers and students read a fundamental work such as Schein (1984) or a textbook such as Moorhead and Griffin (1995) and find quotations from Wilkins (1983) for a Hewlett-Packard value of 'Employees are our most important assets,' they get confused. The confusion arises from the fact that such a statement, according to the definition above, is an assumption – and the connected value telling us what we should do about our employees depends on what is important for (valued by) the employees in question. Another Hewlett-Packard value such as 'We avoid bank debt,' is not a value, but a norm, presumably from a view that you may get into financial trouble if you owe money to the bank which conflicts with a value that it is not good for the firm to run into financial trouble.

There may be many good reasons for the Hewlett-Packard approach – for instance, it is easy to communicate; but for those in the process of managing a culture change that can be communicated throughout the firm, such examples can only serve as an inspiration, not as guidelines for analysing the background for new 'cultural statements'.

This chapter has three related aims:

1. To treat the concepts of culture in an understandable manner so that managers and students can use these concepts to help to solve problems encountered in partnerships.
2. To provide an assessment of assumptions and values in situations where a conscious formulation of new cultural statements is necessary.
3. To identify and examine the consequences of a number of scenarios indicating the kinds of problems connected with forming partnerships.

ORGANISATIONAL CULTURE – MAKING SENSE OF PARTNERSHIP PROBLEMS

Research on organisational culture is greatly influenced by Schein, who has proposed that culture be analysed at three levels: artefacts, values and basic assumptions (Schein, 1985). Basic assumptions are our deepest conceptions of the world, its objects and its people – they are often considered as being unconscious, but nevertheless determine the way we perceive, think and feel (Schein, 1984). The assumptions form our picture of the entities the world consists of (assumptions of content), and they form our understanding of how these entities are connected (assumptions of relations). They may not give us an accurate picture of the real world, but they give us a picture that we think valid – and hence use as the foundation for our actions. This difference between the real world and the one we assume to exist has many similarities to the distinction between the 'objective' and the 'subjective' work situation referred to in job design (Hackman *et al.*, 1975).

Values are our conception of what is 'right or wrong' – 'good or bad'. They are our conceptions about which ideals are desirable or worth striving for. When we are faced with a choice between different action-alternatives, the value tells us which ones ought to be considered and which ones ought to be discarded for some reason or other. What we value need not be considered to be universally good (Keeley, 1983). The important thing is that the values guide our choices in a way that is not very different from the way that the specification of objectives guides the choices made in an economic model. This analogy also makes it clear that not only is our array of values important, but so also is the priority given to each value. If two firms both value employees and customers highly, the one prioritising the employees will be much different from the other (Sathe, 1985).

Artefacts are the objects and behaviours that can be seen or heard. They can be norms, formulated in stories, rituals and symbols, but they can also be technology, control systems and overt behaviour patterns. They are the result of the joint operation of basic assumptions and values and can be regarded as our way of tackling the real world. Our chosen way of grappling with reality may be unsuccessful if our assumptions are wrong and/or our values are out of line with reality, or if our connection of assumptions and values is faulty.

There seem to be two items on the agenda. The description of the artefacts as a result of some joint operation of assumptions and values indicates that culture in some way can be regarded a decision-process – 'the sense-making view' – and the use of words like 'basic' assumptions indicate that culture is something so deeply rooted in us, that we don't make decisions but react 'automatically' to something nearly programmed in us – 'the awareness view'.

The Awareness View

The definitions of organisational culture outlined above suggest that many of our decisions are made more or less unconsciously. That does not necessarily mean that they are made arbitrarily, but rather indicates that the culture comprises a catalogue of proven connections between our mental map of the real world and appropriate decisions. The decision outcomes are still artefacts, actions, behaviours and systems, but we are so familiar with the situation that we do not question the assumptions and values inherent in the decision-making process.

Perhaps the most famous representation of the elements of organisational culture is that of Schein. He identifies three levels, as shown in Figure 10.1, that are connected in the long run. Say, for example, the

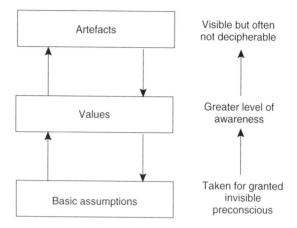

Figure 10.1   A basic approach to organisational culture.

founder of a firm through experience has formed the opinion that the more he advertises, the more he sells. This is equivalent to saying that he has formed a belief or a basic assumption saying that advertising leads to increased sales – he believes it to be a fact. However, if other members of the firm do not have this experience, they can only perceive the founder's basic assumption as the value 'one should always advertise more when one is in trouble' (Schein, 1985). If this works again and again over a long period of time, the firm members will forget the reasoning behind the value and accept it as a fact of life. This means that the value has undergone a cognitive transformation into an assumption. In the same way, a norm can be transformed into a value and ultimately into an assumption if, in the long run, we have seen that it leads to success – maybe that is what happened in the case of the Hewlett-Packard statements referred to above.

Although, Schein's arguments for the linkages between the levels have never been questioned, there have of course been discussions regarding the basic model. Some use other words – substituting the word 'assumptions' for the word 'beliefs' (Nelson and Quick, 1996). More specifically, the number of levels has been disputed. Some think we ought to distinguish between our behaviour and the symbols (artefacts) we use. Others argue that we ought to distinguish between 'terminal values' – desired end-states and 'instrumental values' – desired modes of behaviour (Jones, 1994).

This last proposal is interesting because it changes the perspective from the long-run connections in the original model to the more managerial type of view of how to deal with the world as it is just now. In other words, it gives focus to the problem of a conscious formulation of new norms, behaviours and artefacts, which may be necessary to adjust the organisation to changed circumstances. This is exactly the problem investigated in this chapter.

The Sense-Making View

In normal business language, we would say that assumptions and values are inputs to a decision process, and the artefacts are the outputs. We would also say that the assumptions are decision premises and the values are decision criteria.

This view of the cultural process is illustrated in Figure 10.2, which contains definitions in line with the mainstream literature on cultural processes.

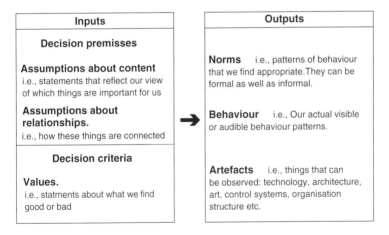

Figure 10.2   Cultural definitions in an input–output relationship.

If, when changing an organisation, it is necessary to change the way we understand and react to the real world then our aim must be to change what are named the artefacts in the cultural mode to become the output of our decision model. The inputs are our assumptions about the world and our criteria for what can be regarded as good or bad.

The input–output connections are illustrated in a simple manner in Table 10.1. Although the examples given in the table are caricatures, it is apparent that the values function as some kind of filter: they distinguish

Table 10.1   Caricatures of norm-forming

Assumption		Value		Artefact/norm
The customers want quality products.	✚	It is good that the customers get what they want	➜	We introduce a TQM (total quality management) system.
People are lazy and don't like to bear responsibility.	✚	It is good when things get properly done.	➜	We prefer a mechanistic organization.
Our firm is too small to make really big profits.	✚	It is good to be independent.	➜	We will try to grow.
Our firm is too small to make really big profits.	✚	It is not good to run risks.	➜	We seek joint ventures with other firms.

between all the possible actions we could take (decisions we could make) and only allow us to do things we feel are of value for our organisation.

In the example in the first row, this is quite obvious – of course, we could supply products of low quality, but we will not do that as we assume the customers would not want to buy them. The second row is an example of a rather old-fashioned view of human nature, showing how a leader may react. The last two rows are slightly different in that they connect the same assumption (that our firm is too small to make really big profits) with two different values; thus they produce two different norms of behaviour. If a firm is too small to make big profits but nevertheless wants to earn a lot of money, we must follow a norm saying that we ought to explore every possibility for growth that will lead to increased profits. If, on the other hand, we are still too small to make big profits but are risk-averse, we can choose to share the risks with others and thus comply with a norm of collaboration with other firms. This kind of reasoning suggests that the same assumptions can lead to different artefacts/norms if they are combined with different values.

This means that the assumptions and the values are not necessarily connected to decision situations, but they can at any given moment be considered independent of each other. Even if in the long run they are connected as in the basic model then it is important to distinguish between the 'assumption element' and 'the value element' when designing changes in organisations.

Figure 10.3 indicates that any artefact or norm originates in our assumptions of how the world is composed. This composition (the business

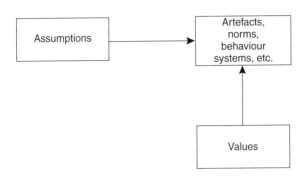

Figure 10.3 The connection between assumptions, values and artefacts.

environment) enables many different lines of action. Conventional contingency theory suggests that we use our values to sort out this set of possibilities to find that particular configuration of artefacts and norms – that is, technical equipment, organisation structure, systems and behavioural norms – that makes a fit between the organisation and its environment.

THE TWO FACES OF ORGANISATIONAL CULTURE

It appears that the two cultural views use the same building blocks – one based on assumptions and values, the other comprising artefacts, norms and behaviour. The definitions of these elements are identical. It is the connections between the elements that differ.

The sense-making approach is relatively short-termed and presupposes knowledge of both assumptions and values to allow conscious decisions about the artefacts. The awareness view focuses on culture formation over the long run and traces the way in which we unconsciously take some reactions for 'granted'.

These two views can coexist. This does not imply that the assumptions are taken more for granted than the artefacts, but that we are aware of some part of both the assumptions, values and artefacts while some other part are unconscious. As shown in Figure 10.4, the unconscious part is probably increasing as we go from artefacts to assumptions.

This means that the primary difference between the two views reflects the way we perceive an organisational situation. The sense-making view represents the situation where we actively perceive our decision premises as well as our decision criteria, while the awareness view unconsciously represents situations where we do not reflect, but take the rationale behind earlier reactions for granted.

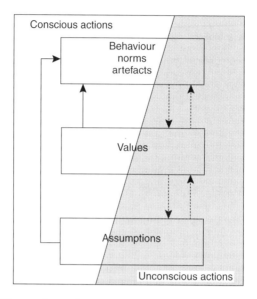

Figure 10.4   The two faces of organisation culture.

THE CULTURAL PROCESS IN BUSINESS MANAGEMENT

The cultural process can be utilised as a 'fit-maker'; that is, it can help identify where partners are 'fit' to be joined and also where errors of perception lead to 'misfit'.

The Cultural Process as a 'Fit-Maker'

Contingency theory suggests that a good 'fit' between the business environment and the organisational arrangements is a prerequisite for success. However, as mentioned frequently in the literature (notably Hackman *et al.*, 1975), and as seen above, people as well as organisations do not respond to the environment as such but respond to the perceived environment, which in turn means that the quality of the fit is related directly to the cultural perception. This implies that managerial reasoning will primarily be connected to a cultural perception of the real world. This leads to an array of decisions about which artefacts to use to deal with the environment. Because it is the artefacts (systems, behaviour, technology and so on) only that react with the real world, it is in the meeting of artefacts and the real world that results are created.

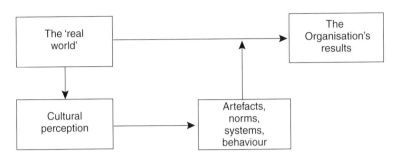

Figure 10.5 Connecting cultural perceptions with reality.

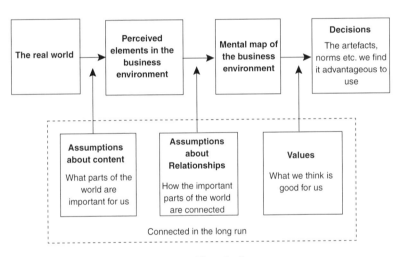

Figure 10.6 The cultural process as a 'fit-maker'.

This is shown in Figure 10.5. The section in bold lines shows the normal fit considerations of contingency theory. The organisation of course operates in the real world, and the better its technology, systems, norms and behaviours fit this environment, the better its results. In other words, the artefacts, systems and norms act as moderators on the connection between the environment and the organisation, and if those moderators are suitable then the results will be good. The route from the 'real' business environment to our choice of artefacts, norms and other ways of coping is shown in Figure 10.6. Our way of coping with the world (the organisation environment) finds its expression in the artefacts and norms, and because these are dependent on the way we interpret the world our coping methods can be proficient only if our assumptions about the world are correct, and if our values reflect a mode of conduct that is considered legitimate. It is a corollary of this that the errors we make when establishing our assumptions, values and artefacts will be errors of perception.

Perceptual Errors and 'Misfits'

Just as the literature on organisational culture operates on three or four levels, almost all textbooks on organisational behaviour describe the perceptual process in four to six stages, where the stimuli (the real world) are sorted and translated until we finally reach our conception of the state of affairs. On the basis of this conception, we then decide what response we will make (what actions we will take) to cope with the reality we perceive.

The following model (building on Dunham, 1984; Northcraft and Neale, 1994; Hellrigel *et al.*, 1995; Kreitner and Kinicki, 1995) is shown in Figure 10.7. In this version, it identifies four stages on the road from stimulus to response. As can be seen, there is a close resemblance between this figure and Figures 10.5 and 10.6. This resemblance can be seen as strengthened by the arguments of authors such as Cohen *et al.* (1995), who argue that there is a feedback loop from the outcomes of our actions to selection and interpreting mechanisms – not unlike the long-term model of organisation culture. There are also indications of the existence of a 'belief-system' that apparently takes care of the connections between beliefs (assumptions) and values. Apparently, the perceptual model assumes the same short-run – longer-run view as does the cultural model (Northcraft and Neale, 1994).

Not surprisingly, this indicates that faulty assumptions and/or values, which are the reasons for misfits between the organisation and its environment, have their roots in perceptual fallacies. Because this is so, the fallacies cited by perception theory must be the ones to avoid when assessing assumptions and values.

PITFALLS IN ASSESSING ASSUMPTIONS AND VALUES

Three possible pitfalls exist that can hamper the correct identification and analysis of cultural assumptions and values:

1. Perceptual selection – problems with assumptions about content.

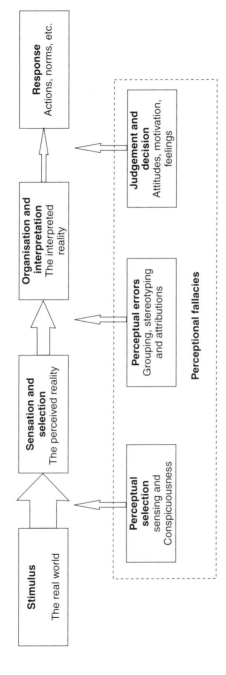

Figure 10.7   A basic perception model.

2. Perceptual errors – problems with assumptions about relations.
3. Judgement and decision – problems with values.

Perceptual Selection

People are not susceptible to influence by everything that is going on because our sensory organs cannot capture all the influences that reach us. Furthermore, some of the information that we maybe could digest is deselected because we, consciously or unconsciously, have decided that they are unnecessary, unpleasant, or otherwise unusable. This means that only part of the stimuli will continue in the process. This gives us a cue to failures in sensing and accepting the stimuli from outside because our sensory equipment may be less than all-encompassing and because some information is so hard to see that we ignore it. In assessing our assumptions about the content of the business environment, we are inclined to see what is most conspicuous and what, for some reason or other, makes an impression on us.

Perceptual Errors

The remaining stimuli (the accepted information on the business environment) are then organised (grouped in clusters) and interpreted (we form our opinion of relationships between the observed and accepted stimuli). Our picture of the business environment is not only limited by our deficiencies in gathering information, but it can also be inaccurate because the arrangement of our observations and the relationship inferences can be faulty. As not all observations can fit into our mental pattern, and as some of the observations may be regarded as stemming from the same source, our final response is normally based on even fewer of the stimuli observed and accepted. This is symbolised by the successively thinner arrows from left to right in Figure 10.7.

Judgement and Decision

In making decisions we not only use our stated criteria because the consequences we draw from our interpretation of the business environment are guided by our feelings, motives, and attitudes. When assessing the rationale behind the assumptions and values that constitute our premises and criteria for creating those artefacts, norms and behaviours that we use in our struggle for achieving results in the business environment, we must keep in mind that these common faults in perception are at play.

Before joining two organisations, a comparison of their assumptions and values ought to be made. This ought to be done in two steps:

First, the logic behind the most visible parts of norms, artefacts and the like ought to be brought into question. Take the logic of the internal planning system as an example: in some firms, the planning originates in the sales department after which the production plan is adapted to the sales forecast. Other firms do it the other way round (adapting sales to production plans), and some firms make a simultaneous optimisation of sales and production possibilities. If the two units to be joined use different logic, it is a sign that the assumptions behind their planning systems differ, and the consequence may well be that the unification will run into trouble at the first joint planning session.

Second, it pays to do some analysis of the more unconsciously layered factors. As the benefits of each planning system depend on the market situation, production capacity and so on, it is reasonable to check if there is still a fit between the firm's situation and the logic behind the planning system. Misfit (in one or both units) is a sure sign of a forgotten rationale leading to an inexpedient planning logic – and as this rationale may be connected to other norms and/or artefacts, it pays to trace its influence throughout the organisation. This is equivalent to a verification of basic assumptions or values.

When a number of conscious and unconscious assumptions and values are found, they ought to be checked for internal consistency. This done, it is time to diagnose what kind of scenario (what types of problems) will follow in the wake of the joining.

POSSIBLE MISFIT SCENARIOS IN JOINING TWO ORGANISATIONAL UNITS

Joining two 'similar' organisational units may seem straightforward and without problems. However, in a number of cases, especially if the organisational units perform the same task, the word 'similar' is taken for granted. The perspective of 'cultural perception' tells us that the two units can be different, even if they apparently generate the same kind of output. If we join two organisational units that apparently generate the same output, their different cultural perceptions can make cooperation difficult. Such different perceptions can of course originate in historical differences, but also in different assumptions of how things ought to be done, or what is important to accomplish. Even units that share the same values can get into problems if they give different priorities to these values; for example, where two units both pursue maximisation of sales and minimising of costs, the one prioritising sales will react very differently to market trouble from the one prioritising low costs.

If we join units with different but connected jobs, they will often face different sub-environments. Their success is dependent on how well they match their individual environments, and when they try to obtain this match they will drift apart. The result is that a fit with the environment (which will be a success) is obtained at the expense of the internal fit between organisational sub-units (which will also be a success). In other words, there may be situations where it is impossible to share all assumptions and values. Such situations are undoubtedly the reason why Lawrence and Lorsch could show that such organisations needed an elaborate internal coordination mechanism involving quite a lot of meetings and other personal contact (Lawrence and Lorsch, 1969).

Given the assumptions and values inherent in the two organisational units, Figure 10.8 draws a picture of the nine different scenarios that can arise if their assumptions and/or values are identical or overlapping or disjunctive.

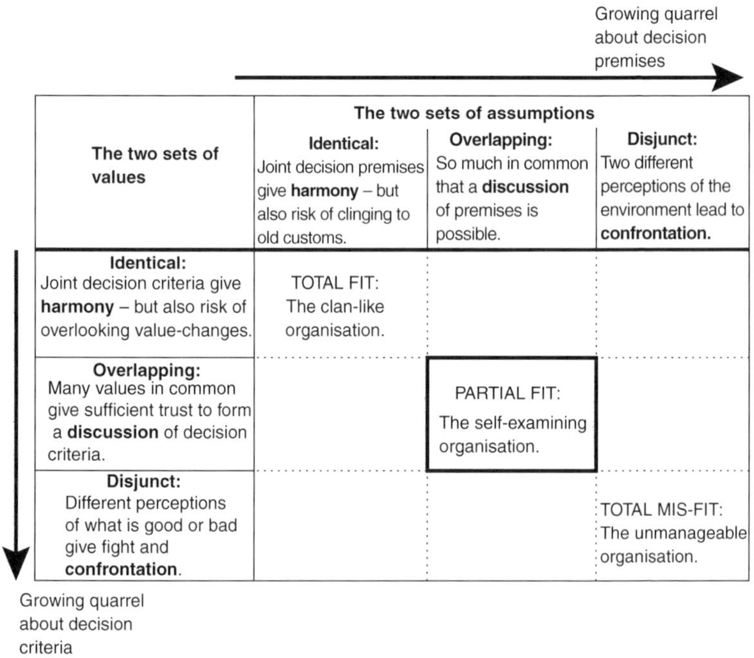

Growing quarrel about decision premises →

| The two sets of values | The two sets of assumptions | | |
	Identical: Joint decision premises give **harmony** – but also risk of clinging to old customs.	**Overlapping:** So much in common that a **discussion** of premises is possible.	**Disjunct:** Two different perceptions of the environment lead to **confrontation.**
Identical: Joint decision criteria give **harmony** – but also risk of overlooking value-changes.	TOTAL FIT: The clan-like organisation.		
Overlapping: Many values in common give sufficient trust to form a **discussion** of decision criteria.		PARTIAL FIT: The self-examining organisation.	
Disjunct: Different perceptions of what is good or bad give fight and **confrontation**.			TOTAL MIS-FIT: The unmanageable organisation.

Growing quarrel about decision criteria ↓

Figure 10.8 Scenarios arising from different combinations of assumptions and values.

The northeast corner is a picture of the clan-like organisation; the sub-units are in total harmony, which is good when the environment is stable and when the assumptions are right and the values do not differ from what is seen as legitimate. In the southwest corner we find an organisation consisting of culturally unconnected sub-units that do not understand each other and do not find the same conditions satisfying. This is of course an unmanageable organisation. In between, we find organisations with different degrees of shared assumptions and/or values.

It is not possible to say which of the constellations is the most successful in economic terms, but it is evident that the clan-like situation is the easiest to manage. All others cause internal frictions, which will have to be straightened out. Probably the most transformable organisation will be the one in the middle, because the sub-units have enough overlap between both values and assumptions to make trust and understanding possible, while containing enough differences to secure a process of self-examination.

CONCLUSION

A more detailed account indicating the foreseeable types of problems encountered in joining two organisational units is shown in Figure 10.9.

The identification of problem types rests on:

- the realisation that assumptions (whether conscious or unconscious) act as decision premises and that values can be regarded as decision criteria, and
- a statement and comparison of the assumptions and values in the two organisational units.

As in Figure 10.8, the northwest corner indicates no reasons for problems unless the shared assumptions and values are in misfit with the business environment.

The three lightly shaded areas are all characterised by overlapping assumptions or values or both. As there is common ground, there should be no reason to expect complete hostility, and it should be possible to sort differences out by discussion. Probably the situation with discussion around both premises and criteria signifies the most viable and flexible organisation if there is both common ground and different points of view, which means that the new unit is ready to question different trends in the business environment. It would seem that any problems could be solved by interventions from the organisation development toolbox.

The two sets of values (Decision criteria)	The two sets of assumptions (Decision premises)		
	Identical: Joint decision premises give **harmony** – but also risk of clinging to old customs	Overlapping: so much in common that a **discussion** of premises is possible	Disjunct: Two different perceptions of the environment lead to **confrontation**.
Identical: Joint decision criteria give **harmony** – but also risk of overlooking value-changes.	No problems – if the organisation is in balance with its job and environment.	Discussion of decision premises.	Confrontation about decision premises.
Overlapping: Many values in common give sufficient trust to form a **discussion** of decision-criteria.	Discussion of decision criteria.	Discussion of decision criteria. Discussion of decision premises.	Discussion of decision criteria Confrontation on decision premises.
Disjunct: Different perceptions of what is good or bad give fight and **confrontation**.	Confrontation on decision premises.	Confrontation on decision criteria. Discussion of decision premises.	Confrontation on decision criteria Confrontation on decision premises.

Organisation development interventions   Strategic interventions

Figure 10.9   Expectations from forming partnerships.

The five more darkly shaded areas are characterised by assumptions or values or both being disjunctive, which means possible confrontation. This calls for a major alignment resembling strategic interventions. The area in the southeast corner could cause most trouble, but in those cases, the organisation members will most likely be prepared for the differences. Probably the situation where values are identical and assumptions are disjunctive is the most threatening, especially if the members of the two units adhere to the same decision criteria, but to different perceptions of the world. This is a sign of two completely different sets of logic, which may be very hard to reconcile.

Even this rather mechanistic way of resolving matters, that are qualitative in many ways, misses some points. First, the conclusion treats assumptions as a single entity and has not taken account of the fact that there are two kinds of assumptions (about content and about relations). This is a matter of convenience, and could easily be done by drawing a cubic figure instead of a two-dimensional table. Of course, the difference between these two kinds of assumptions should be taken into account when diagnosing real-world situations, but for illustrative purposes the present treatment of the problem will suffice. The third dimension will assist in choosing exactly the requisite interventions.

Second, the treatment ignores the additional problems that arise if the assumptions and values of one unit are right and those of the other wrong, nor has it been mentioned what can happen if both joined units are at fault in their assessments.

This could of course be dealt with. I am confident that it is possible to trace the diagnosis of which specific types of organisational development interventions to use by listing the most important assumptions and values, then checking them for relevance and next for fits/misfits between the two units to be joined, and finally checking for situational characteristics of the newly joined unit. It would be complicated, but in principle not much different from the fault-finding diagrams anyone uses when they have trouble with their car or their refrigerator.

References

COHEN, A.R., FINK, S.L., GADON, H. and WILLITS, R.D. (1995) *Effective Behavior in Organizations*. Irwin, Chicago.

DUNHAM, R.B. (1984) *Organizational Behavior*. Irwin, Homewood, IL.

HACKMAN, J.R., OLDHAM, G., JANSON, R. and PURDY, K. (1975) New strategy for job enrichment. *California Management Review*, summer, *17*, 57–71.

HELLRIGEL, D., SLOCUM, J.W. and WOODMAN, R.W. (1995) *Organizational Behavior*. West, St. Paul, MN.

HUCZYNSKI, A.H. and BUCHANAN, D. (1991) *Organizational Behavior: On Introductory Text*, Prentice-Hall, New York.

JONES, G. (1994) *Organization Theory*. Addison-Wesley, Reading, MA.

KEELEY, M. (1983) Values in organizational theory and management education. *Academy of Management Review*, *3*, 376–86.

KREITNER, R. and KINICKI, A. (1995) *Organizational Behavior*. Irwin, Chicago, IL.

LAWRENCE, P.R. and LORSCH, J.W. (1969) *Organizational and Environment*. Irwin, Chicago, IL.

MOORHEAD, G. and GRIFFIN, R.W. (1995) *Organizational Behavior: Managing People and Organizations*. Houghton Mifflin, Boston, MA.

NELSON, D.L. and QUICK, J.C. (1996) *Organizational Behavior: The Essentials*. West, St Paul, MN.

NORTHCRAFT, G.B. and NEALE, M.A. (1994) *Organizational Behavior: A Management Challenge*. Dryden Press, Fort Worth, TX.

ROBBINS, S.P. (1991) *Organizational Behavior*. Prentice-Hall, Englewood Cliffs, NJ.

SATHE, V. (1985) *Culture and Related Corporate Realities*. Irwin, Chicago, IL.

SCHEIN, E.H. (1984) Coming to a new awareness of organizational culture. *Sloan Management Review*, Winter, *28*, 3–16.

SCHEIN, E.H. (1985) *Organizational Culture and Leadership: A Dynamic View.* Jossey-Bass, New York.
WILKINS, A. (1983) Organizational stories as symbols which control the organization. In Pondy, L.R., Frost, P.J., Morgan, G. and Dandridge, T.C. (eds.) (1991) *Organizational Symbolism*, Greenwich, CT, JAI Press.

11 Managing Effective Partnerships

Jens Genefke and Frank McDonald

THE PROBLEMS OF COLLABORATION

As already indicated in the introduction and as demonstrated repeatedly in these chapters, attaining effective organisational collaboration is not an easy endeavour. The advice in the chapter by Huxham and Vangen – 'Don't do it unless you have to!' – provides a timely warning of the possibility that some partnerships are impossible in the sense that they are doomed to a short life and/or low efficiency.

This possibility is also clearly indicated in the chapters on power relationships and on culture. In Chapter 9, it is shown that even if the more powerful members of a collaboration try to apply an optimal rather than maximal pressure on the partners they may well end up in an inefficient solution. The explanation has two components: the transaction costs associated with monitoring the 'optimal pressure' are high and very hard to measure with any precision, and the partners' institutional and motivational frameworks can be hard to reconcile. This latter possibility is explored in Chapter 10, where it is suggested that certain partnerships can be regarded as unmanageable.

This being said, our summing up takes as its starting point the situation where a number of organisations have decided to embark on a collaborative venture.

OPEN AND CLOSED PARTNERSHIPS

All partnerships run into difficulties of structuring, coordination, trust-forming and the like, but the chapters on 'formation of partnerships' indicates that there is the possibility of choosing the time and place to find solutions for these difficulties. Two general types of partnership can be identified: closed and open.

- *Closed partnerships:* In situations that are thoroughly analysed and where the prospective partners have met each other before the collaboration is formed there is a possibility for the partners to check for common intents, egocentricity, distribution of incentives, mutual trust, cultural differences and so on. We do not argue that such pre-planning will eliminate all potential problems, but at least it will establish some common expectations of a meta-domain, that is, the collaborative system as a whole. This makes it possible to sort out the operating problems within a general set of basic rules.

This is no easy matter, but it has the strength of separating discussions of the running of the partnership from the intent – that is, the goals and aspirations of the collaboration.

- *Open partnerships:* In cases where it is impossible to pinpoint the prospective partners in advance – especially if the partnership is broad in scope or if some of the prospective partners refuse to commit themselves until they can see 'how things develop' – all sorts of matters will become subject to discussion. In these circumstances, it is almost impossible to separate problems of intent from operation problems. Furthermore, to build trust for later entrants it may be necessary not only to fulfil the needs for information but also to adjust the overall domain. As this in all likelihood has to be done across managerial and cultural borders, it becomes a complex and time-consuming process leading to an inclination by influential partners to use power to solve these problems.

This does not imply that partnerships of the first type should be the only ones pursued, because many worthwhile endeavours cannot be defined beforehand. However, as we said in the introduction, we are convinced that the distinctions between open and closed partnerships are more important than the often mentioned differences between public and private or big and small. Moreover, we will show that it is important for collaborating partners to keep an eye on tendencies that indicate a drift from one type towards the other.

One of the corollaries to the distinction between open and closed partnerships seems to be the choice of time when the bulk of work connected to partnership formation and development is undertaken. In closed partnerships most of the trouble is in the formation phase, while the harvest of the benefits comes in the form of a smooth-running operational phase. In open partnerships, the formation period is relatively easy and may be exciting, but this can be at the expense of uncertainty, trouble and costs later on.

The questions, then, are: 'What are the obstacles to closure?' and 'How to avoid collaborative drift if closure is not obtained?'

In this summary, we follow the sequence outlined in Figure 11.1. Chapters 1 to 10 contain elements that make it possible to follow the partnership from

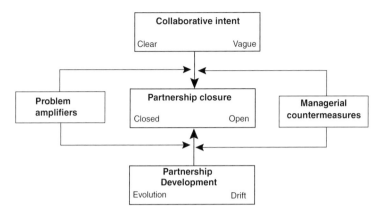

Figure 11.1 Aim of collaboration.

the first formulation of the intent (whether clear or vague) to the end of the formation process where it can be established if the partnership is closed or open. Additionally we can make some educated guesses on the prospective development of the partnership – whether it evolves into something better than expected or it drifts along towards erosion. In addition, we have signs that some characteristics within and between the partners can amplify the problems and thereby increase the possibility for collaborative drift – and we find grounds for proposing some management remedies that can counteract such a drift.

Of course, this account is limited in scope. Chapters 1 to 10 do not cover all contingencies, but as they originate from very different management disciplines and as they fit into the common pattern sketched above, we are confident that we present a way of thinking that is both realistic and useful.

THE MANY FACES OF COLLABORATIVE INTENT

This book disputes directly the sufficiency of the common distinction between cooperative intent (striving for synergy) and competitive intent (striving for acquiring key skills and/or competencies). The argument in Chapter 4 by Martin and Matthews presents a continuum from total long-term commitment to hostile competition. Along the same lines, in Chapter 2 Stiles makes a strong case that cooperative and competitive intent can coexist in the same partnership while in Chapter 3 ul-Haq and Morison show that in the banking sector the alliances cluster in two out of three possible types – neither of which have competitive intent.

The evidence presented indicates two lines of thought:

If the partners are symmetric in the sense that each has some resources or skills that are of value to all, that their cultures are compatible and that they trust each other then the partnership tends to be cooperative, and an added dimension of competitive intent will tend to make the partnership learning-oriented.

If, on the other hand, there are asymmetries in the partnership then a tendency towards erosion will arise as the stronger partners seek to appropriate the bulk of the benefits of collaboration. These asymmetries may draw the partnership in the direction of an evolutionary process, ending in a merging of firms.

This point of view signifies that some constellations of intent and organisational compatibility are predisposed for cooperation, while others are susceptible to more hostility between the partners. The evidence gathered from Chapters 1 to 10 provides a useful guide to what to look for during the process of partnership formation.

As the type of asymmetries, as well as their magnitude, influences the intent of collaboration, the lesson is that some alliances have inbuilt tendencies towards 'collaborative drift'. This leads to a tendency for stronger partners to use these asymmetries to promote their own interests at the expense of the weaker and notably to undermine the initial collaborative goals of the partnership. This erosion of mutual benefits is one of the main problems that partnerships encounter. This means that the partnership from the outset ought to take measures to counter such a development. In case of gross asymmetries it may be necessary to create forces that can be applied during the partnership formation process, or be held in readiness for later deployment, should the need arise.

META-SYSTEMS AND COLLABORATION

There is a tendency to interpret partnerships at two different levels. One level focuses on the dependencies between the collaborating partners or, as phrased in Chapter 5 by Sink, the meta-domain. The other level consists of the operational systems.

At the meta-level, conventional optimising techniques are of little help because coalition-forming is strongly influenced by feelings, culture and the like. It is not enough to focus on the collective intent because operating systems have to meet goals set by the individual partners. Indeed, collaboration is often a means to advance these separate ends. This implies that incentives affecting the distribution of benefits are instruments of balance and, as such, they deserve careful attention if the partnership is to endure.

Though this is often mentioned throughout the book, only three chapters approach the problem directly: Martin and Matthews (Chapter 4) and Sink (Chapter 5) discuss the building of complex collaborations between many partners while Butler and Gill (Chapter 7) elaborate on the formation process in a focused two-partner collaboration. Two factors appear strongly to influence the outcome from the multitude of variables that make up the meta-system: the level of preparation before the collaboration is formed and the permeability of the collaboration borders.

It is recognised that all partnerships enjoy benefits from preparation. The more prepared the partners and the more aligned their expectations, the easier it is to find out if the partnership is workable or not. This calls for a thorough preparation before entering into collaborative arrangements. However, it is not always possible to pinpoint the prospective partners in advance, and some of them may refuse to commit themselves until they can see 'how things develop'. This, of course, is at least partly dependent on the clarity of the intent of the partners and partly on the level of trust.

These three chapters indicate that while a small number of partners with goals that complement each other by careful planning can form and run a tight partnership, this is not practicable in complex multi-partner collaborations where many conflicting goals can exist. The corollary to this is that small partnerships with clear and consistent goals can manage themselves by elaborate joint search and planning, as shown in Chapter 7 by Butler and Gill. On the other hand, big partnerships with goals of mixed consistency need quite a lot of leadership, even if the goals are clear. This view is argued in Chapter 4 by Martin and Matthews, who find it necessary to supplement a model of interdependencies and distribution of incentives with an 'inclusive leadership'. If the intent is unclear, Sink (Chapter 5) considers that some kind of neutral 'bridging organisation' is imperative. Moreover, if the overall goals are unclear then the partnership may attract the attention of many organisations that see the possibility to further their own interests without caring much about the overall aims of the partnership. Inevitably, this will give rise to quite a lot of sub-coalition formation, unless the overall aims are used as mechanisms for sorting out free riders and potential troublemakers. This is a job for the leadership of the partnership.

FROM INTENT TO CLOSURE

The main factors involved in moving from intent to closure are illustrated in Figure 11.2. The forces drawing the partnerships towards an unwanted drift are vague intent and many disparate partners. Each of these forces is

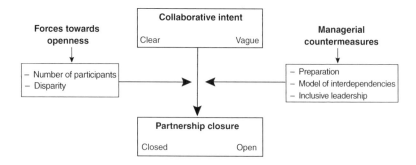

Figure 11.2   From intent to closure.

enough to disturb the cooperative climate – but together they can make things very difficult. The remedy is to make things clear and to introduce a neutral and comprehensive overview of the partnership. This requires knowledge in the form of well-prepared modelling of interdependencies and limitations of any attack on a settled system of incentives. It also takes an accepted, strong and neutral leadership to secure a realistic model and a fair distribution of benefits.

POWER IS A WEAPON AND TRUST IS A TOOL

The whole idea behind collaboration is that together the participants can do their jobs in a more efficient way than if they operated separately. This requires a mutual respect between the partners. McDonald (Chapter 9) shows that if stronger partners 'attack' weaker partners the stronger can wind up more profitable, but the partnership can easily deteriorate and become ineffective. This chapter makes two contributions to our conclusion. First, it illustrates some of the mechanisms that lead to collaborative drift, and second, it indicates methods that could be used by the leadership to clarify the consequences of egocentrism and by increasing the transparency of the collaborative system.

Clearly, transparency is not easily accomplished, because we all have personal barriers to understanding other people and the obstacles are often felt to be higher if we think that the gains by partners are blocking our own prospects.

This serious problem is addressed in three chapters. In Chapter 10, Genefke treats culture as a filter for perception with an emphasis on the distinction between cause-and-effect relationships (which form the basis for every planning system) and value-judgements (which function as criteria in every decision process). From this platform, it is possible to deduce what kind of organisation development techniques can remedy the partner's different views of what is important for planning and decision-making. This kind of reasoning is also used in Chapter 8 by Erdener and Torbiörn, who show how staffing is a means to use people as a tool to bridge the gap between different values in firms and countries. In Chapter 6, Winch and Sauer use IT-systems to shed light on the cause-and-effect relationships that exist between diverse partners in multiple-partner networks.

While the shape of these four chapters are rather mechanistic, their content certainly is not, since each addresses an aspect of the transparency-creating process that is perhaps the most important remedy against the stronger partners' more or less natural inclinations to feather their own nests. At the core of this is of course trust.

Apart from situations characterised by infatuation, the feeling of trust is impossible without openness and common understandings. This theme, that emerges repeatedly in almost every chapter, appears to be tackled in two different ways. First, trust is regarded as the antidote to the fear of being exploited by partners that are more powerful. Second, trust is recognised as a tool that can replace a multitude of bureaucratic arrangements. Taking account of attempts to consider trust and distrust as two separate concepts, it is possible to look upon trust as a managerial instrument that can further coordination by rendering red tape superfluous. Such a thought may seem to be rather strange, because it is difficult to see how a feeling can be an instrument. However, consideration of the expectancy theory of motivation convinces us that feelings are already thought of as management tools. Leaders delegate work on the expectancy that a person can do a job and the person doing the job works on the expectancy that they will receive a reward when the job is accomplished. Seen as an organisational tool for coordination, trust is not much different. It could be defined as the expectancy that a person will do what they say they will do. Therefore, trust is an instrument for reducing uncertainty.

FROM PARTNERSHIP CLOSURE TO COLLABORATIVE DRIFT

The summing up of these tendencies is shown in Figure 11.3, where the box labelled 'unresolved asymmetries' indicates the variety of partner differences in terms of factors such as size, resources, knowledge, flexibility,

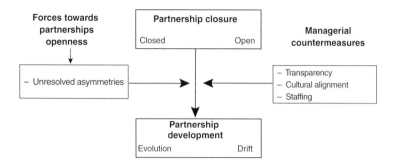

Figure 11.3   From partnership closure to collaborative drift.

market connections and quality production. The overall message is that open partnerships are liable to have many differences that ought to be taken into account and resolved in the formation phase of the partnership. If these differences are suppressed, they could later on be sources of power for an egocentric behaviour that may drive the partnership towards erosion. A few, albeit important, managerial remedies are outlined in the chapters. Transparent rules for partnerships based on systems such as IT-models for sharing information, or cultural alignment and human linkages created by a careful selection of staff, may provide useful means of counteracting problems that arise in partnerships. It is not enough to say 'Peter is good at his job, let him be our representative towards the partners;' rather, it should be asked, 'What can Peter supply that the partners would see as a real contribution to the partnership?' Professional capacity is only rarely the major factor necessary for the successful management of partnerships.

A MODEL OF COOPERATION

Although Chapters 1 to 10 stem from a diversity of sources, the common elements outweigh the differences. The same problems are mentioned whether the focus is on public or private ownership, the manufacturing or service sectors, or big or small organisations. The same kind of recommendations for remedial action emerge whether the approach stems from transaction cost theory, resource-based theory or organisation theory. As we do not find this to be a coincidence, we outline a model that incorporates the main issues that are highlighted by Chapters 1 to 10. This model is presented in Figure 11.4. The axes show the three main variables that

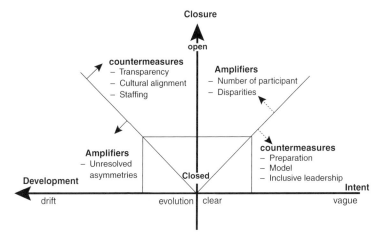

Figure 11.4 A model of management issues connected to partnerships.

describe the three main characteristics of partnerships. These are the purpose or the intent of the collaboration, the degree to which the partners find the partnership closed and an indication whether the development of the partnership will lead to evolution or a drift towards erosion. These three main variables are connected by lines showing that increased vagueness of intent leads to open borders to the partnership and that the confusion caused leads to collaborative drift and possibly erosion. As these connexions are valid only under the clause of ceteris paribus, we have shown two groups of amplifiers that make the prospects of the partnership even more pessimistic. Two possible remedies that can counterbalance the gloomy picture are shown.

Figure 11.4 can be read at two different levels. The right quadrant illustrates that at a general level the more vague the intent, the more the partnership will be open. This means that changes to goals can attract new partners that bring along new possibilities, which lead to further spreading of the collaborative arena. The left quadrant shows that the consequences of this vagueness is a growing possibility for collaborative drift – that is, the tendency for the partnership to fall apart because of misunderstanding and conflict.

At a more specific level, these tendencies can be modified by adopting policies that alter the slope of the lines. If vague intent attracts new partners in great numbers and if the partners are very different then these act as amplifiers that force the line in the right quadrant to become steeper and therefore the partnership to become more open. To curb problems caused by such developments a variety or remedies are available, for example, a thorough preparation for prospective partnerships, the use of models that highlight the dependence between the partners and an inclusive leadership. These remedies can decrease the slope of the line and thus keep the partnership at a tolerable level of openness, that is, a level that will not lead to collaborative drift.

The line in the left quadrant shows the consequences of growing openness. If the openness results in many unresolved asymmetries, these will draw the partnership towards collaborative drift. In the model, this will result in a decreasing slope of the line. There are countermeasures to these problems. The partnership can be made transparent, cultures can be aligned and staff can work more closely across organisational borders to obtain a clearer picture of the partnership as a whole. This will reduce conflicts and misunderstandings, thereby counterbalancing or even removing the temptations to exploit egocentric possibilities. In the model, this is shown as a force moving the line in the left quadrant upwards.

CONCLUDING COMMENTS

The overall conclusion from chapters 1 to 10 as summarised in the above model is not pessimistic. In most cases, there will be medicine to cure a sick patient. The main problem is diagnosis. When a collaborator in a partnership experiences unforeseen problems it is important to ascertain the factors that influence the slope of the lines in Figure 11.4 and to reflect on which countermeasures to employ in order to neutralise or exploit the situation.

The main lessons that emerge from the investigations reported in this book are that collaboration between organisations is often a good solution to problems faced by private and public sector and large and small organisations, but the task of managing effective partnerships is considerable. Careful preparation in the formation stage can, in some cases, alleviate these problems, especially if the number of partners is small and the goals of the collaboration can be clearly identified. However, even when careful preparation is possible, difficulties arising from cultural, power and goal asymmetries mean that effectual operations of partnerships require the deployment of high-level management inputs. Moreover, because many of the problems that afflict partnerships emerge as the collaboration evolves, high-quality managerial inputs are needed at all stages of partnerships not only at the beginning. In cases where there are many partners and where the goals of collaboration are not clear, partnerships attaining effective operations become even more difficult. Management systems that are capable of engendering trust between what are often very different organisational cultures and, in the case of international partnerships, national cultural differences, appear to be at the heart of finding solutions to these problems. We hope that the analysis and conceptual frameworks outlined in this book will contribute to a better understanding of these issues.

Index